Prosecution of Adult Felony Defendants

Prosecution of Adult Felony Defendants

A Policy Perspective

Peter W. Greenwood
Sorrel Wildhorn
Eugene C. Poggio
Michael J. Strumwasser
Peter De Leon
The Rand Corporation

Lexington Books
D.C. Heath and Company
Lexington, Massachusetts
Toronto   London

Library of Congress Cataloging in Publication Data

Main entry under title:

Prosecution of adult felony defendants.

    Bibliography: p.
    1. Criminal statistics—California—Los Angeles Co. 2. Criminal justice,
Administration of—Los Angeles Co., Calif. 3. Prosecution—Los Angeles
Co., Calif. I. Greenwood, Peter W.
KFC1199.L62C768   345'.79493'02   75-36893
ISBN 0-669-00389-1

Copyright © 1976 by The Rand Corporation

Published simultaneously in Canada

Printed in the United States of America

International Standard Book Number: 0-669-00389-1

Library of Congress Catalog Card Number: 75-36893

CONTENTS

LIST OF FIGURE AND TABLES

PREFACE

This book is unusual in that it presents both the results of a research study (on the prosecution of adult felony defendants in Los Angeles County) and a description of the public policy and operational impacts of the study occurring after its release.

The research study—undertaken in cooperation with the Los Angeles County District Attorney's Office—is presented in the Summary and Chapters I through VIII and in the supporting Appendixes. It was funded by a grant from the National Institute of Law Enforcement and Criminal Justice, the research arm of the Law Enforcement Assistance Administration of the U.S. Department of Justice.

The broad objectives of the study were: (1) to demonstrate the value of on-going operational analysis in revealing to policymakers how well policies of the Los Angeles County District Attorney's Office were working; and (2) to describe how felony proceedings were functioning throughout Los Angeles County.

After the study was released in the spring of 1973, the District Attorney instituted a number of policy and management changes in response to the study's findings and recommendations. Chapter IX briefly describes these changes and traces their subsequent effects on the court agencies of Los Angeles County, in general, and on the District Attorney's Office, in particular.

Although the context of this study is Los Angeles County felony proceedings, we believe it has wide application. It should be of specific interest to practicing professionals and administrators in police departments, prosecutors' offices and the criminal courts throughout the United States and to criminal justice researchers, as well as being of general interest to informed lay persons.

Points of view or opinions stated in this book are those of the authors and do not necessarily represent the official position or policy of the U.S. Department of Justice or of the Los Angeles County District Attorney's Office.

ACKNOWLEDGMENTS

For encouraging us to undertake the research study and providing complete access to the people and the records of his Office, we owe a special debt of gratitude to the late Joseph P. Busch, the Los Angeles District Attorney at the time of our study. We also wish to thank the many deputies and management personnel who cooperated with us in interviews and with whom we discussed our work. Special Assistant District Attorney Robert Martin provided invaluable assistance throughout the project in guiding us to appropriate personnel and helping us to maintain our policy perspective of the Office. Deputy District Attorney Raymond Sinetar was also extremely accommodating in helping us to interpret our findings and in answering a multitude of procedural questions. Edrena Alexander and Marilyn Plutae of the District Attorney's Record Section were particularly helpful in fulfilling our data needs.

We are grateful to Ronald Beattie, William Hutchins, and David Miller of the California Bureau of Criminal Statistics for the assistance they provided us in working with their data.

Many of our colleagues at Rand have also contributed valuable assistance to this project. Kathleen Scofield and Naomi Ainslie were responsible for much of our data collection. Misako Fujisaki, Barbara Horner, Leola Cutler, Robert Young, and Robert Eggleton all provided computer programming support for the analyses. Joel Edelman (formerly of Rand) and Professor Norman Abrams of the University of California, Los Angeles, School of Law provided valuable assistance in the formulation of our research approach. Jan Chaiken and Marvin Lavin reviewed an earlier draft of the research study.

We are particularly grateful to our colleague Irving Cohen for his invaluable reviews and critiques throughout the project.

SUMMARY

This research has been undertaken in cooperation with the Los Angeles County District Attorney to:

- Demonstrate the value of analysis as an ongoing activity to inform policy-makers about how the policies of the District Attorney's Office are working.
- Describe how the criminal justice process currently functions throughout Los Angeles County.

Concentration has been on following what happens to adult felony defendants from the time of their arrest until they leave the adjudicatory system or are sentenced. The basic steps involved can include (1) the decision by the District Attorney on whether or not to file felony charges; (2) the decision by the Municipal Court as to whether the defendant should be held to answer on felony charges, should be dismissed, or should be treated as a misdemeanant; (3) the offering of inducements by the prosecutor or the court to encourage a guilty plea; (4) the decision by the defendant on whether to plead guilty, to submit on the transcript, or to go to trial before a judge or jury; and (5) the finding of the court as to the defendant's guilt and the appropriate sentence. In addition to the effects of factors peculiar to the defendant (offense, prior record, race, etc.) and background factors such as type of defense counsel and pretrial custody status, we explore variations in this flow which can be attributed to different policies among police, District Attorney Branches, courts, or individual judges.

We believe that our analysis raises grave doubts as to the consistency or equity with which defendants are treated in Los Angeles County. This phenomenon, we observe, is not unique to Los Angeles County. For example, a recent series of articles in the *New York Times* (September 25-October 5, 1972) discusses the inconsistency with which defendants are treated by the State and Federal Courts within New York City and in the rest of New York State. Although we have not been able, in this first analysis, to explore all of the causes for the variations in treatment, we have attempted to suggest plausible explanations for examination. We have refrained from making detailed recommendations for change, believing that these can only come from the agencies concerned, after our findings have been carefully assessed. The recommendations offered in Section VIII are made primarily to stimulate consideration of the appropriate actions to be taken.

Previous studies of the prosecution function have concentrated on describing the areas in which wide discretion exists and how it is exercised, based on interviews and direct observations. Court studies that are somewhat related have captured only the aggregate flow pattern of defendants as they move through the adjudicatory process.

The present study is particularly novel in that it combines the techniques of empirical analysis and observation to identify and analyze those factors within the system that affect the treatment of individual defendants. Since the Los Angeles County Superior Court and the District Attorney's Office each consists of a number of large Branches, often operating under different management policies, we were able to examine the effect of a variety of management policies on the performance of the Office.

A summary follows of our findings on various aspects of how adult felony defendants are handled by the prosecution and the courts.

FINDINGS

Lack of Performance Measures

There are no objective performance measures consistently applied by criminal justice administrators to evaluate the performance of their employees or policies. Unlike other areas of business or social endeavor in which an agency's performance can be gauged by historical performance standards such as sales, profits, reading achievement, or cure rate, criminal justice officials are judged mainly on the basis of their individual actions rather than on the overall performance of their agencies.

Furthermore, no information system or data source currently exists that can provide administrators with the data used for the analyses displayed in this report.

We believe that by monitoring arrest rates, rejection rates, dismissal rates, methods of disposition, and conviction and sentencing rates, and using the kinds of statistical controls developed in this report, criminal justice administrators would greatly increase their capability to detect and diagnose problem areas, as well as to evaluate new programs. Such performance measures should be monitored for each individual Deputy District Attorney and each major organizational unit, as well as for the entire Office.

Differences in Treatment of Defendants in Los Angeles County and in Other Jurisdictions in the State

Los Angeles County has one of the largest and most complex criminal justice systems in the country, involving more than 40 arresting agencies, 24 Municipal Court Districts, and 8 Superior Court Districts—all of which are serviced by the District Attorney. When we compare the performance of each agency against that of agencies in other parts of the state, we find significant disparities. These disparities are not observed when agencies in counties such as San Francisco, San Diego, or San Mateo are compared with their counterparts other than Los Angeles County.

The following findings are indicative of the differences in treatment:

- An arrest is more likely to be based on felony charges in Los Angeles than elsewhere in the state.
- The District Attorney in Los Angeles is much less likely to file felony charges. He rejects 53 percent of the cases brought in by the police, compared to only 29 percent for the rest of the state.
- The Municipal Courts in Los Angeles are much less likely to reduce felony charges to misdemeanors than lower courts elsewhere in the state.
- In Los Angeles, many more defendants submit their cases for judgment on the preliminary hearing transcript (SOT) than elsewhere: 31 percent in Los Angeles versus 3 percent elsewhere. The SOT is apparently used in place of guilty pleas, since plea rate plus SOT rate in Los Angeles is roughly equal to the same total elsewhere in the state.
- A felony defendant who is arraigned in Los Angeles Superior Court has an 0.81 chance of being convicted, versus 0.88 for defendants elsewhere.
- If a felony defendant is convicted, he is much less likely (0.41) to receive a felony sentence than defendants elsewhere (0.73).

The overall result is that the difference between the number of defendants arrested by the police on felony charges and the number of defendants found by the courts to be deserving of felony sentences is much larger in Los Angeles than elsewhere in the state. The fraction receiving felony sentences in Los Angeles is 12 percent compared to 28 percent in the rest of the state.

This large difference leads to several effects which may be undesirable from the community's point of view:

- Many citizens who are subsequently found not guilty of behavior deserving felony punishment are subjected to the anxiety, costs, and loss of freedom associated with a felony arrest, as opposed to the much more limited costs and inconveniences associated with a misdemeanor arrest.
- The credibility of the criminal justice system suffers considerably in the eyes of habitual offenders who believe they can consistently get off with much lighter sentences than those prescribed for their arrest charge.
- The criminal justice system must bear the wasted costs of processing many felony cases that could have been settled much less expensively in the lower courts with the same results.

Whether the difference is due to excessive arrest charges by the police or to more lenient findings by the court cannot be ascertained solely from our data.

The Effects of Pretrial Custody Status, Defense Counsel, and Race

Felony defendants can spend their time awaiting trial in jail, can be released on bail, or can be released on their own recognizance (OR), depending on their circumstances and the skill of their attorneys. Our data show that defendants who remain in jail have a much lower chance of being either dismissed or acquitted and a greater chance of receiving a felony sentence if convicted. Several hypotheses can be constructed to explain this finding. First, the system may tend to prejudge defendants, more often granting release to those who have weaker cases against them. Second, defendants who are not able to secure bail or OR may be less competent or less motivated to avoid being found guilty. Finally, the characteristics that make a defendant unacceptable for release (no funds, no community ties) may also lead to higher conviction rates and harsher sentencing rates by the court. None of these explanations sounds particularly just.

Any given defendant may be represented by a private attorney if he has funds, by a public defender if he does not, or by a court-appointed attorney if a public defender is unacceptable. The data show that clients of private attorneys are much more likely to make bail, more likely to plead guilty, less likely to demand a jury trial, and more likely to receive a felony sentence upon conviction than clients of public defenders and court-appointed attorneys. Court-appointed attorneys are more likely to seek a jury trial and more likely to have their defendants acquitted. The public defender, although less likely to win either a dismissal or an acquittal for his client, is most likely to avoid a felony sentence upon conviction.

Since the data support many arguments that refute explanations of these differences solely on the basis of defendant characteristics, we may assume that these findings reflect some differences among types of attorneys in economic incentives, strategy, or knowledge of the system.

When we examine the treatment of defendants by ethnic group, we find a number of small to moderate disparities. Of all persons arrested on felony charges, black defendants are more often ultimately acquitted than are Anglo-Americans. But black defendants also are more likely to plead not guilty. Of all defendants who plead not guilty, Anglo-Americans are more often acquitted than blacks. When blacks are convicted, they are more likely than Anglo-Americans to be convicted of a lesser charge than that for which they were originally arrested and are also more likely to receive a misdemeanor sentence. The treatment of Mexican-American defendants falls between that of black and Anglo-American defendants. These findings tend to suggest that either a double standard is applied to Anglo-American and minority group defendants, or that cases against minority groups tend to be weaker, reflecting over-arrests by the police or weaker evidence (over-prosecution) against minority groups. Given the data at our disposal we could not resolve the question of which hypothesis best explains the observed differences.

Police Arrest Practices

Although arrests in Los Angeles County are more likely to be based on felony charges than elsewhere in the state, there is considerable variation when we look at major police departments across the county. Although the Los Angeles (City) Police Department and Los Angeles County Sheriff's Office accounted, respectively, for 51 percent and 23 percent of roughly 100,000 felony arrests made in Los Angeles County in 1970, six other departments also made more than 1,000 felony arrests.

In Long Beach, the ratio of felony to misdemeanor arrests is only 0.22; for the Los Angeles Sheriff's Office and the Compton Police Department, it is 0.48 and 0.77, respectively. Looking at the ratio of felony to misdemeanor arrests for drug offenses shows an even more extreme variation: 0.66 for the Long Beach Police Department; 10.4 for the Los Angeles Sheriff's Office; 35.5 for the Pasadena Police Department; and 114.3 for the Compton Police Department. These large differences cannot be accounted for by differences in crime patterns; they flow mainly from differences in police arrest policies.

When we look at what happens to these arrests, we find District Attorney rejection rates in cases involving possession of dangerous drugs varying from 26 percent for the Whittier Police Department, to 39 percent for the Pomona Police Department, to 59 percent for the Los Angeles Police Department, to 69 percent for the Long Beach Police Department. Even for robbery, rejection rates vary from 6 percent in Compton, to 30 percent in Long Beach, to 53 percent for the Los Angeles Sheriff's Office. These differences tend to support our conclusion that police departments vary greatly in their own screening of felony cases.

Complaint Filing by the District Attorney

The District Attorney refuses to file felony charges against over half of the defendants arrested by the police: 7 percent are released to other jurisdictions, 18 percent are referred for misdemeanor filing, and 28 percent are released without charge. This pattern varies widely across offenses because of differences in the seriousness of the offenses and in evidentiary requirements.

For some offenses, the District Attorney may recommend either felony or misdemeanor proceedings, depending on the facts. During 1971, when we were examining filing actions, the District Attorney attempted to modify practices in the Office by prescribing the circumstances under which these "alternative felonies" should be filed as misdemeanors. Included in this category are such offenses as possession of dangerous drugs and possession of marijuana. Rejection rates for these offenses changed from 34 to 53 percent for possessing dangerous drugs, and from 41 to 61 percent for possessing marijuana. While only 17 percent of the rejected dangerous-drug felony cases were referred for misdemeanor filing prior to the policy change, 51 percent were referred during the subsequent period.

Individual District Attorney Offices differ greatly both in their filing actions and in their responses to the filing policy change. Prior to the policy change, rejection rates for dangerous drugs varied from 25 percent in the Whittier Area Office and in Los Angeles Central, to 56 percent in the San Pedro Area Office. After the change, rejection rates jumped to 57 percent in the Central Office but remained fairly constant in San Pedro and Whittier. The Long Beach rejection rate jumped from 30 to 68 percent, while Pasadena's remained constant.

As expected, most of the increase in drug possession case referrals for misdemeanor filing can be attributed to the small amount of contraband involved, since the District Attorney's policy memo prescribed the amount of contraband below which such referrals should be made. However, many branches apparently began referring cases for misdemeanor filing which they had previously been rejecting outright.

Terminations in the Municipal Court

One indication of the quality of the District Attorney's complaint screening occurs in the Municipal Court, which must hold the defendant to answer in Superior Court if the case is to continue as a felony. At this point 13 percent of the felony cases filed are dismissed and 6 percent are reduced to misdemeanors. With the change in filing policy discussed above, we might expect to see some reduction in the fraction of felony cases that are reduced to misdemeanors in the lower court, but, in fact, all Branches showed a substantial increase.

When we look at dismissals in the lower court, we find an inexplicable increase after the filing policy change. In all Branches, the dismissal rate after the change was equal to or greater than the prior rate. For dangerous drugs cases, the dismissal rate varied from 2 percent in Long Beach to 34 percent in Central. For grand theft, auto, the rate varied from 0 in Santa Monica and Pomona, to 16 percent in Pasadena. The lack of uniformity in termination rates among Branches most likely reflects differences in the thoroughness of their complaint screening.

Superior Court Dispositions

Out of the 33,000 defendants arraigned in the Los Angeles Superior Court during 1970, 13 percent were dismissed, 45 percent pleaded guilty, 31 percent were SOT, and 11 percent went to trial; one-third of the trials were before a jury. A further refinement of dismissal rates shows that 4.8 percent of the cases are diverted from the system because the defendant is unavailable for prosecution or the case is to be combined with another; 3 percent are dismissed on a §995 PC motion (to set aside the information) by the defense; 1.3 percent are dismissed on a §1538.5 PC motion (to suppress illegally obtained evidence); and 3.9 percent are dismissed "in the interests of justice."

Conviction rates for 1970 were 81 percent for SOT, 62 percent for court trials, and 69 percent for jury trials. Overall, 81 percent of the defendants were convicted.

Figures for 1971 show a reduced number of dismissals, as well as fewer SOTs. Guilty pleas rose to 55 percent.

As in all other matters, the pattern of disposition varies considerably across offenses:

- The dismissal rate for marijuana possession is 20 percent, compared to 10 percent for burglary and 9 percent for robbery.
- Robbery cases go to a jury trial 10 percent of the time, compared to 1 or 2 percent for most drug offenses.
- Jury conviction rates vary from 35 percent for forgery to 86 percent for sale of narcotics.

The prior record of the defendant can have a considerable effect on the disposition of his case. Defendants with extensive prior records tend to have a smaller chance for dismissal, a greater chance of having a jury trial, and a higher probability of conviction, regardless of procedure.

Across branches there is also considerable variation in how cases are handled. For all felony dispositions in 1970, the following differences are observed:

- The average dismissal rate varies from 20 percent in Pasadena to 9 percent in Long Beach.
- Torrance disposes of 56 percent of its caseload by SOT, compared to 12 percent in Pasadena.
- The percentage of cases that actually go to trial varies from 6 percent in Van Nuys to 14 percent in Long Beach.

- Jury conviction rates vary from 63 percent in Central to 83 percent in Long Beach.
- The overall conviction rate varies from 74 percent in Pasadena to 89 percent in Long Beach.

Some of these differences, such as those among dismissal rates, reflect differences in policy among Branches. Others, such as the high use of SOT in Torrance, are the result of historical practices among a group of judges.

Sentencing

In order to investigate how sentencing is affected by a number of factors, we have used two measures of sentencing severity—felony sentence rate and prison rate. The felony sentence rate is simply the percentage of a specified group of convicted defendants who receive felony sentences. The prison rate is the percentage who receive a state prison sentence. A felony sentence need not involve prison, but a prison sentence is always a felony sentence.

Across offenses, the felony sentence rate varies from 20 percent for possession of marijuana to 75 percent for robbery or possession of narcotics. The prison rate varies from less than 1 percent for possession of marijuana or dangerous drugs to 6 percent for burglary and 26 percent for robbery.

In accordance with law and sensible practice, defendants who have more extensive prior records consistently receive more severe sentences than those who do not. The felony sentence rate for burglary defendants with major prior records is 52 percent compared to 28 percent for defendants with no prior records.

Across all categories of offense and prior record, defendants who plead guilty or SOT are sentenced more leniently than defendants who are convicted by trial. Defendants convicted in jury trials are sentenced much more harshly than any others. This finding supports the generally accepted theory that the court system extracts a greater price from defendants who refuse to cooperate.

Looking across Branches we find the same disparities in sentencing that we found in dispositions. Both felony sentence rates and prison rates in Long Beach are often twice the rates in some of the more lenient Branches.

This disparity in sentencing is also found among judges in any given district. In the Central District, the felony sentence rate for possession of dangerous drugs varies among judges from 8 to 54 percent; in Torrance, it varies from 17 to 48 percent. In the Central District, the prison rate for robbery varies among judges from 7 to 57 percent.

This wide variation in outcomes among different courts and judges should be cause for concern. It implies that justice is an uneven affair in which the disposition of the defendant depends greatly on who handles his case. And it suggests that defense attorneys have compelling incentives to maneuver their cases before the more lenient judges in order to secure a more favorable outcome.

Models of Prosecutorial Behavior

The following table attempts to summarize qualitatively the Branch Office differences in felony disposition. In an attempt to determine to what degree these

BRANCH OFFICE VARIATIONS IN FELONY DISPOSITIONS: A QUALITATIVE SUMMARY[a]

Disposition Measures	Branch Office							
	L.A. (central)	Long Beach	Santa Monica	Van Nuys	Torrance	Norwalk	Pomona	Pasadena
D.A. felony rejection rate	Avg	L	VH	VH	Avg	(b)	VL	Avg
Termination rates in Municipal Court:								
Dismissal rate	VH	VL	Avg	Avg	L	(b)	Avg	VL
Reduction to misdemeanor rate	VL	VL	H	VH	VL	(b)	VH	Avg
Superior Court Dismissal rate								
Interests of justice	H	L	H	L	L	VL	Avg	VH
§995 PC (insufficient evidence)	Avg	VL	Avg	Avg	Avg	L	H	VH
§1538.5 PC (unlawful search and seizure)	Avg	Avg	Avg	VL	VH	L	H	H
Method of disposition rate								
SOT	Avg	L	L	VL	VH	H	L	VL
Plea of guilty	L	H	H	VH	VL	H	H	H
Court trial	H	H	L	VL	H	VL	Avg	VH
Jury trial	H	VH	L	L	VL	L	VL	Avg
Conviction rate								
SOT	L	VH	L	L	H	H	L	VL
Court	Avg	VH	VL	H	L	H	L	Avg
Jury	VL	VH	VH	H	H	H	H	Avg
Overall (includes guilty plea)	L	VH	Avg	H	Avg	VH	Avg	VL
Sentencing								
Felony sentence rate	Avg	VH	L	L	Avg	H	Avg	Avg
Prison sentence rate	Avg	VH	Avg	Avg	Avg	Avg	Avg	H

NOTE: VH = very high, H = high, Avg = average, L = low, VL = very low.

[a] District Attorney felony complaint rejection rates, and dismissal and reduction rates in Municipal Court, are for the period from January to May 1971; Superior Court dispositions (dismissal rates, conviction rates, method of disposition rates, and sentencing severity rates) are for calendar year 1970. Entries are for several felony offense categories or for all felonies taken together.

[b] Not applicable because the Norwalk Branch does not file felony complaints or conduct preliminary hearings in Municipal Court.

differences reflect different underlying patterns or models of police, prosecutorial, and judicial decisionmaking, we can hypothesize two *polar* prosecutorial models: the *Rigorous Model* and the *Laissez-Faire Model.* The Rigorous Model represents an independent, "tough," closely managed prosecutorial office whose management style, procedures, and philosophy are characterized as follows:

- Close management supervision over complaint issuance, preliminary hearings, plea bargaining, and trials.
- Well-articulated (formal or informal), strict filing standards and guidelines.
- Resistance to police pressure to file marginal cases.
- Discouragement of complaint deputy-shopping by police officers who seek to secure complaints.
- Positive efforts to influence and affect police arrest and charging standards and to upgrade the quality of police investigations.
- A strong preference for adversary proceedings (court and jury trials) over bargaining (pleas and SOT), especially if caseload per deputy is not excessive.
- Little influence by the courts over prosecutorial procedures and personnel assignments to individual courts.
- Positive efforts to make the prosecutor's views known at probation and sentencing hearings.

In terms of outcome measures, the Rigorous Model implies the following: (1) moderate to low complaint rejection rates if the quality of police investigation is high and if police arrest and charging standards are similar to those of the prosecutor (and high rejection rates if police investigation quality is low and arrest standards are different); (2) low termination rates in Municipal Court and low dismissal rates in Superior Court because complaint filing standards are high; (3) above-average court and jury trial rates; (4) above-average plea rates; (5) high conviction rates, especially for jury and court trials; and (6) more severe sentencing because of prosecutorial participation in probation and sentencing hearings, although sentencing outcomes are mainly products of judicial and Probation Department decisions.

The Laissez-Faire Model essentially embodies the opposite characteristics and would tend to exhibit opposite outcome measures.

The Long Beach Branch's management style and statistical outcome measures fit the Rigorous Model quite well. The management style and outcome statistics of other Branch Offices are less consistent with either of the two polar models. In some cases, management style may be more consistent with one model, while outcome measures may be more consistent with the other model. In the Pasadena Branch, for example, management style is more consistent with the Laissez-Faire Model: relatively permissive filing standards, scant influence over police arrests and investigatory standards, no resistance to deputy-shopping by the police, and considerable control by the court over the Deputy District Attorney personnel assignments in the court.

The Pasadena outcome statistics, however, are mixed: average rejection rates; low to average termination rates in Municipal Court; high dismissal rates in Superior Court; above-average rate of adversary proceedings; above-average plea rate but very low SOT rate; very low overall conviction rate but above average sentencing severity.

From the table it appears that outcome statistics for the Norwalk Branch are fairly consistent with the Rigorous Model—high conviction rates, low dismissal rates in Superior Court, and average or above-average sentencing severity. The management style, however, is not consistent with the Rigorous Model: loose control and supervision and no strong willingness to engage in adversary proceedings are characteristic of that Office. (Because the Norwalk Branch does not file complaints, but merely prosecutes felony complaints filed in other Area Offices, filing standards and policies toward police are not relevant in this case.)

In the Torrance Branch, management style is more consistent with the Rigorous Model (close supervision, moderately strict filing standards, and discouragement of deputy-shopping, but there is little influence over police charging standards and no strong willingness to engage in adversary proceedings). The statistical outcome measures, on the other hand, are mixed, as the reader may observe from the table.

*   *   *   *   *

In summary, there are large disparities within Los Angeles County in the exercise of prosecutorial discretion and in the disposition of adult felony defendants. These differences may be only partially "explained" by appealing to different prosecutorial management styles. But the large differences themselves should be cause for concern on the part of police chiefs, the District Attorney, and the judiciary, because they mean that justice is not meted out evenhandedly in the county.

I. INTRODUCTION

Members of the legal community, as well as the general public, feel a growing concern over the functioning of our criminal justice system. Some of this concern has been created by reports from special study groups and the news media, depicting deplorable conditions and practices existing in many of our courts and correctional institutions. Some has resulted from unresolved conflict between the deterrence, punishment, and rehabilitation functions of the system. And some has come from distressing statistics showing widespread failure of criminal justice agencies to make significant reductions in crime. The pattern perceived is that most offenders are not arrested, most arrestees are never prosecuted, most convictions are accomplished by accepting guilty pleas to lesser offenses, and most defendants who are sentenced to correctional institutions return to criminal behavior soon after they are released.

Public respect for criminal justice institutions is often reduced by the contact that citizens have with them as complainants, witnesses, jurors, or defendants. Expecting to find careful, deliberative proceedings, they are often confronted by a mass-production process, with each official spending only a short time on any one case, with the defendant or victims as perplexed bystanders, and with decisions based on expediency.

Many problems in contemporary criminal justice proceedings result directly from the massive size of criminal justice agencies and the large number of cases they must deal with. The size of the system creates serious problems for administrators as well as for the general public in ensuring fair and consistent treatment for all defendants. Elected officials, in particular, have difficulty introducing policy changes and then ensuring that these policies are carried out.

RESEARCH OBJECTIVES

The District Attorney of Los Angeles County asked The Rand Corporation to study management and decision practices within his Office in order to suggest potential improvements. During the exploratory phases of the project, we elected to concentrate on the prosecution of adult criminal defendants whose cases originate with a police arrest, because this function constitutes the major workload of the Office and was the most amenable to analysis within the terms of our grant. Al-

1

though our focus excludes the investigation and prosecution activities associated with child support, juvenile offenses, organized and white collar crime, as well as the appellate functions of the Office, we do not understate the importance of these activities.

Our research concerned both the internal operations of the District Attorney's Office and its relationship with other criminal justice agencies, primarily the police and the courts. Our objectives were (1) to demonstrate the value of analysis as an ongoing activity to inform policymakers about how the system is functioning and (2) to describe how the Los Angeles system operates at the present time.

As our work progressed we calculated a number of statistical performance measures such as rejection rates, dismissal rates, and jury conviction rates, which we used to indicate areas for exploration in our interviews. Many attorneys we contacted showed little interest in such statistical data, usually offering one of the following arguments against its value:

- No two cases are really alike; therefore, any performance measure that results from averaging a number of cases, no matter how similar they may appear, may neglect some essential differences.
- Data from two different offices or agencies can never be meaningfully compared because differences in definition or recording procedure almost always make the two sets of data incompatible.
- Even if the data are reliable, they cannot be usefully interpreted because no statistical standard for a "good" prosecutor's office exists.

Because this report is aimed at many readers who may share similar views, we address these arguments now.

First, we concede that many factors affecting the outcome of any particular case are somewhat beyond the prosecution's control: the defendant's characteristics, his past record, the specific nature of the offense, the quality of the evidence, the methods by which it was procured, the defense attorney, the jury composition, and the judge's temperament and philosophies. In comparing the performance of two different offices we would like to be sure that we are comparing them only on cases with similar characteristics. Yet, when we attempt to select a sample of cases that hold all these factors constant, we find that many such elements are not recorded for each case, and if they are, the resulting sample sizes are so small that the results lack statistical reliability.

The analysis of prosecution data does require careful statistical treatment to eliminate spurious biases while retaining adequate sample sizes. When the data have been carefully treated and do show some clear difference in outcome between two offices or two procedures, one can discount these differences on the grounds that they are attributable to the normal variations between cases only if he has shown that they are not caused by differences in the average population of cases handled by the two offices.

The argument that the rules for collecting data vary between agencies is sufficiently true that a major portion of any comparative study must be spent resolving these differences, as we have done in this study. We were fortunate to obtain raw data from the California Bureau of Criminal Statistics (BCS), which probably has the most consistent set of data on Superior Court dispositions in the nation. However, due to a limited data processing capability within the BCS, these data are usually not available on a timely basis for agency officials, nor are they published in a form that would allow others to make many of the comparisons we made. Until greater attention is given to developing standard definitions for various measures and to ensuring accurate data collection, meaningful statistical analyses will be hampered.

Most Deputy District Attorneys we talked with preferred to evaluate other deputies on the basis of their apparent professional competence: how they handle a witness, what questions they ask before filing, how they perform in court. Yet the prosecution process, as it operates in a large office such as Los Angeles, is made up of many such individual tasks. Judging an office solely by how well each task is performed, rather than by looking for some objective measure of output or performance, appears to result in highly subjective evaluations colored by the priority that the evaluator places on certain tasks.

This is not to argue that by itself a set of statistics kept over some extended period *will* tell the whole story. Changes in policy or procedure within other agencies can affect almost every D.A. activity. Rather, statistical performance data of the type developed here[1] should be used to look for causes of inconsistencies both within the office being studied and within the agencies that office deals with. These data will be much more likely to signal gradual changes in activity, such as a loosening of filing standards, than will periodic observation of individual deputy performance. In short, although qualitative and statistical evaluations both have their own shortcomings, using both is likely to provide more insight than either alone.

In describing how the criminal justice process currently works in Los Angeles, our second objective, we aim at two sets of readers. First are the policymakers within that system. Because they are all aware of how the system is supposed to work and what the official policies are, our intent is to focus on practices that deviate considerably from the norm. Here we are especially sensitive to policy issues over which the District Attorney can exercise some control. Our second audience is the criminal justice research community, which has lacked access to the type of comparative empirical data provided by the eight Districts of the Los Angeles Superior Court.

Throughout this report our objective is to describe things as they are. When the data suggest several hypotheses, we examine each to the best of our ability. Although in a few instances we have made value judgments, we have largely refrained from judging how things should be or from attempting to decide which of various policies in force in different offices is best. These tasks will require considerable dialogue among many members of the legal and political community. This report could be one impetus to such a dialogue.

The report is organized as follows. Section II describes the Los Angeles County criminal justice system for those readers unfamiliar with it. Section III discusses the basic pattern of dispositions countywide, including relationships among method of disposition, defendant's prior record, and sentence severity. Section IV discusses some background sources of variation in the treatment of defendants, such as race, type of defense counsel, and pretrial custody status. Section V examines the complaint issuance process in the District Attorney's Office and the termination process in Municipal Court.

---

[1] Appendix B discusses in greater depth the uses of statistical measures of prosecution effectiveness.

Sections VI and VII examine disparities among Branch Offices of the District Attorney. Section VI discusses departures from uniformity in office management styles, procedures, and workload. Section VII discusses in detail the pattern of dispositions across Branches, from police arrest to sentencing, and attempts to explicate the relationships among various statistical outcome measures and the factors controllable by the police, the District Attorney, and the courts. Finally, Section VIII summarizes the findings and recommendations.

RESEARCH APPROACH

Our final research strategy was determined after an initial survey of the District Attorney's Office. We decided to concentrate on the routine prosecution of felony defendants, both because that activity is the largest in the Office and because it was susceptible to empirical analysis through various data sources.

During our initial survey we became aware of many policy differences between individual offices. We resolved to document as many of the major differences as we could and then look for the effects of these policy differences in the empirical analysis. This type of exploratory analysis provides the basis for this report.

Our primary source of data[2] was the California Bureau of Criminal Statistics Superior Court Disposition File,[3] which contains a record for every defendant appearing in Superior Court. The record contains data on the defendant, the handling of the case, and the ultimate disposition. We used 1970 and 1971 data on over 70,000 felony defendants. Secondary sources of data were the District Attorney's Felony Filing and Felony Rejection Indexes, which list all cases filed or rejected. For our study of rejections and dismissals, we used the case records themselves to extract additional data concerning these actions. We also used Judicial Council figures and information from various divisions of the Los Angeles County Clerk's Office. These data give a picture of how individuals are handled as they move through the system. When aggregated by Office, they tend to reveal the actual practices of that Office.

To obtain a better account of the various factors that might influence Office performance, we conducted numerous interviews with senior personnel in each Office. The interviews solicited four types of information:

- The policies of the Office.
- The performance of the police agencies with which the Office deals.
- The conduct of the local judges.
- The nature of the local defendants, witnesses, and jurors.

These interviews provided insights into reasons why various performance measures differed among the Branch Offices.

Unlike most other studies of the prosecution process we have not dealt with problems of court delays because Los Angeles Superior Courts are not experiencing extensive backlogs. Granting of continuances—a stalling tactic in many other jurisdictions—does not appear to be a significant factor. Since neither court nor prosecu-

---

[2] Appendix A discusses our data sources in greater detail.

[3] These raw data were provided to us in the form of computer tapes.

tion administrators have to be overly concerned with reducing delays, we did not choose to consider this factor in our study.

PREVIOUS RESEARCH

Previous studies of the prosecution process have tended to provide either observer-based descriptions of how particular matters are handled or statistical descriptions of defendant flows.

Among those studies based primarily on observation, Kaplan (1965)[4] provides an inside view of prosecutorial discretion based on his own experiences in that capacity, and Newman (1966) looks at the plea bargaining process across several states. Miller (1969) discusses variations in charging practices between a number of jurisdictions. Grossman (1969) describes the exercise of discretion by the prosecutor in Canada. Graham and Letwin (1971) describe preliminary hearing procedures in Los Angeles. Each of these studies demonstrates that the prosecutor is allowed a broad range of discretion in performing his function; that the use of this discretion is difficult to monitor; and that there is considerable variation in how that discretion is exercised.

The empirical studies of defendant flows have been used to demonstrate the nature of the screening function performed in each step in the criminal justice process and the relatively small proportion of defendants who are ever convicted as originally charged. Subin (1966) provides such a picture of the courts in Washington, D.C., as does the President's Crime Commission (1967) for the nation as a whole. Oaks and Lehman (1966) describe the processing of indigent defendants in Cook County while Bing (1970) studies Lower Criminal Courts of Boston, and Jennings (1971), adult defendants in Manhattan Criminal Courts.

Perhaps the most elaborate flow model of criminal defendants is that developed by Blumstein and Larson (1969). By using empirical data to generate estimates of the branching probabilities along each link, and the resources required to perform each task, the model could be used to predict resource requirements, assuming various processing policies. Unfortunately, criminal justice agencies do not currently produce the type of data necessary to support such a model. For illustrative purposes Blumstein and Larson were forced to use a combination of estimates and aggregate data from different jurisdictions.

Our study differs from its predecessors in a number of aspects. It makes much greater use of statistical controls to eliminate biases in the measures considered. It focuses on variations in practice that are susceptible to policy control. Particularly novel is the exploration of the causes of variation in practice that can be attributed to organizational factors and policies *within* the criminal justice system of a single county—in this case, Los Angeles County.

---

[4] See Bibliography beginning on p.155.

II. THE LOS ANGELES COUNTY CRIMINAL JUSTICE SYSTEM

The first step in understanding the criminal justice process in any jurisdiction involves learning the basic steps and procedures used to deal with defendants and the characteristics of the agencies that carry them out. This section provides that basic information about the Los Angeles County system.

THE POLICE

There are more than forty arresting agencies in Los Angeles County that seek felony complaints from the District Attorney. At least eight of these departments average more than 1000 felony arrests per year. The two largest are the Los Angeles Police Department (LAPD) and the Los Angeles County Sheriff's Department (LASO) which made 52,435 and 23,338 adult felony arrests, respectively—or about three-fourths of the total of 101,899 for the county—in 1970. The LASO covers the unincorporated county areas and a number of contract cities.

County geography makes it necessary for both the LAPD and the Sheriff to operate from a number of decentralized divisions or substations that are largely contained in a single Judicial District. Thus the performance and practices of these major departments may vary considerably between D.A. Branches due to local management practices.

THE COURTS

The Municipal Courts and the Superior Court are two separate entities. Municipal Courts are local agencies defined by the County Charter, and the Superior Court is a County Department. For felonies, the Municipal Court handles the initial arraignment and preliminary hearing. The Superior Court handles pleas, motions, and trials. The Municipal Court of the Los Angeles Judicial District is by far the largest in the county, handling over half of the county's cases. Table 1 shows the felony filings in FY 1970-1971 for all of the Los Angeles Municipal Courts.

Table 1

FELONY FILINGS IN LOS ANGELES COUNTY
MUNICIPAL COURTS, FY 1970-1971

Judicial District	Total Filings
Alhambra	559
Antelope	314
Beverly Hills	1,095
Burbank	374
Citrus	1,859
Compton	2,834
Culver	230
Downey	1,306
East Los Angeles	1,787
El Monte	1,869
Glendale	667
Inglewood	1,726
Long Beach	2,256
Los Angeles	26,345
Los Cerritos	953
Newhall	245
Pasadena	1,428
Pomona	911
San Antonio	1,455
Santa Anita	487
Santa Monica	672
South Bay	2,290
South Gate	863
Whittier	1,288

SOURCE: Judicial Council of California, *Annual Report of the Administrative Office of the California Courts*, January 1972, p. 119.

The Los Angeles County Superior Court is staffed by approximately 134 judges sitting in the Hall of Justice and in seven Branch sites: Long Beach, Norwalk, Pasadena, Pomona, Santa Monica, Torrance, and Van Nuys. At any one time about sixty judges will be handling criminal matters, and about fifty do so exclusively.

THE DISTRICT ATTORNEY

The Los Angeles District Attorney's Office is the focal point of this study. The largest prosecutor's office in the country, it employs approximately 430 Deputy District Attorneys and covers the seven million residents of Los Angeles County. The District Attorney is an elected official with the power to fill by appointment only the top two positions in his Office. All other positions are subject to civil service control. Deputies generally enter the Office as Grade I or II and may gradually work their way up through Grades II, III, IV, and higher supervisory positions. The deputy in charge of each Branch Office is a Grade V, while the administrators in charge of the three major subdivisions of the Office carry the title of Director.

State law and the County Charter establish the District Attorney's duties and responsibilities. Specifically, he initiates and prosecutes all felony cases arising in the county, as well as misdemeanors arising in unincorporated county areas and in cities of the county that do not maintain a City Prosecutor. Table 2 shows the recent prosecutorial resources and caseloads the District Attorney is responsible for.

Table 2

TRENDS IN BUDGET, AUTHORIZED MANPOWER, AND CASELOAD
FOR THE LOS ANGELES COUNTY DISTRICT ATTORNEY,
1967-1971

Year	Budget ($ million)	No. of Deputy District Attorneys Authorized	Felonies Filed
1967-1968	7.95	253	30,381
1968-1969	9.56	280	37,942
1969-1970	12.61	409	44,455
1970-1971	15.79	430	48,216
Percent increase of 1970-1971 figures over 1967-1968	98.6	81.8	58.7

As shown in Fig. 1, the staff is organized both functionally and geographically to carry out its wide range of responsibilities. In this study we concentrate exclusively on the work of the Bureau of Branch and Area Operations and the Bureau of Central Operations, the two units whose sole responsibility is prosecuting adult criminal defendants whom the police present to them. These two Bureaus account for about 340 deputies or two-thirds of the Office's professional work force.

Central Operations, located in the Hall of Justice, prosecutes all felony cases arising in the Central Judicial District—more than one-third of the total Office caseload. To handle this large number of cases, deputies are divided into three specialized units: the Complaints Division—responsible for screening and preparing the formal complaint; the Preliminary Division—responsible for initial arraignments and preliminary hearings; and the Trials Division—responsible for all arraignments, motions, trials, and sentencing in the Superior Court.

The remainder of the county is serviced by seven Branch Offices, located adjacent to the Superior Court Branches, and fourteen Area Offices, located near Municipal Courts. The average staff for a Branch Office is twenty deputies; that for an Area Office is four.

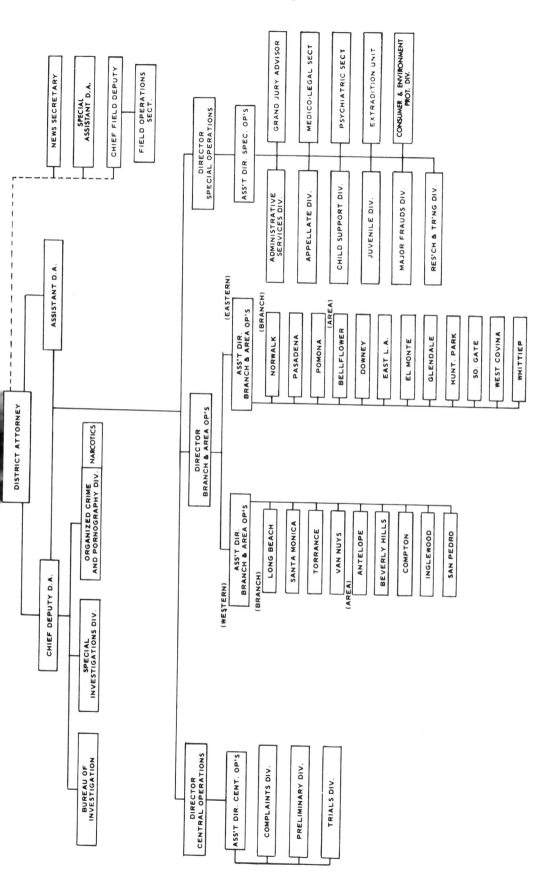

Fig. 1—Organization chart—Office of the District Attorney

Since Area Offices serve only Municipal Courts, they handle misdemeanor trials, felony arraignments, and preliminary hearings, but no felony trials. The deputy in charge, usually a Grade IV, handles most of the filing. A felony case originating in an Area Office is transferred to a Branch Office when the defendant is held to answer (i.e., bound over to the Superior Court). Table 3 shows the relationship between Branch and Area Offices, the police who send them cases, and the courts that they serve.

Table 3

RELATIONSHIP AMONG LOS ANGELES COUNTY DISTRICT ATTORNEY BRANCH AND AREA OFFICES, POLICING AGENCY, AND MUNICIPAL AND SUPERIOR COURTS IN PROCESSING CASES

District Attorney's Office	Areas Serviced	Surrounding Judicial District	Place of Felony Trial	Policing Agency	Misdemeanor Prosecuting Attorney	
					State Law	Local Ordinance
Antelope Valley	Lancaster	Antelope	Van Nuys	Sheriff:	DA[a]	DA
	Palmdale	Antelope	Van Nuys	Lancaster	DA	DA[b]
	Unincorporated	Antelope	Van Nuys	Lancaster	DA	DA
Bellflower	Artesia	Los Cerritos	Norwalk	Sheriff:	DA	DA[b]
	Bellflower	Los Cerritos	Norwalk	Lakewood	DA	DA[b]
	Cerritos	Los Cerritos	Norwalk	Lakewood	DA	DA[b]
	Hawaiian Gardens	Los Cerritos	Norwalk	Lakewood	DA	DA[b]
	Lakewood	Los Cerritos	Norwalk	Lakewood	DA	DA[b]
	Unincorporated	Los Cerritos	Norwalk	Lakewood	DA	DA
Beverly Hills	Beverly Hills	Beverly Hills	Santa Monica	Beverly Hills PD	DA	CA[c]
	Sunset Strip	Beverly Hills	Santa Monica	Sheriff:	DA	DA
	West Hollywood	Beverly Hills	Santa Monica	West Hollywood	DA	DA
Compton	Compton	Compton	Los Angeles	Compton PD	DA	CA
	Lynwood	Compton	Los Angeles	Lynwood PD	DA	CA
	Paramount	Compton	Los Angeles	Sheriff:	DA	DA[b]
	Carson	Compton	Los Angeles	Firestone	DA	DA[b]
	Unincorporated	Compton	Los Angeles	Lakewood	DA	DA
Downey	Downey	Downey	Norwalk	Downey PD	DA	DA[b]
	La Mirada	Downey	Norwalk	Sheriff:	DA	DA[b]
	Norwalk	Downey	Norwalk	Norwalk	DA	DA[b]
	Unincorporated	Downey	Norwalk	Norwalk	DA	DA
East Los Angeles	Montebello	East Los Angeles	Norwalk	Montebello PD	DA	DA[b]
	Commerce	East Los Angeles	Norwalk	Sheriff:	DA	DA[b]
	Unincorporated	East Los Angeles	Norwalk	East Los Angeles	DA	DA
El Monte	El Monte	El Monte	Pomona	El Monte PD	DA	DA[b]
	South El Monte	El Monte	Pomona	Sheriff:	DA	DA[b]
	Rosemead	El Monte	Pasadena	Temple City	DA	DA[b]
	Unincorporated	El Monte	Pomona	Temple City	DA	DA[b]
	La Puente	El Monte	Pomona	Industry	DA	DA[b]
Glendale	Glendale	Glendale	Los Angeles	Glendale PD	DA	CA
	Burbank	Burbank	Los Angeles	Burbank PD	CA&DA[d]	CA
	Unincorporated	Glendale	Los Angeles	Sheriff: Montrose	DA	DA
Huntington Park	Huntington Park	San Antonio	Norwalk	Huntington Park PD	DA	DA[b]
	Bell	San Antonio	Norwalk	Bell PD	DA	DA[b]
	Maywood	San Antonio	Norwalk	Maywood PD	DA	DA[b]
	Vernon	San Antonio	Norwalk	Vernon PD	DA	CA
	Cudahy	San Antonio	Norwalk	Sheriff:	DA	DA[b]
	Unincorporated	San Antonio	Norwalk	Firestone	DA	DA
	Bell Gardens	San Antonio	Norwalk	East Los Angeles	DA	DA[b]
Inglewood	Inglewood	Inglewood	Torrance	Inglewood PD	CA	CA
	El Segundo	Inglewood	Torrance	El Segundo PD	DA	DA[b]
	Hawthorne	Inglewood	Torrance	Hawthorne PD	CA	CA
	Unincorporated	Inglewood	Torrance	Sheriff: Lennox	DA	DA

NOTE: See footnotes on p. 12.

Table 3--Continued

District Attorney's Office	Areas Serviced	Surrounding Judicial District	Place of Felony Trial	Policing Agency	Misdemeanor Prosecuting Attorney State Law	Misdemeanor Prosecuting Attorney Local Ordinance
Long Beach[e]	Long Beach	Long Beach	Long Beach	Long Beach PD	CA	CA
	Signal Hill	Long Beach	Long Beach	Signal Hill PD	DA	DA[b]
	Avalon	Catalina	Long Beach	Sheriff: Lennox	DA	DA[b]
Newhall	Newhall	Newhall	Van Nuys	L.A. Sheriff	CA	DA
	Saugus	Newhall	Van Nuys	Valencia	CA	DA
	Valencia	Newhall	Van Nuys	Valencia	CA	DA
	Placerita	Newhall	Van Nuys	Valencia	CA	DA
	Unincorporated	Newhall	Van Nuys	Valencia	CA	DA
Norwalk[e]	Bellflower	Bellflower	Norwalk	Los Angeles SO		
	Bell Gardens	Bellflower	Norwalk	Los Angeles SO		
	Downey	Downey	Norwalk	Downey PD		
	East Los Angeles	East Los Angeles	Norwalk	Los Angeles SO		
	Huntington Park	Huntington Park	Norwalk	Huntington Park PD		
	South Gate	South Gate	Norwalk	South Gate PD		
	Whittier	Whittier	Norwalk	Whittier PD		
Pasadena[e]	Pasadena	Pasadena	Pasadena	Pasadena PD	CA	CA
	Alhambra	Alhambra	Pasadena	Alhambra PD	CA	CA
	Arcadia	Santa Anita	Pasadena	Arcadia PD	DA	CA
	Monrovia	Santa Anita	Pasadena	Monrovia PD	DA	CA[b]
	Monterey Park	Alhambra	Pasadena	Monterey Park PD	DA	DA[b]
	San Gabriel	Alhambra	Pasadena	San Gabriel PD	DA	CA
	San Marino	Pasadena	Pasadena	San Marino PD	DA	CA
	Sierra Madre	Pasadena	Pasadena	Sierra Madre PD	DA	CA
	South Pasadena	Pasadena	Pasadena	South Pasadena PD	DA	CA[b]
	Duarte	Santa Anita	Pasadena	Sheriff: Temple City	DA	DA[b]
	Bradbury	Santa Anita	Pasadena	Temple City	DA	DA[b]
	Temple City	Alhambra	Pasadena	Temple City	DA	DA[b]
	Unincorporated	Alhambra	Pasadena	Temple City	DA	DA
	Altadena	Pasadena	Pasadena	Altadena	DA	DA
	Unincorporated	Pasadena	Pasadena	Altadena	DA	DA
Pomona[e]	Pomona	Pomona	Pomona	Pomona PD	DA	CA[b]
	Claremont	Pomona	Pomona	Claremont PD	DA	DA[b]
	La Verne	Pomona	Pomona	La Verne PD	DA	CA[b]
	San Dimas	Pomona	Pomona	Sheriff: San Dimas	DA	DA[b]
	Walnut	Pomona	Pomona	Industry	DA	DA[b]
	Unincorporated	Pomona	Pomona	Industry & San Dimas	DA	DA
San Pedro	San Pedro	Los Angeles	Long Beach	Los Angeles PD	CA	CA
	Wilmington	Los Angeles	Long Beach	Los Angeles PD	CA	CA
Santa Monica[e]	Santa Monica	Santa Monica	Santa Monica	Santa Monica PD	CA	CA
	West Los Angeles	Los Angeles	Santa Monica	Los Angeles PD	CA	CA
	Culver City	Culver City	Santa Monica	Culver City PD	CA	DA
	Unincorporated	Malibu	Santa Monica	Sheriff: Malibu	DA	DA
	Unincorporated	Culver City	Santa Monica	Lennox	DA	DA

NOTE: See footnotes on p. 12.

Table 3--Continued

District Attorney's Office	Areas Serviced	Surrounding Judicial District	Place of Felony Trial	Policing Agency	Misdemeanor Prosecuting Attorney	
					State Law	Local Ordinance
South Gate	South Gate	South Gate	Norwalk	South Gate PD	DA	DA[b]
	Unincorporated	South Gate	Norwalk	Sheriff: Firestone	DA	DA
Torrance[e]	Redondo Beach	South Bay	Torrance	Redondo Beach PD	CA	CA
	Hermosa Beach	South Bay	Torrance	Hermosa Beach PD	CA	CA
	Manhattan Beach	South Bay	Torrance	Manhattan Beach PD	DA	DA
	Torrance	South Bay	Torrance	Torrance PD	CA	CA[b]
	Gardena	South Bay	Torrance	Gardena PD	DA	DA[b]
	Palos Verdes	South Bay	Torrance	Palos Verdes PD	DA	DA[b]
	S.W. Los Angeles	Los Angeles	Torrance	Los Angeles PD	CA	CA[b]
	Lawndale	South Bay	Torrance	Sheriff:	DA	DA[b]
	Rolling Hills	South Bay	Torrance	Lennox	DA	DA[b]
	Rolling Hills Estates	South Bay	Torrance	Lennox	DA	DA[b]
	Lomita	South Bay	Torrance	Lennox	DA	DA[b]
	Unincorporated	South Bay	Torrance	Lennox	DA	DA
Van Nuys[e]	Los Angeles	Los Angeles	Van Nuys	Los Angeles PD	CA	CA
	San Fernando	Los Angeles	Van Nuys	San Fernando PD	DA	CA
	Hidden Hills	Calabasas	Van Nuys	Sheriff:	DA	DA
	Unincorporated	Calabasas	Van Nuys	Malibu	DA	DA
	Unincorporated	Newhall	Van Nuys	Newhall	DA	DA
West Covina	West Covina	Citrus	Pomona	West Covina PD	DA	DA[b]
	Covina	Citrus	Pomona	Covina PD	DA	DA[b]
	Baldwin Park	Citrus	Pomona	Baldwin Park PD	DA	DA[b]
	Irwindale	Citrus	Pomona	Irwindale PD	DA	DA[b]
	Azusa	Citrus	Pomona	Azusa PD	DA	DA[b]
	Glendora	Citrus	Pomona	Glendora PD	DA	DA[b]
	Industry	Citrus	Pomona	Sheriff:	DA	DA[b]
	Unincorporated	Citrus	Pomona	Industry	DA	DA
Whittier	Whittier	Whittier	Norwalk	Whittier PD	DA	DA[b]
	Santa Fe Springs	Whittier	Norwalk	Sheriff:	DA	DA[b]
	Pico Rivera	Whittier	Norwalk	Norwalk	DA	DA[b]
	Unincorporated	Whittier	Norwalk	Norwalk	DA	DA

SOURCE: *District Attorney's Operation Manual.*

[a]District Attorney.

[b]Contract city. For a fee, the District Attorney performs city prosecution services.

[c]City Attorney.

[d]Burbank City Attorney prosecutes state code violations if the investigating agency is the Burbank Police Department; all misdemeanor offenses arising in Burbank and not investigated by the Burbank Police Department are prosecuted by the District Attorney.

[e]Branch Office. Note that the Norwalk Branch Office does not service a Municipal Court.

Assignment of deputies within each Branch Office varies according to the scheduling of local courts and the philosophy of the Branch Head Deputy. The normal pattern is to assign three deputies to each Superior Court Department, with the remainder of the staff assigned to complaints or Municipal Court duties. Table 4 shows a typical assignment pattern for a 20-man Branch serving four Superior Court Departments, three Municipal Courts, and one Juvenile Court. These assignments are usually for an extended time (several months) but are subject to day-to-day changes according to court workload.

In the normal pattern, the senior Grade IV in each Superior Court Department is designated the Calendar Deputy. After reviewing each case, he assigns it to one

Table 4

TYPICAL BRANCH ASSIGNMENT OF DEPUTY DISTRICT ATTORNEYS
IN LOS ANGELES COUNTY

Assignment	Grade II	Grade III	Grade IV	Grade V	Total
Superior Courts (4)	4	4	4		12
Municipal Courts (3)	2	1			3
Juvenile Courts (1)		1			1
Complaints and Administration		1		1	2
Other		1	1		2
Total	6	8	5	1	20

of his junior deputies. The senior deputy approves any plea bargaining that goes on in his court, and the junior man handles simpler trials and motions. When a deputy is not engaged in trial, he is preparing cases or possibly handling complaints.

The most junior men handle Municipal Court cases. The first matter a deputy is allowed to handle on his own is a routine misdemeanor case or a preliminary hearing. In several Branches, Municipal Court deputies must travel to different Municipal Courts which operate on alternate days of the week.

Complaints are normally handled by experienced deputies—at least a Grade III for any nonroutine case. Deputies assigned as "Other" may be on leave or on some special assignment.

The Director of Branch and Area Operations and his two deputies supervise the Branch and Area Offices. The Director issues policy directives, assigns manpower, and reviews their paperwork on a sample basis. A police department that wants to contest the rejection of a specific case by a Branch appeals to the Director. Certain actions with political overtones by the Branch Head require the Director's approval, such as a decision to affidavit a judge.

The Area Office is not subservient to the Branch Office that must eventually handle its cases.[1] This is an important point since many deputies feel that the most crucial decision affecting the performance of the Office is the decision to file. In several Branches more than half of their felony cases are initially filed by an independent Area Office, and one Branch actually files none of its own. The effect of these relationships is examined later when the Branches are compared.

---

[1] Although in some cases the deputy in charge of an Area Office will seek the advice and counsel of the Branch Head Deputy in matters involving complaint issuance.

THE SYSTEM AT WORK

Arrest

The entry point into the system for most defendants is by police arrest. For adults, there is a critical distinction between a misdemeanor and a felony arrest. For a misdemeanor, there is an automatic schedule for bailing out at the police station, and the maximum penalty that can be imposed is a 1-year jail sentence. For a felony, the defendant must usually appear before a magistrate to make bail or gain release on his own recognizance (OR).[2] This may often be as long as 48 hours (or more on weekends) after the arrest, so the defendant may spend up to several days in the police lockup, even if no charges are subsequently filed.

Many local police, including the LAPD, do not release felony defendants or reduce charges without attempting to seek a review and evaluation of the case from the District Attorney. The usual justification for this policy is that it removes any incentive the defendant might have for bribing the police to let him off. It also eliminates any chance to charge the police with bias in exercising this discretion.

After a felony arrest is made and the arrestee is booked, any subsequent investigation is usually handled by the department's detectives. Although the level of investigation depends partly on the seriousness of the crime and the complexity of the case, for many cases it is quite cursory. At a minimum, the police look for a local rap sheet and request a prior record from the Bureau of Criminal Identification and Investigation (CII) in Sacramento.

One aspect of police performance in Los Angeles County can be examined by comparing its departments with those in other parts of the state regarding the ratio of felony to misdemeanor arrests and the percentage of felony arrests resulting in a felony charge. Table 5 presents the ratio of adult felony to adult misdemeanor arrests for all crimes and for two specific categories—assault and drug violations. For assault, the ratio of felonies to misdemeanors in Los Angeles County is twice that for the rest of the state, while for drugs it is slightly less. The total figures show that Los Angeles arrests are more likely to be for felonies than are arrests elsewhere in the state.

Table 6 gives the outcomes of one type of interaction between the District Attorney and the police: the percentage of felony arrests that the District Attorney selects to prosecute. In Los Angeles County almost twice as many defendants are released without charges as compared with the rest of the state. Less than half are charged with felonies, whereas 71 percent are so charged elsewhere in California.

Four propositions may be advanced to explain the disparities shown in Tables 5 and 6:

1. The pattern of criminal behavior is more serious in Los Angeles County, with a higher proportion of felony behavior.

---

[2] Release on his own recognizance permits the arrestee to be released on his promise to return for trial without having to post bond. Although the judge has the right to release a person summarily on OR, this is rarely done. Rather, the request is routed through the OR Division of the Superior Court. Although the Division is attached to the Superior Court, it handles all OR investigation in both Municipal and Superior Courts. In 1971, 12,826 OR investigations were carried out, resulting in 3218 recommendations for OR. The Court actually granted OR release in 2848 cases.

Table 5

RATIO OF ADULT FELONY ARRESTS TO ADULT MISDEMEANOR
ARRESTS IN CALIFORNIA BY AREA, 1970

Area	All Crimes	Assault	Drug Law Violations
Los Angeles County	0.35	1.67	4.42
State less Los Angeles County	0.25	0.79	4.72
San Francisco Bay Area	0.29	0.80	6.64

SOURCE: California Bureau of Criminal Statistics, *Crime and Arrests*, 1970.

Table 6

ADULT FELONY ARRESTS AND DISPOSITIONS IN CALIFORNIA BY AREA, 1970

Area	Total Felony Arrests	Released Without Charge (%)	Rerouted to Another Jurisdiction (%)	Charged with Misdemeanor (%)	Charged with Felony (%)
Los Angeles County	101,899	28	7	18	47
State less Los Angeles County	112,937	16	3	10	71
San Francisco Bay Area	45,304	20	1	11	68

SOURCE: California Bureau of Criminal Statistics, *Crime and Arrests*, 1970.

2. The Los Angeles police concentrate more of their efforts on felony behavior.
3. The Los Angeles police tend to overcharge defendants when they make arrests.
4. The Los Angeles District Attorney tends to be stricter in screening cases than District Attorneys elsewhere in the state.

We know of no other evidence to support Proposition 1. Some support for Proposition 2 may be found in the fact that the LAPD and LASO account for most of the felony arrests and both departments maintain specialized divisions such as Bunco, Major Frauds, Major Crimes, etc., which deliberately focus on sophisticated felony behavior. Also, we have interviewed a number of personnel who would support Propositions 3 and 4. The accuracy of these propositions is considered later in this report.

Issuing a Complaint

Within 48 hours after an arrest (excluding weekends and holidays), the police must obtain a complaint from the District Attorney or release the defendant. In most cases the police officer seeking an evaluation of a case will either be the investigating officer assigned to the case or a "legman" who performs this function for most cases. The former practice prevails primarily in serious cases, while the latter applies to more routine cases.

When the police officer arrives at the appropriate Branch or Area Office (it is always the same one for a given police unit), the receptionist tells him which deputy to see. Sometimes this assignment is based on a prearranged pattern; sometimes she consults with a senior deputy; and sometimes the police can seek out a specific individual. At this point an assignment card is filled out for each case.

The deputy handling the case reviews the police reports, the defendant's prior record, and talks with the officer about the case. If he thinks the case should be filed, he fills out a complaint information form, from which a clerk typist then prepares a formal complaint and the case proceeds. If he thinks the case should not be filed, he can reject it outright. He may also refer the case to the City Attorney for misdemeanor filing consideration. A third option is to suggest that some further investigation be performed and the case be resubmitted for filing. As shown in Table 6, only 47 percent of the felony arrests made by the police in Los Angeles County were subsequently filed as felonies by the District Attorney in 1970.

Most felony arrests are rejected for lack of evidence connecting the defendant to the crime or indicating that a crime was committed, or because the offense is not serious enough to warrant felony prosecution, even though it meets the statutory definition of a felony. Some offenses can be defined as either misdemeanors or felonies at the D.A.'s discretion.[3] In this class of cases, even if the District Attorney files a felony, the Municipal Court judge can reduce it to a misdemeanor at the preliminary hearing.[4] With drugs, for example, the D.A.'s Office has established that a defendant must have in his possession at least 11 pills or 6 marijuana cigarettes; otherwise only misdemeanor charges are filed if the defendant has not been previously convicted of an offense subject to a felony sentence.[5]

When he is deciding whether or not to file a case, the deputy is not applying some absolute standard. Most deputies would agree that careful consideration should be given to the chances of winning the case in court. Of course, some deputies may worry that someone may complain if they do not file.

The police also attempt to anticipate the District Attorney, much as he in turn anticipates the judge. It is not unusual to hear an investigating officer tell a deputy when he first walks in that he has two good cases and four rejects—cases he knows from experience the deputy will not file. The present record systems, however, do not allow us to infer what percentage of the rejects the police recognized as such before they were submitted. Estimates by deputies range from 10 to 30 percent.

The complaint filing function is one of the most sensitive because it sets a case on one of two largely irreversible tracks. If the complaint is rejected and the police

[3] California Penal Code §17(b)(4).

[4] California Penal Code §17(b)(5).

[5] Special Directive from John Howard, Chief Deputy District Attorney, Los Angeles County, May 10, 1971.

agree, it is lost from the system without much chance for review or second thoughts. Once it is filed, the system exerts considerable pressure to proceed.

In determining exactly how to carry out the complaint process in a given office, the District Attorney has a number of policy choices to make:

1. *What filing standards will be employed to screen cases?* In Los Angeles these standards are moderate to tough. In New York almost every case is filed as the police prefer. In establishing strict standards, the District Attorney often must be prepared to withstand the resistance of the police, both investigators and management, who may not take kindly to having a sudden rise in rejections. Strict District Attorneys will screen not only the offense but also the completeness of investigation so that the case may be rejected if some specific steps have not been completed. The arguments for screening are that it saves court resources and that, in poor cases, a rejection means that the defendant will avoid the stigma of a felony complaint and all that it implies. The argument against it is that probably some guilty defendants go free.

2. *Should the filing standards be public?* Although publication of the standards would reduce the chance of arbitrary application, it might also reduce whatever deterrent effect the law still retains.

3. *Who can file and what training does he receive?* In Los Angeles the practice is to allow only experienced trial deputies to file, expecting them to pick up the knowledge they need through an apprenticeship in other parts of the Office. The U.S. Attorney's Office in Washington, D.C. (which handles the District's criminal cases) also attempts to screen cases, but has a much higher turnover of deputies and therefore less time for on-the-job training. In that Office a detailed filing manual provides a checklist of factors to be considered for each type of case.

4. *Is deputy-shopping by the police to be allowed or discouraged?* Invariably the police find some deputies more competent or more sympathetic than others in their willingness to file and, when possible, they will seek them out. Where permitted, this practice lessens conflict between individual police and deputies, but tends to circumvent strict filing policy.

5. *What degree of review or quality control will be exercised over filing deputies?* As professionals making decisions within their competence, deputies might consider it demeaning to have their work checked or questioned. Because the discretion inherent in the filing decision gives the deputy so much power, the operative question is the degree of review of this discretion. In Los Angeles the degree of review varies among Offices, but in no Office are all filings reviewed routinely by management.

These questions have received considerable attention in the professional literature and are a source of continual debate within the Office. In Sections VI and VII of this report we examine the range of policies currently in use and attempt to determine their effect.

Municipal Court Arraignment and Preliminary Hearing

The defendant's first encounter with the court system comes at his initial arraignment in Municipal Court where he is brought before a magistrate who informs him both of the charges against him and of his Constitutional rights. At this hearing the defendant can apply for bail (usually set according to a fixed schedule) or for release on his own recognizance. Although the defendant is not required to plead either way at this time, and it is unusual for him to do so, he can enter a plea. If he pleads guilty, he is certified directly to the Superior Court for sentencing. If he enters a not guilty plea, a date is set, usually one week hence, for a preliminary hearing.

In Los Angeles, the People are usually represented by the investigating officer, not the District Attorney, at the initial arraignment because the merits of the case are not tested at this point. A deputy is usually available on short notice to act for the People should the need arise, and he would be present for the most serious cases to argue his position on bail or OR.

Of 38,526 cases filed in the Los Angeles Superior Courts in 1970 (includes multiple filings for a single defendant), 98.9 percent were by information resulting from a preliminary hearing, 0.5 percent by indictment, and 0.6 percent by certification. Grand Jury indictment is reserved almost exclusively for cases involving public officials, cases where the District Attorney desires to protect the anonymity of some witnesses until the trial, or cases of unusual complexity (major trials).

Before preliminary hearings commence, the deputy assigned to the court prepares his cases by reading the complaint deputy's worksheet and the police reports. If he has any questions he may interview the investigating officer or a civilian witness. When the magistrate calls the case, the deputy tries to present a fairly complete case, usually calling all of his important witnesses. The defense usually exercises its right to cross-examine witnesses, but normally does not call any witnesses of its own at this time. When the testimony is complete, the defense usually moves for dismissal on the grounds that the prosecution has failed its burden of proof. Each side then presents oral arguments on this point. The average hearing lasts less than 30 minutes.

The Municipal Court preliminary hearing can result in the following forms of dispositions: the defendant can be bound over to the Superior Court for felony prosecution; the judge can declare or reduce the charge to a misdemeanor; the case can be referred to Juvenile Court; or the charges can be dismissed.

In comparing the results of Los Angeles preliminary hearings with those of the rest of the state, we are faced with several sets of irreconcilable data as shown in Table 7. Column 1 shows the number of adult felony arrests that resulted in felony complaints for 1970. Column 2 shows the number of cases terminated in Municipal Court, and Column 3 shows the number of cases dismissed. The differences between Columns 2 and 3 represent felony cases reduced to a misdemeanor. Columns 4 and 5 show the resulting Municipal Court termination rates and dismissal rates. These data show that the rest of the state settles a much higher percentage of cases in Municipal Court than Los Angeles County does, primarily by reducing them to misdemeanors.

Unfortunately, the accuracy of these termination data is doubtful because there is no sure way to cross-check them, and random checks by the BCS turn up many

Table 7

DISPOSITIONS OF ADULT FELONY CASES IN CALIFORNIA MUNICIPAL COURTS BY AREA, 1970

Area	(1) Adult Arrests Resulting in Felony Complaints[a]	(2) Cases Terminated in Lower Courts[b]	(3) Lower Court Dismissals[b]	(4) Cases Terminated in Lower Court (%)	(5) Cases Dismissed in Lower Court (%)	(6) Felony Filings in Superior Court[c]	(7) Implied Terminations[d]	(8) Implied Terminations (%)
State	129,046	40,393	16,101	31	12	71,850	57,196	44
Los Angeles County	48,216	9,927	6,875	21	14	38,526[e]	9,690	20
State less Los Angeles County	80,830	30,466	9,226	38	11	33,324	47,506	59

[a]California Bureau of Criminal Statistics, *Crime and Arrests*, 1970.

[b]California Bureau of Criminal Statistics, *Felony Defendants Disposed of in California Courts*, 1970, Table 6.

[c]Ibid., Table 8.

[d]Total obtained by subtracting Column 6 from Column 1.

[e]Includes multiple filings for a single defendant.

missing cases. An alternative procedure for estimating the terminations is to subtract the Superior Court filings (Column 6 in Table 7) from the arrests that resulted in felony complaints (Column 1). These differences are shown in Column 7. The estimate derived for Los Angeles County (9690) is quite close to the 9927 figure stated by the BCS, but for the rest of the state there is a discrepancy of some 17,000 cases or 50 percent more than the BCS figures shown in Column 6.[6] Column 8 shows the resulting percentage of cases terminated using this alternative basis.

On either basis, it appears that defendants in other parts of the state are much more likely to have their cases reduced to a misdemeanor than are defendants in Los Angeles. (Unfortunately, deficiencies in the Municipal Court records system make it impossible to reliably determine what happens to cases after they are reduced.) One or more of the following three hypotheses may explain these findings:

1. The Los Angeles District Attorney does a better job of initially screening cases than do other District Attorneys in the state.
2. Los Angeles Municipal Court judges or Deputy District Attorneys are more reluctant to accept misdemeanor pleas for felonies or to reduce felonies under §17(b)(4) or §17(b)(5) of the Penal Code.
3. Defendants in Los Angeles see less benefit in reducing their charges to a misdemeanor than do defendants elsewhere in the state.

Even if a case is dismissed, the defendant is not necessarily acquitted. Although there is no appellate review of the magisterial decision holding the evidence insufficient (Graham and Letwin, p. 700), the District Attorney can apply to the Grand Jury or refile with the court on different or identical charges (§999 PC) in hopes of more success. The District Attorney can also refer the case to the City Attorney for misdemeanor prosecution. The District Attorney reviews each case dismissed as a matter of Office policy. If the deputy perceives an error or negligence on the part of the court, a vital missing witness, a technicality, or any other factor that he thinks could be remedied by a rehearing, the District Attorney may refile the case. In Los Angeles County, however, most dismissals are not refiled.

Superior Court Arraignment and Trial

Criminal cases that reach the Los Angeles Superior Court are calendared in one of two ways. In some Branches, a master calendar department handles all arraignments and then assigns cases to other departments for trial. In other Superior Court Branches, the Municipal Courts are instructed to assign cases to each department on a rotating basis so that each Superior Court department handles its own calendar from arraignment through sentencing.

At his arraignment the defendant is assigned counsel if he has none; has the "information" read to him (usually waived); is given a copy of the preliminary transcript; is again advised of his rights (only in some courts); and is asked to plead (this step is usually continued so the defendant can consult with his counsel). Efforts to arrange a plea at this stage range from routine conferences in chambers to refusal by some judges to discuss the matter with attorneys outside of open court.

---

[6] If one man is arrested three times in one year, it will add three to the total arrest figures, but if the charges are combined by the court into a single case, it will show up as a single disposition.

After his arraignment, the defendant can move for the suppression of illegally obtained evidence under §1538.5 PC, or make a variety of other, less common motions. Each motion is normally set for a separate hearing. If all motions fail, and the defendant continues to plead not guilty, a trial date is set.

Cases reaching the Superior Court can be terminated with one of four types of disposition: *diversion, dismissal, guilty,* or *acquittal.*

Diverted cases are those removed from Court jurisdiction without any decision on their merits. This may occur if a particular case is combined with another, or referred to the Juvenile Court, or if the defendant is released into the custody of another jurisdiction where he has committed a more serious offense. In 1970, 4.8 percent of the Superior Court cases were terminated in this fashion.

A *dismissal* can occur at any point in the proceedings, although it most usually occurs before trial. The BCS records distinguish dismissals in three separate categories: §995 PC (insufficient evidence), §1538.5 PC (suppression of illegally obtained evidence), and "in the interests of justice." In 1970, 8.2 percent of the cases were dismissed, with 3.0 percent for §995, 1.3 percent for §1538.5, and 3.9 percent in the interests of justice.

Guilty or *acquittal dispositions* are obtained by four different methods: *plea, submission on the transcript of the preliminary hearing (SOT), court trial,* or *jury trial.* The BCS distinguishes pleas of guilty at the time of arraignment from changes in plea from not guilty to guilty later in the proceedings. The 1970 data show 45.2 percent of the defendants eventually plead guilty, with 8.7 percent pleading guilty at arraignment[7] and 36.5 percent switching their pleas later on. This proportion of changes in plea most probably reflects a strategy of exhausting all options short of trial (motions, continuances) and finally pleading guilty if the case is not dismissed.

When *plea bargaining* occurs, the senior deputy in court usually handles it. The consideration a defendant receives in return for his guilty plea might include any of the following prosecutorial agreements:

- To drop some counts.
- To accept a plea to a lesser included offense.
- To not file prior convictions.
- To omit allegedly habitual offender pleadings.
- To recommend against consecutive sentences.
- To recommend against prison time.
- To recommend commitment to the California Rehabilitation Center.
- To refrain from opposing probation at the probation and sentencing (P&S) hearing.

The *SOT submissions* are very much like a plea in that the ultimate disposition of the judge is not often in doubt—81.0 percent of all SOT cases resulted in guilty findings by the judges in 1970. For this reason, the SOT is often called a slow plea (of guilty), and some courts require that the defendant be given all warnings and make all waivers he would make if he were going to plead.[8] In addition to such slow pleas, the SOT also covers the following:

---

[7] Includes defendants who plead guilty to felony charges in Municipal Court.

[8] Some defense attorneys favor the use of an SOT because it allows them to briefly interrogate their client before the judge and bring out the client's good points which might mitigate the sentence.

- Slow plea bargains in which the District Attorney does not accept a guilty plea to a lesser offense, despite his knowing that the latter will be the judge's finding.
- Slow dismissal in which the judge states he will find the defendant not guilty on an SOT.

In the course of an SOT, additional evidence can be presented, but this is usually not the case. Some of the transcripts are so routine that the judge is able to conclude matters quickly. The SOT is a procedure somewhat unique to Los Angeles County, where it was used to settle 30.8 percent of the Superior Court cases in 1970. The comparable figure for the rest of the state was less than 3 percent.

Using the BCS estimates of SOTs, pleas, and total defendants (not including those diverted), we find that, in 1970, the total percentage of cases settled by either a plea or an SOT was 79.9 percent for Los Angeles County and 78.6 percent for the rest of the state. This suggests persuasively that the SOT is really a substitute for a guilty plea. The common reasoning holds that the motivation for going SOT is that the defendant does not have to make a potentially embarrassing confession in open court and thus can still protest his innocence, although he does not intend to contest the matter.

Another potential motivation can be found in the records of criminal appeals. Table 8 shows appeal rates and reversal rates for all crimes in California, by various methods of disposition for two 2-year periods, 1964-1965 and 1966-1967. Although figures for the two periods differ, mostly in reduced reversal rates, we see that SOT defendants are much more likely to appeal and to win a reversal than defendants who plead guilty. Therefore, the SOT can also be looked on as a means of preserving future options.

In Section III of this report, when we examine the relationship between the method of disposition and the final sentence, we show that SOT defendants consistently get slightly more lenient sentences than defendants who plead guilty in Los Angeles County. Under these circumstances, the usual question of why SOTs are so heavily used here seems somewhat unnecessary. The more logical question is why

Table 8

CRIMINAL APPEALS AND THEIR OUTCOMES IN CALIFORNIA SUPERIOR COURTS,
1964-1965 AND 1966-1967

Court Action	Plea of Guilty		SOT		Court Trial		Jury Trial	
	1964-65	1966-67	1964-65	1966-67	1964-65	1966-67	1964-65	1966-67
Total defendants convicted	44,158	47,647	6,152	10,323	4,455	4,142	3,905	4,571
Appeals as % of convicted	0.9	0.5	6.3	6.9	14.8	17.0	33.8	38.4
Reversals as % of appeals	3.7	5.8	13.8	6.8	15.4	7.6	18.1	8.1
Reversals as % of convicted	0.03	0.02	0.9	0.5	2.3	1.3	6.4	3.1

SOURCE: California Bureau of Criminal Statistics, *Criminal Appeals in California, 1964-1968.*

more defendants do not go SOT both in Los Angeles and in the rest of the state. Because we have been unable to examine the relationship between sentencing severity and disposition method for the rest of the state, we cannot answer this question.

Few cases ever actually go to *trial.* In 1970, 3.4 percent were tried before *juries* and 7.6 percent were tried before *judges.* By the time cases reach this point, the defendants have exhausted most of the legal maneuvers that could win a dismissal and they know the strength of the prosecutor's case. Therefore, many are reluctant to go through a trial if they expect to lose.

Table 9 compares the 1970 results of all jury and judge trials in Los Angeles County with the rest of the state. The figures show that defendants in Los Angeles are much more likely to choose a judge rather than a jury trial. In both Los Angeles and the rest of the state, the conviction rates before juries are higher than before judges. How much of this difference is due to the deliberation of judges and juries and how much is due to the nature of the cases they see, we cannot say at this time. One might expect that the cases going before a jury are stronger from the prosecution side and the defendant is attempting to increase his chances for a lucky acquittal. This approximately 10-percent higher conviction rate holds true for individual crime types as well as for the total caseload.

Table 9

RESULTS OF ALL TRIALS IN CALIFORNIA, 1970

Area	Ratio of Jury to Court Trials	Jury Conviction Rate	Judge Conviction Rate
Los Angeles County	0.45	0.70	0.62
State less Los Angeles County	3.22	0.80	0.73

A major study of American juries by Kalven and Zeisel (1966) found that judges tended to convict much more frequently (83 percent) than juries (67 percent) when they both heard the same cases. This basic pattern held for a wide variety of crimes. Further clarification of motives leading to the selection of a judge trial over a jury trial and the reasons for the higher jury conviction rate will require more detailed examination of individual cases and interviews with defendants and defense attorneys.

In summary, of cases adjudicated in 1970, 81.3 percent resulted in convictions in Los Angeles County and 87.8 percent resulted in convictions elsewhere in the state.

Probation and Sentencing Hearings

The final step in adjudication for the guilty defendant is a probation and sentencing hearing,[9] usually scheduled for 3 weeks after his guilt is determined. A probation and sentencing report is prepared to assist the judge. An Area Office of the Probation Department services each of the County's Municipal and Superior Courts. Whether the defendant is permitted to be at large or is held in custody during the interim is left to the judge's discretion. The defendant's bail status during the trial and the type of crime he was convicted of are determining factors in the decision.

The Probation Department estimates that each case requires about 6 to 8 hours of a deputy's time over this 3-week span. The county describes the investigation process as follows:

> An investigation always includes interviews with the defendant, his family, and others who can contribute to [an] understanding of the individual and of the circumstances of the offense. A complete record of arrests is obtained and records of law enforcement and other investigative or enforcement agencies are reviewed... The officer provides for the court his professional evaluation and analysis of the defendant, of the meaning and seriousness of the offense, and of the kind of treatment program which is required.[10]

The court can accept or reject the Probation Department recommendation as it sees fit. Table 10 shows the percentage of defendants investigated who were placed on probation, as identified by the Department of Probation recommendations. These data show that Los Angeles judges tend to behave the same as judges elsewhere in following the Probation Department's recommendations.

There are essentially seven different sentencing options from which the judge can choose for a given defendant, subject to the constraints of the Penal Code section covering the offense for which the defendant was convicted. These options are: death,[11] state prison, California Youth Authority (CYA), probation, jail, fine, or civil commitment. Some can be combined, e.g., probation and jail, or jail and a fine. The variety of sentences actually imposed also includes suspended sentences and a summary (or bench) probation that may let the defendant retain his liberty, with some restrictions, but allows the court to retain jurisdiction if he violates the terms of his probation.

Table 11 shows the distribution of sentences for defendants originally held to answer on felony charges in 1970. These data show that defendants in Los Angeles County are more likely to receive probation or county jail sentences, as opposed to state prison, than defendants in other parts of the state.

Convicted defendants can leave the Superior Court as either convicted felons or misdemeanants. Felonies where no alternative for state prison is prescribed may never be reduced. Felonies that do provide for alternative punishment may be reduced at the time of sentence or later. Such felonies are reduced routinely at the

---

[9] In many cases in which the guilty plea resulted from plea bargaining, this hearing is waived and sentence is pronounced immediately following the plea.

[10] County of Los Angeles Probation Department, *Information Series*, No. 5: *Adult Services*, revised, September 1971.

[11] This option, imposed on a defendant under §190 PC, has been found to be unconstitutional under the authority of *People v. Anderson*, 6 Cal.3d 628 (1972), and *Furman v. Georgia*, 408 U.S. 238 (1972).

Table 10

PERCENTAGE OF DEFENDANTS RECEIVING PROBATION
IN CALIFORNIA, 1970

Area	Percent Granted Probation by Court When –	
	Probation Recommended	Probation Not Recommended
Los Angeles County	97	43.0
State less Los Angeles County	96.2	45.8

SOURCE: California Bureau of Criminal Statistics, *Adult Probation*, 1970.

successful completion of probation. Table 12 shows the relationship between conviction level and sentence imposed for all defendants convicted in 1970. As in Table 11, defendants in Los Angeles County appear more likely to get lighter sentences (misdemeanor sentences) than elsewhere in the state.

The Judicial Council has suggested that this is not so much due to greater leniency on the part of Los Angeles judges as it is to deficiency of the screening processes.[12] In other words, the various stages of the arrest-complaint-preliminary hearing processes should act as filters; cases that are misdemeanors should be identified and prosecuted as such in the Municipal Courts and not be permitted to reach the Superior Court level. If this selective process does not operate efficiently, one would expect a larger percentage of misdemeanor-type crimes heard in the Superior Court and, concomitantly, a larger percentage of misdemeanor sentences handed down. The Judicial Council lays most of the blame for this Los Angeles situation on the bifurcated city and county District Attorney arrangement; it argues that complaints are filed as felonies if the cases have *any* elements of a felony.[13] While this factor cannot be entirely discounted, it must also be observed that a given arrest is more likely to be labeled a felony by the Los Angeles police, and the Los Angeles Municipal Courts are less likely to reduce a charge at the preliminary hearing. The Los Angeles District Attorney apparently rejects a much larger proportion of the offenses presented to him than do other District Attorneys in the state.

A final note of interest is the amount of time expended in the disposition of a case. The Bureau of Criminal Statistics has calculated time (in months) for the disposition of cases in the Superior Court from the time the case is filed with the court until the defendant is sentenced. These figures *exclude* (and are not calculated for) defendants who are acquitted or whose cases have been dismissed or diverted. Obviously these periods can vary as widely as the range for those convicted. Generally, however, the average conviction will be reached more quickly than the average

[12] Judicial Council of California, *Annual Report of the Administrative Office of the California Courts,* San Francisco, California, January 1971, pp. 123-124.
[13] Ibid.

Table 11

DISTRIBUTION OF SENTENCES FOR CONVICTED FELONS IN CALIFORNIA, 1970

(In percent)

Area	Total Felons Convicted	Criminal Commitment								Civil Commitment	
		Department of Corrections		Youth Authority	Probation			County Jail	Fine	CRC[a]	Mental Hygiene
		Death	Prison		Total	Straight	With County Jail				
Los Angeles County	25,642	0.02	5.97	3.19	69.99	49.34	20.65	14.79	3.12	2.61	0.31
State less Los Angeles County	24,308	0.05	14.30	4.34	65.28	27.14	38.14	9.56	0.77	5.07	0.67

SOURCE: California Bureau of Criminal Statistics, *Felony Defendants Disposed of in California Courts, 1970*.

[a]California Rehabilitation Center.

Table 12

CONVICTION LEVEL[a] FOR FELONY DEFENDANTS CONVICTED AND SENTENCED IN SUPERIOR COURTS OF CALIFORNIA, 1970

(In percent)

Area	Total Defendants Convicted	Felony as Charged		Lesser Felony		Misdemeanor	Total	
		Felony Sentence	Misdemeanor Sentence	Felony Sentence	Misdemeanor Sentence		Felony Sentences	Misdemeanor Sentences
Los Angeles County	25,642	31.24	41.27	9.29	9.12	9.07	40.53	59.46
State less Los Angeles County	24,308	59.25	16.32	13.70	3.19	7.54	72.95	27.05

SOURCE: California Bureau of Criminal Statistics, *Felony Defendants Disposed of in California Courts*, 1970.

[a]See Sec. III.

acquittal or dismissal because guilty pleas require a minimum amount of time. However, the 3-week probation investigation (obviously not needed for those not convicted) would extend the time span for those found guilty. These estimates also *exclude* the time spent during the Municipal Court portion of the prosecution. Given the various time constraints placed upon the process by the penal codes, one could estimate that Municipal Courts add another 5 to 6 weeks in processing defendants up to the Superior Court. This reflects only defendants who are bound over to the Superior Court. The Municipal Courts dispose of a certain percentage of cases (either the case is dismissed or handled as a misdemeanor); these cases obviously require much less disposition time. Table 13 displays disposition time.

An important factor to consider in attempting to measure the prosecutor's workload is the proportion of cases he settles by various means short of a full jury trial. Table 14 shows estimates, developed by the Administrative Office of the Los Angeles Superior Court, of the average time required to complete various Superior Court actions. From these figures we can infer that a bench trial takes two to three times longer in court than a plea or an SOT, whereas a jury trial is ten times as costly.

The approximate direct cost of operating a single Superior Courtroom, including the participation of Court, County Clerk, Sheriff, District Attorney, Public Defender, and Probation personnel, is $9.00 per minute. Using this unit cost, Table 15 obtains the approximate total cost of processing defendants by the major disposition routes.

THE SYSTEM COMPARED

The data in Table 16 allow us to compare the results of the criminal justice process in Los Angeles County with the rest of the state. The numbers are all probability estimates, derived from 1970 data, for the outcomes of the most essential steps in the process.

- Row 1 shows that in distinguishing between the severity of an offense in making an arrest, the Los Angeles police are more likely to arrest for a felony.
- Row 2 shows that the Los Angeles District Attorney rejects a much higher fraction of the offenses brought to him. As we showed earlier, most of these rejections are subsequently filed as misdemeanors.
- Row 3 shows a much greater likelihood that defendants charged with felonies by the District Attorney will be held to answer or bound over to the Superior Court in Los Angeles than elsewhere in the state.
- Row 4 shows a somewhat lower probability of conviction in the Los Angeles Superior Court than elsewhere in the state.
- Row 5 shows a much lower probability that convicted defendants in the Los Angeles Superior Court will receive a felony sentence.
- Rows 6 and 7 present cumulative probabilities obtained by multiplying the probabilities for the sequence of actions preceding them. The probability that a felony arrest will result in a felony sentence in Los Angeles is 50

Table 13

TIME REQUIRED TO DISPOSE OF FELONY DEFENDANTS IN CALIFORNIA
FROM FILING DATE TO SENTENCING DATE, 1970

Area	Total Defendants	Percentage of Cases Disposed of in—							Median Time (mo)
		Less Than 1 Month	1-9 Months	2-2.9 Months	3-5.9 Months	6-11.0 Months	12-24 Months	More Than 24 Months	
Los Angeles County	25,642	7.66	16.70	24.28	37.19	12.74	1.34	0.09	3.1
State less Los Angeles County	24,308	23.16	21.24	21.94	23.34	9.08	1.18	0.06	2.3

SOURCE: California Bureau of Criminal Statistics, *Felony Defendants Disposed of in California Courts*, 1970.

Table 14

AVERAGE TIME REQUIRED BY SUPERIOR COURT
TO COMPLETE VARIOUS ACTIONS

Superior Court Action	Ave. Time[a] (min)
Arraignment	2
§995 PC or §1538.5 PC hearing	51
Change of plea/dismissal	19
SOT	30
SOT with testimony	74
Pretrial hearing	6
Court trial	96
Jury trial	1000

SOURCE: Unpublished study by the Administrative Office of the Los Angeles Superior Court.

[a]One court day equals approximately 255 min or 4.25 hr.

Table 15

TIME REQUIRED AND COST TO COMPLETE ACTIONS FOR ALTERNATIVE
DISPOSITION METHODS IN SUPERIOR COURT

Method of Disposition	Arraign- ment (min)	§995 PC or §1538.5 PC (min)	Change of Plea (min)	SOT (min)	Court Trial (min)	Total Time (min)	Cost[a] ($)
Plea (change NG to G)	2	---	19	---	---	21	189
SOT	2	---	---	30	---	32	288
Court trial	2	51	---	---	96	149	1341

[a]Cost of disposition method = ($9/min) × total time required to process each step.

Table 16

PROBABILITY ESTIMATES FOR OUTCOMES OF CRITICAL STEPS
IN ADJUDICATION PROCESS[a]

	Probability Estimate	
Outcome	Los Angeles County	State Less Los Angeles County
1. Arrest will be a felony	0.62	0.57
2. Felony arrest will result in felony charge	0.47	0.71
3. Felony defendant will be held to answer or bound over to Superior Court	0.79	0.62
4. Felony case in Superior Court will result in conviction	0.81	0.88
5. Felony defendant will be given felony sentence upon conviction	0.41	0.73
6. Felony arrest will eventually result in felony sentence	0.12	0.28
7. Person charged with felony will receive felony sentence	0.26	0.40

[a]Derived from 1970 data.

percent less than in the rest of the state. The probability that a defendant charged with a felony by the District Attorney will receive a felony sentence in Los Angeles is one-third less than in the rest of the state.

Before commenting on these figures, the first question we should settle is the likely source of the variations. The BCS data[14] show that the proportion of the various crime categories making up the felony total is essentially the same across Los Angeles and the rest of the state, so the differences cannot be attributed to divergences in the proportion of offenses.

Another possible explanation for these disparate probability estimates could be differences in the characteristics of the population from which defendants, victims, witnesses, and juries are drawn. Since Los Angeles County is entirely urban, with a large minority population, we might expect the system to work differently in more rural areas with more homogeneous populations. Of the 113,000 California arrests in other than Los Angeles County during 1970, 72,000 were in Orange, San Diego, or one of the San Francisco Bay Area counties, which are also urban. Data from these other counties agree closely with the statewide averages when Los Angeles County is excluded. Therefore, the data cannot be discounted because of a rural bias.

[14] California Bureau of Criminal Statistics, *Crime and Arrests*, 1970, p. 21.

The only reasonable explanation is that the source of variation lies in the system itself: Things are done differently in Los Angeles County. We cannot say whether this variation is caused by one particular agency, because the statistics we have cited are affected by the behavior of several agencies. The data for Los Angeles seem to suggest that the policies of some agencies or decisionmakers conflict with others. In particular, the Superior Court seems to have a much more restricted definition of what behavior justifies felony treatment than any other agency. In a later discussion of variations in practice *within* Los Angeles County, we clarify this particular issue.

The summary data cited above should raise two policy questions about the performance of any criminal justice system:

1. What amount of coordination between criminal justice agencies is appropriate to prevent conflicting policies from rendering the system grossly inefficient or unfairly inconsistent?

2. What should the objectives of such coordination be? What are reasonable standards for performance? More specifically:

    *   How high must the rejection rate go before police judgment in making arrests is questioned?
    *   At what dismissal rate should the adequacy of D.A. screening be questioned?
    *   At what acquittal rate is the quality of D.A. case preparation open to question?
    *   At what rate of dismissal or reduction to misdemeanor in Superior Court does the quality of Municipal Court performance become questionable?
    *   At what difference in average sentences between pleas and trial does one conclude that the system is placing an unjust burden on defendants to plead?

III. THE BASIC PATTERN OF DISPOSITIONS IN LOS ANGELES COUNTY

In this section we examine the basic pattern of disposition for all types of crime, and the fundamental sources of variation in treatment that are common to any prosecutor's office: the nature of the offense, the defendant's prior record, and the method of adjudication selected by the defendant. Determining how these variables interact to affect the outcome of a case will help us measure the system's differentiation and equity performance. We expect to see defendants who are convicted of more serious or threatening offenses treated more harshly than those convicted of lesser crimes. We also expect to see defendants with extensive prior records treated more harshly than those with fewer criminal justice contacts, especially when the prior record and current offense indicate that the defendant is a serious threat to society. However, large differences in sentencing severity between bargained dispositions and jury trials are assumed to place an unfair burden on the defendant to plead guilty and thus escape the much more serious consequences of a trial.

We consider only those defendants who fall into one of the eight offense categories shown in Table 17, as determined by the offense the District Attorney charges them with. Each category is an aggregation of similar categories defined by the California Penal Code and California Health and Safety Code, grouped to form desirable sample sizes.

Our identification of defendants by *charged* offense rather than by arrested charge or by convicted offense may require some explanation. First, the policies of *one* single agency, the District Attorney, govern the charging of these defendants, whereas arrest or conviction charges result from actions by *numerous* independent police agencies or judges who may not be applying equivalent standards. Therefore, by using the charge specified by the District Attorney, we have the best chance of ensuring that two defendants, charged with the same type of offense, are indeed suspected of similar criminal activities.

A second reason for using the charged offense is that we wish to examine the effects of the criminal justice system on various types of cases. For many defendants, the convicted charge, reflecting the terms of the negotiated plea, bears little resemblance to the actual offense.

Table 17

OFFENSE CATEGORIES

Offense	BCS Code	California Code	
Assault	300	§664/187 PC[a]	Attempted murder
	310	§217 PC	Assault with intent to murder
	320	§245a PC	Assault with a deadly weapon
	330	§203 PC	Mayhem
	340	§245b PC	ADW on peace officer, with prior record
	341	§245b PC	ADW on peace officer
	342	§243(242) PC	Battery on peace officer
	343	§149 PC	Assault by officer
	344	§241 PC	Assault on peace officer
	345	§69 PC	Resisting executive officer
	346	§148 PC	Resisting police officer
Robbery	200	§211 PC	Robbery
Burglary	400	§459 PC	Burglary
Forgery	580	§470 PC	Forgery
		§472 PC	Possession of counterfeit seal
		§475 PC	Passing forged notes
		§475a PC	Possession of fraudulent checks
		§477 PC	Counterfeiting coins
		§480 PC	Possession of counterfeit plates
Possession of narcotics	801	§11500 HS[b]	Possession of narcotics
Possession of dangerous drugs	823	§11910 HS	Possession of dangerous drugs, with prior record
	825	§11910 HS	Possession of dangerous drugs
Possession of marijuana	810	§11530 HS	Possession of marijuana
	815	§11530 HS	Possession of marijuana, with prior record
		§11530.1 HS	Cultivating marijuana, with prior record
Sale of drugs or narcotics	802	§11501 HS	Selling narcotics
	803	§11500.5 HS	Possession of narcotics for sale
	811	§11531 HS	Selling marijuana
	812	§11530.5 HS	Possession of marijuana for sale
	820	§11913 HS	Sale of dangerous drugs to minors
	821	§11912 HS	Sale of dangerous drugs
	822	§11911 HS	Possession of dangerous drugs for sale,
	824	§11911 HS	Possession of dangerous drugs for sale, with prior record

[a]Penal Code.

[b]Health and Safety Code.

METHOD OF DISPOSITION

Within our method-of-disposition categories, we have included the various means by which the defendant can exit from the system, with or without adjudication, as well as the outcome of adjudication when it occurs. Table 18 defines these categories.

Table 19 shows the pattern of dispositions for all 1970 felony defendants arraigned in the Los Angeles Superior Court for our eight categories of offense. The conviction rates shown for a particular method of disposition are the percentage of defendants convicted of the total disposed of by that method.

Table 18

METHODS OF DISPOSITION

Type	Definition
Diverted	Cases diverted from the system for reasons other than merit, such as those combined with another case or those in which the defendant is turned over to another jurisdiction.
Dismissed (§995 PC)	Cases dismissed on the granting of §995 PC motion (to set aside the information or indictment) by the defense.
Dismissed (§1538.5 PC)	Cases dismissed on the granting of §1538.5 PC motion (illegally obtained evidence) by the defense.
Dismissed (Interests of Justice)	Cases dismissed for reasons other than those above.
SOT	Cases adjudicated by a judge on the basis of the preliminary hearing transcript, with or without additional testimony.
Jury trial	Cases adjudicated by a jury trial.
Court trial	Cases adjudicated by a judge or bench trial.
Plea (original)	Cases in which the defendant pleads guilty when he is first required to enter a plea.
Plea (change NG to G)	Cases in which the defendant changes an earlier plea of not guilty to guilty.

Table 19

DISPOSITION OF FELONY DEFENDANTS IN EIGHT OFFENSE CATEGORIES,
LOS ANGELES SUPERIOR COURT, 1970[a]

(In percent)

Number of Cases, Disposition, Conviction Rates	Offense							
	Assault	Robbery	Burglary	Forgery	Possession, Narcotics	Possession, Dangerous Drugs	Possession, Marijuana	Sale of Drugs/ Narcotics
Number of cases	1566	1736	4703	1561	709	6162	5042	2423
Disposition[b]								
Diverted	5.5	3.1	4.7	5.7	2.8	5.3	5.8	3.9
Dismissed (§995 PC)	1.8	1.5	2.1	1.1	3.1	2.7	5.5	3.2
Dismissed (§1538.5 PC)	0.1	0.1	0.3	0.1	2.8	2.3	3.7	1.7
Dismissed (Int of Jus)	5.0	4.2	2.6	1.7	7.2	3.4	5.1	4.1
SOT	29.1	22.9	29.7	25.0	31.0	32.9	33.2	37.3
Jury trial	7.0	10.1	3.7	1.7	2.8	1.2	1.3	4.2
Court trial	13.5	11.4	6.4	4.2	9.6	5.8	6.0	9.5
Plea (original)	1.7	3.7	9.0	15.8	4.5	11.2	9.8	3.5
Plea (change NG to G)	36.3	43.1	41.6	44.7	36.1	35.2	29.5	32.9
Conviction rates[c]								
SOT	81.8	86.7	87.8	81.5	80.0	80.7	73.1	90.5
Jury trial	53.2	72.6	69.7	35.2	85.0	76.0	50.0	86.1
Court trial	59.4	67.5	71.0	68.2	61.8	63.4	51.0	76.1
Overall[d]	77.8	84.2	87.9	90.4	75.9	81.9	71.5	84.1

[a]Based on data from California Bureau of Criminal Statistics, *Felony Defendants Disposed of in California Courts*, 1970.

[b]Percentage of all defendants charged with the indicated offense.

[c]Percentage of defendants convicted of total disposed of by each method.

[d]Excludes cases that were diverted.

From Table 19 the following observations can be made.

- There is less diversity in the disposition of various crime types than one might first expect. They all follow the same basic pattern.
- For six of the eight offense categories, more than 88 percent of the caseload is disposed of without recourse to trial.
- Drug offenses show a greater likelihood of dismissal, especially on a §995 PC or a §1538.5 PC motion.
- Drug offenses show a greater tendency to use SOT and a lower tendency to use jury trials than the other offenses do.
- The percentage of defendants choosing jury trials does not appear to be correlated with the differences between jury and court conviction rate for any particular offense.
- Assault and robbery cases are about twice as likely to go to trial as other offenses.

Table 20 shows the disposition pattern for the total felony caseload in 1970 and 1971, which leads to the following observations.

- The pattern of dispositions is relatively consistent between the years.
- Dismissals in two major categories, §995 PC and Interests of Justice, are down in 1971 while dismissals under §1538.5 are up.
- There is a large decrease in the use of SOT and an increase in pleas resulting in a higher overall conviction rate.
- There is a significant decrease in jury and court conviction rates, which may be accounted for by a smaller, and potentially harder to win, trial caseload.
- The jury conviction rate remained higher than the court conviction rate.

Sentencing Patterns

We consider two distinct aspects of the severity of a sentence. First is the nature and harshness of the penalty. The BCS data distinguish the following categories, in each of which the terms can still vary considerably:

Sentence

Death
Prison
California Youth Authority
Probation (supervised)
Probation and jail (supervised)
Summary· or court probation (nonsupervised)
   or probation and jail (nonsupervised)
Jail
Probation and jail
Fine
Indeterminate sentence as sexual
   psychopath
California Rehabilitation Center (§3051 W&I)

Table 20

SUPERIOR COURT DISPOSITION OF TOTAL FELONY
DEFENDANTS IN ALL OFFENSE CATEGORIES,
1970 AND 1971[a]

(In percent)

Number of Cases, Disposition, Conviction Rates	1970	1971
Number of cases	33,142	35,009
Disposition[b]		
Diverted	4.8	4.3
Dismissed (§995 PC)	3.0	2.5
Dismissed (§1538.5 PC)	1.3	1.7
Dismissed (Int of Jus)	3.9	2.3
SOT	30.8	25.0
Jury trial	3.4	2.9
Court trial	7.6	5.3
Plea (original)	8.7	16.2
Plea (change NG to G)	36.5	39.1
Conviction rates[c]		
SOT	81.0	79.0
Jury trial	69.8	64.9
Court trial	62.2	55.0
Overall[d]	81.2	83.4

[a]Based on data from California Bureau of Criminal Statistics, *Felony Defendants Disposed of in California Courts*, 1970 and 1971.

[b]Percentage of all defendants charged.

[c]Percentage of defendants convicted of total disposed of by each method.

[d]Includes pleas.

The second aspect is the stigma attached to the defendant after release. Here the distinction is primarily between felons and misdemeanants. A felon loses certain rights and is usually subject to more severe treatment if convicted again. The BCS data use the following breakdown.

Level of Conviction

Felony as charged, felony sentence
Felony as charged, misdemeanor sentence
Felony as charged, §17 PC
Lesser felony, felony sentence
Lesser felony, misdemeanor sentence
Lesser felony, §17 PC
Lesser misdemeanor

Our measures of these two aspects of sentencing are (1) *prison rate* —the percentage of defendants sentenced to prison, and (2) *felony sentence rate*—the percentage of defendants receiving a felony sentence.[1] Our justification is as follows:

- To make many comparisons, we require single-dimensional measures.
- The two categories selected, prison and felony sentence rates, have a clear meaning unto themselves.
- Our sample sizes are large enough that these measures will detect significant differences for the crimes of interest.

Another important variable affecting the severity of a given defendant's sentence (in addition to current offense) is his prior criminal record. In fact, some offenses carry mandatory increases in the minimum allowable sentence if the defendant is a repeater. To describe the defendant's prior record, we used aggregated categories shown in Table 21 based on BCS definitions.

Table 22 shows the prison rates and felony sentence rates for the eight types of offenses (Table 17) and four categories of prior record (Table 21). Correlation between the two measures appears quite good, i.e., an offense and prior record category ranking high on one measure also ranks high on the other. Other observations supported by these data are as follows:

- Robbery defendants are treated much more harshly than are defendants charged with other crimes. The robbery prison rate is two-and-a-half times that for the next most severe offense.
- The burglary and sale sentences seem somewhat lenient in comparison with other offenses.
- The miniscule prison rates for possession of marijuana or dangerous drugs may indicate that more of these offenses might be prosecuted in Municipal Court.
- Sentencing severity consistently increases with the degree of prior record.
- Gradients tend to be lower for more serious offenses (robbery, sale) and higher for offenses representing less threat to the general public, indicating a judicial willingness to be very lenient with inexperienced defendants and more severe with defendants with long prior records, no matter what their *current* offense is.

Effect of Prior Record on the Method of Disposition

Table 23 shows the method of disposition for all 1970 felony defendants as a function of their prior criminal record. The pattern observable in these aggregate figures also holds true for individual crime categories as well. We can make the following observations:

- As severity of prior record increases, the likelihood of diversion or dismissal decreases.

---

[1] The BCS uses another measure of sentencing outcome called the *sentence weight,* a weighted index for each case that combines into a single number the amount of fines, length of probation, and jail and prison terms. Early in this project a number of D.A. officials observed that they felt such weights are artificial, so we eliminated the sentence weight as a sentencing measure. Apparently, most administrators prefer to see the raw data themselves and apply their own weighting.

Table 21

CATEGORIES OF PRIOR RECORD

Record	Description
None/No prior record	1. No prior arrests. 2. One or two arrests only--no disposition given.
Minor prior record	1. Three to seven arrests--no dispositions or one or two convictions of less than 90 days jail or probation of less than 2 years. 2. Eight or more arrests--no dispositions or three, four, or five convictions of less than 90 days or probation of less than 2 years. 3. Six or more convictions of less than 90 days or probation of less than 2 years.
Major prior record	1. One or two convictions of 90 days in jail or more or probation of 2 years or more. 2. Three or more convictions of 90 days in jail or more or probation of 2 years or more.
Prior prison record	1. One prison commitment, and no more than one major prior record. 2. One prison commitment, with two or more major prior records. 3. Two prison commitments. 4. Three or more prison commitments.

- As severity of prior record increases, there is some increase in the likelihood of a jury or court trial.
- As severity of prior record increases, the probability of being convicted in a trial of any type increases significantly, as does the overall conviction rate. (Jury trials of defendants with no prior record are a peculiar exception to this rule.)
- As severity of prior record increases, those with more severe records are more likely to plead not guilty at their arraignment and then change their plea at a later time, although the guilty plea rates are similar for each prior category.

In summary, defendants with more serious prior records are less likely to be released without adjudication, more likely to contest their guilt in a trial, and more likely to be convicted.

Table 22

PRISON AND FELONY SENTENCE RATES FOR FELONY DEFENDANTS BY PRIOR RECORD AND
CHARGED OFFENSE, LOS ANGELES SUPERIOR COURT, 1970[a]

(In percent)

Offense	Prior Record				Total[b]	Gradient[c]
	None	Minor	Major	Prison		
A. Percentage of Defendants Receiving Prison Sentences						
Assault	3	5	11	13	7	0.77
Robbery	10	15	27	50	26	0.80
Burglary	1	2	6	15	6	0.93
Forgery	1	2	7	21	7	0.99
Possession, narcotics	1	5	6	17	8	0.94
Possession, dangerous drugs	0	.1	1	2	1	1.00
Possession, marijuana	0	0	1	2	.3	1.00
Sale of drugs/narcotics	2	4	13	28	9	0.93
B. Percentage of Defendants Receiving Felony Sentences						
Assault	25	35	38	37	33	0.32
Robbery	67	73	78	80	75	0.16
Burglary	28	38	52	54	44	0.48
Forgery	33	42	54	62	47	0.47
Possession, narcotics	55	79	82	79	75	0.30
Possession, dangerous drugs	19	26	39	36	26	0.47
Possession, marijuana	14	19	31	31	20	0.55
Sale of drugs/narcotics	65	74	81	83	74	0.22

[a]Based on data from California Bureau of Criminal Statistics, *Felony Defendants Disposed of in California Courts*, 1970.

[b]Average rate across all defendants regardless of prior record.

[c]Measure of difference between sentencing severity for defendants with no prior record and those who have been to prison. Calculated by dividing the difference in rates between "Prison" and "None" by the "Prison" rate.

RELATIONSHIP BETWEEN DISPOSITION METHOD AND SENTENCE

The final relationship of interest in this section is that between method of disposition and sentence severity. To examine this relationship, we selected six groups of defendants in the 1970 records who had the following charged offense and prior record combinations:

Charged Offense	Prior Record
Robbery	Major
Burglary	Major'
Burglary	Prison
Sale of Narcotics or Drugs	None
Sale of Narcotics or Drugs	Major
Possession of Dangerous Drugs	Major

Table 23

METHOD OF DISPOSITION OF ALL FELONY DEFENDANTS AS A FUNCTION
OF PRIOR CRIMINAL RECORD, LOS ANGELES SUPERIOR COURT, 1970[a]

(In percent)

Disposition and Conviction Rates	Prior Record				Total[b]
	None	Minor	Major	Prison	
Disposition[c]					
Diverted	5.90	4.60	3.70	3.03	4.15
Dismissed (Int of Jus)	3.85	3.81	3.35	3.37	3.56
Dismissed (§1538.5 PC)	1.68	1.15	1.13	1.05	1.20
Dismissed (§995 PC)	3.59	2.85	2.43	2.19	2.68
SOT	31.06	31.01	32.17	28.89	31.07
Jury trial	2.86	3.11	3.53	5.89	3.74
Court trial	6.63	7.82	8.33	8.19	7.92
Plea (original)	9.97	8.87	7.50	6.53	8.08
Plea (change NG to G)	34.48	36.78	37.85	40.84	37.60
Conviction rate[d]					
SOT	77.03	81.82	83.81	86.16	82.67
Jury trial	75.49	64.85	71.64	79.20	72.52
Court trial	58.47	64.73	63.49	71.65	64.81
Overall	79.08	81.86	83.21	85.39	82.64

[a]Based on data from California Bureau of Criminal Statistics, *Felony Defendants Disposed of in California Courts*, 1970.

[b]Average rate across all defendants regardless of prior record.

[c]Percentage of all defendants in each prior record category.

[d]Percentage of defendants convicted of total disposed of by each method.

For each group we computed the sentencing severity by disposition method using two different measures: percentage receiving felony sentences and percentage sentenced to prison. These results are shown in Table 24.

Defendants who plead guilty at arraignment often receive harsher sentences than those who prolong their cases by originally pleading not guilty and then changing their plea or submitting their case on the transcript. In fact, their sentences are about equal in severity to those received by defendants demanding a court trial. One explanation for this phenomenon may be that defendants who plead guilty the first time a plea can be entered suffer from poorer legal representation than other defendants. Another may be that defendants are more likely to plead guilty sooner when the evidence against them is very strong. Sentence severity increases from change of pleas and SOTs to court trials and then to jury trials, however, which fits well within the accepted view that the system extracts some greater price from those who force it to go through all of the steps of formal adjudication. Yet, the

Table 24

RELATIONSHIP OF DISPOSITION, PRIOR RECORD, AND SEVERITY OF
SENTENCE, LOS ANGELES SUPERIOR COURT, 1970 SAMPLE[a]

(In percent)

Charged Offense	Prior Record	Method of Disposition				
		Original Guilty Plea	Not Guilty to Guilty Plea	SOT	Jury Trial	Court Trial
A. Percentage of Defendants Receiving Felony Sentences						
Robbery	Major	75	78	70	97	90
Burglary	Major	60	53	44	61	55
Burglary	Prison	71	54	46	77	54
Sale of drugs/ narcotics	None	68	7C	58	82	67
Sale of drugs/ narcotics	Major	86	82	78	93	85
Possession, dangerous drugs	Major	39	41	34	65	39
B. Percentage of Defendants Receiving Prison Sentences						
Robbery	Major	25	25	17	67	31
Burglary	Major	8	5	6	15	13
Burglary	Prison	26	9	10	62	20
Sale of drugs/ narcotics	None	0	1	1	32	0
Sale of drugs/ narcotics	Major	0	12	13	19	23
Possession, dangerous drugs	Major	2	1	1	0	0

[a]Based on data from California Bureau of Criminal Statistics, *Felony Defendants Disposed of in California Courts*, 1970.

slightly more lenient sentences attributed to SOT as compared to pleas is still surprising, since the SOT does not always reflect a deal and is usually more time-consuming than a straight plea. As will be shown in Section VII, to some extent this apparent tendency toward leniency on the SOT may be attributed to more lenient sentencing practices in Offices that use SOT most heavily, notably Central Los Angeles and Torrance.

Because our comparison of 1970 and 1971 dispositions (Table 20) showed that the percentage of defendants pleading guilty doubled in 1971, we analyzed sentencing severity by method of disposition for 1971 as well, to see if there were changes in the basic pattern. In summary, we found that the apparent discrepancy between the harshness of sentences for those who plead immediately and those who later change their plea or request a court trial had disappeared. Apparently, more plea bargaining is taking place earlier in the process as an inducement for early pleas. As before, the consistent leniency toward SOT defendants continues to exist.

We can gain some insight into possible plea bargaining practices by examining how the distribution of defendants falls across the BCS categories for various types of offenses and disposition methods. Part A of Table 25 shows this matrix for convicted burglary defendants with prior prison records. As in Table 24, this table shows that defendants who change their plea to guilty, go SOT, or choose a court trial are much more likely to receive misdemeanor sentences than those who plead guilty immediately or ask for a jury trial. Such actions also often result in misdemeanor sentences, even though the defendants are convicted of the original felony charge.

Part B of Table 25, which shows the distribution of sentences for these same defendants, indicates that those who ask for a jury trial greatly reduce their chances for any type of probation and substantially increase their chances of going to prison. Also, defendants who change their pleas or go SOT have a substantially better chance of doing jail time rather than prison time than do defendants who plead guilty initially.

Part A of Table 26 shows that although most defendants with no prior record who are charged with sale of drugs, marijuana, or narcotics are convicted of some felony charge, the charge is much more likely to be decreased from the original for a change in plea, SOT, or court trial than for other methods of disposition. Part B of Table 26 shows that only jury trial defendants have a substantial chance of serving prison time.

In summary, these are our major findings in this section:

- As in other jurisdictions, more than 90 percent of the cases filed in Superior Court are settled without trial.
- The unusual practice in Los Angeles of using SOT for a quick disposition is found in all categories of offense; however, the use of SOT diminished significantly in 1971.
- Less than 1 percent of all defendants charged with the possession of dangerous drugs or marijuana are sentenced to prison.
- There is a strong positive correlation between sentencing severity and prior record.
- Defendants who SOT are sentenced much more *leniently* than other defendants.
- Defendants convicted by a jury are sentenced much more *severely* than other defendants.

Table 25

LEVEL OF CONVICTION AND SENTENCE, BY METHOD OF DISPOSITION,
FOR CONVICTED BURGLARY DEFENDANTS WITH PRIOR PRISON
RECORDS, LOS ANGELES SUPERIOR COURT, 1970[a]

(In percent)

Level of Conviction and Sentence	Method of Disposition				
	Original Guilty Plea	Not Guilty to Guilty Plea	SOT	Jury Trial	Court Trial
A. Level of Conviction					
Felony as charged, felony sentence	60	42	39	75	43
Felony as charged, misdemeanor sentence	15	26	32	17	35
Felony as charged (§17 PC)	0	1	1	0	0
Lesser felony, felony sentence	11	11	7	2	11
Lesser felony, misdemeanor sentence	4	13	5	4	4
Lesser felony (§17 PC)	0	0	0	0	0
Lesser misdemeanor	10	7	16	2	7
B. Sentence					
Prison	26	10	10	62	20
California Youth Authority	3	2	2	0	2
Probation (supervised)	8	9	16	4	2
Probation and jail (supervised)	21	24	20	8	26
Summary or court probation (nonsupervised) or probation and jail (nonsupervised)	4	8	13	2	7
Jail	23	37	35	23	39
Probation and jail	3	2	0	0	2
Fine	0	1	0	0	0
Indeterminate sentence as sexual psychopath	0	0	0	0	0
California Rehabilitation Center (§3051 W&I)	12	7	4	2	2

[a]Based on data from California Bureau of Criminal Statistics, *Felony Defendants Disposed of in California Courts*, 1970.

Table 26

LEVEL OF CONVICTION AND SENTENCE, BY METHOD OF DISPOSITION,
FOR DRUG/NARCOTIC SALE DEFENDANTS WITH NO PRIOR RECORD,
LOS ANGELES SUPERIOR COURT, 1970[a]

(In percent)

Level of Conviction and Sentence	Method of Disposition				
	Original Guilty Plea	Not Guilty to Guilty Plea	SOT	Jury Trial	Court Trial
A. Level of Conviction					
Felony as charged, felony sentence	60	51	33	73	49
Felony as charged, misdemeanor sentence	12	8	7	14	7
Felony as charged (§17 PC)	4	1	0	0	2
Lesser felony, felony sentence	8	19	25	9	19
Lesser felony, misdemeanor sentence	16	17	29	5	19
Lesser felony (§17 PC)	0	3	4	0	5
Lesser misdemeanor	0	2	1	0	0
B. Sentence					
Prison	0	1	1	32	0
California Youth Authority	12	4	1	5	0
Probation (supervised)	40	42	57	27	51
Probation and jail (supervised)	20	45	34	36	42
Summary or court probation (nonsupervised) or probation and jail (nonsupervised)	12	4	4	0	5
Jail	0	2	1	0	2
Probation and jail	0	0	0	0	0
Fine	0	0	2	0	0
Indeterminate sentence as sexual psychopath	0	0	0	0	0
California Rehabilitation Center (§3051 W&I)	16	2	1	0	0

[a]Based on data from California Bureau of Criminal Statistics, *Felony Defendants Disposed of in California Courts*, 1970.

IV. BACKGROUND SOURCES OF VARIATION IN THE TREATMENT OF DEFENDANTS

In Section III we examined the countywide pattern of dispositions for felony defendants in the Los Angeles Courts, and how it is affected by several factors: the specific offense the defendant is charged with, his prior record, and method of disposition. This section summarizes our findings concerning the impact of other background variables on the eventual disposition of cases.

The general public, as well as serious students of the criminal justice process, generally presumes that both the defendant's financial status and his race can affect how he is treated. Because the data base we worked with contains no reference to financial status, we examined two other variables, in addition to *race*, that are somewhat related to financial status: *pretrial custody status* and *type of attorney*. The BCS data allow us to distinguish among three different classes of pretrial custody status: (1) released on bail, (2) released on own recognizance (OR), and (3) remaining in jail. Defendants categorized as "released on bail" spend at least part of their pretrial waiting period released on bail and can be presumed to have greater financial resources, on the average, than defendants in the other two groups, as we explain later. Defendants classified as "released on own recognizance" spend at least part of their pretrial waiting period released under the auspices of the Superior Court's OR Unit. This release requires no cost outlay on their part but presumably indicates that they have stronger community ties than defendants who are not released. The last group includes defendants who spend their entire pretrial waiting period in detention.

We distinguish the following types of attorneys retained for the defense: (1) private attorneys—retained at the defendant's own expense and therefore presumed to represent defendants of more substantial means than the average; (2) Public Defenders—members of the Los Angeles County Public Defender's Office assigned by the court to counsel defendants who claim to be indigent; and (3) court-appointed attorneys—private attorneys[1] appointed by the court to represent indigent defendants for whom the Public Defender is disqualified by reason of a conflict.[2]

---

[1] Each court maintains a list of attorneys from which it selects counsel in a particular case.

[2] For purposes of this rule, the Public Defender's Office is treated as one large firm and therefore cannot represent more than one codefendant in multiple defendant prosecution when a conflict occurs. Likewise, a conflict can occur when the Public Defender is representing the victim in some other matter. Consequently, in such cases, the court appoints a private attorney to represent defendants for whom the conflict exists.

For convenience and statistical reliability, we limited our analysis to four groups of theft defendants in the 1970 countywide felony defendant file, identified by their charged offense and prior record. We selected these particular groups because they represent fairly serious crimes, provide large sample sizes, and allow us to observe the effects of prior criminal records. There is no obvious reason to believe that the results found in examining these groups would not apply to a broader sample of defendants.

Group	Offense	Prior Record	Number of Cases
1	Robbery	None	206
2	Robbery	1 or 2 convictions of 90 days or more in jail	506
3	Burglary	None	659
4	Burglary	1 or 2 convictions of 90 days or more in jail	1246
Total			2617

THE EFFECTS OF PRETRIAL CUSTODY STATUS

In our total sample of 2617 defendants, 38.3 percent were released on bail, 16.9 percent were released on their own recognizance (OR), and 44.9 percent remained in jail. There appears to be a significant relationship between the defendant's custodial status while his case is pending and the method which he and his attorney choose to dispose of his case.

Table 27 shows the distribution of disposition methods, broken down by the defendants' custodial status. Defendants released on their own recognizance are shown to have a much better chance of having their cases dismissed than defendants who are either out on bail or remaining in jail. This difference can possibly be attributed to judges' bias in the decisions that favor persons who qualify for OR— the middle class, employed defendants with roots in the community. However, there is very little evidence of such bias in the dismissal rate according to any defendant attributes that we can measure. Therefore, an alternative explanation appears required.

The basis for such an explanation might be a feeling among judges that defendants against whom the evidence is particularly weak should not be penalized even to the extent of paying the premium of bail.

It is rather surprising that defendants who have been released on OR have the highest dismissal rate, since OR is most frequently won by the Public Defender, who, on the average, has the poorest record of winning dismissals for his client, as we shall see subsequently. However, the higher frequency of dismissals among defendants released on OR occurs for clients of all three types of attorneys. One final explanation for these differences might be that defendants who have won release, no matter by what method, are better able to demonstrate their ability to stay clean, and thereby earn some leniency from the court in the disposition of their cases.

Table 27

METHOD OF DISPOSITION BY PRETRIAL CUSTODIAL STATUS[a]

(In percent)

Custodial Status	Disposition				
	Dismissed	SOT	Jury Trial	Court Trial	Guilty Plea
Released on bail	11.1	29.8	3.3	7.9	47.8
Released on OR	15.8	29.1	1.8	9.9	43.3
Remained in jail	6.0	28.3	4.8	6.3	54.7
All defendants	9.6	29.0	3.7	7.5	50.1

[a]Sample of 2617 theft defendants in 1970 countywide felony defendant file.

Among defendants who do decide to contest their cases, those jailed while their cases are pending are considerably more likely to insist on a jury trial than those who have been released. Only 25 percent of the defendants out on OR or bail who contest their prosecutions ask for a jury trial, compared to 43 percent of the defendants left in jail. Sixty percent of the jury trials in Los Angeles County involving theft offenses in 1970 were conducted for defendants who were incarcerated until their cases were tried.

Whether or not the denial of pretrial release influences trial outcomes is a hotly debated issue among lawyers, sociologists, criminologists, and civil libertarians. Our knowledge of the procedures employed in Los Angeles County Courts is simply inadequate for us to answer *if* custodial status influences the outcome of trials. But the following discussion should provide useful information and a basis for measuring the issue's amenability to analysis, as well as give us hypotheses for subsequent, more rigorous analysis.

We attempted to find statistically significant relationships between custodial status and trial outcomes. Those we found and reported here should be considered in terms of at least two theoretical models of the effect of custodial status on judicial outputs: one model states that custodial status influences trial outcomes; the other suggests that the expected trial outcomes affect bail status. If either or both models possess some accuracy, they portend serious problems for the judicial system. If custodial status seriously affects outcomes, the judicial system must assume a far greater burden for justifying denials of pretrial release and even of supporting convictions of defendants who are incarcerated during their trials. If the second model is correct, it reflects an unconstitutional violation of the presumption of innocence.

We have, then, two kinds of inquiries in the present discussion: Does pretrial release influence outcomes? And does the means by which release is secured influence outcomes? We address these two questions in order.

Table 28 shows the relative acquittal rates for defendants released and unreleased while their cases are pending. While unreleased defendants were acquitted

Table 28

ACQUITTAL RATES FOR RELEASED AND UNRELEASED
DEFENDANTS WHILE CASE PENDING[a]

(In percent)

Custodial Status	Acquitted	Convicted
Released	19.4	80.6
Unreleased	10.1	89.9

[a]Sample of 2617 theft defendants in 1970 countywide felony defendant file.

only 10.1 percent of the time, released defendants were acquitted 19.4 percent, or nearly twice as frequently.

Naturally, one could argue that this difference merely manifests differences in the kinds of defendants and is not a feature of the judicial system itself. For instance, that the types of people who do not secure release (who would presumably be persons too poor to make bail and who lack the community roots necessary to be a candidate for OR) simply tend to be guilty more frequently than persons who qualify for one or the other form of pretrial release. But there is no evidence in the data to support this contention. When we examine cases separately for each type of defense attorney (and we know that type of defense attorney is determined exclusively by economic status), we find the effect to be uniform: Clients (regardless of what type of attorney they have) who secure pretrial release have almost twice the acquittal rate of clients (with the same type of attorneys) who are unable to gain pretrial release. Furthermore, this effect seems independent of the disposition of the case. Regardless of whether a defendant submits on the transcript, tries his case before a court, or takes his case to a jury, his chances of acquittal are roughly doubled if he is able to get bail or OR.

The effects of pretrial release are considerably slighter if we measure judicial outputs by the conviction level of defendants who are convicted. Table 29 shows a statistically significant but rather slight tendency for released defendants to be convicted of less serious offenses.

This trend toward slightly lower convictions for released defendants is also evident when we consider separately the kinds of attorneys the defendants have. Comparison of the acquittal rates of released and unreleased defendants for each of the three types of attorneys shows that released defendants had a statistically significant advantage, although this advantage was small, and smallest of all for Public Defender clients.

Examining separately each method of disposition showed a somewhat ambiguous effect. The effect was present for both methods of contested disposition: Among jury trial defendants, those who had gained pretrial release had 9.1 percent higher acquittal rates; and among court trial defendants, those who had gained pretrial release had 10.1 percent higher acquittal rates. Only a slight advantage (1.2 percent)

Table 29

DISTRIBUTION OF CONVICTION LEVELS FOR RELEASED AND
UNRELEASED DEFENDANTS WHILE CASE PENDING[a]

(In percent)

Custodial Status	Conviction Level		
	Felony Charged	Lesser Felony	Misdemeanor
Released	61.6	27.2	11.2
Unreleased	63.5	28.7	7.8

[a]Sample of 2617 theft defendants in
1970 countywide felony defendant file.

accrued to released defendants who pleaded guilty, and there was no discernible difference between released and unreleased defendants who submitted on the transcript.

This difference between contested and uncontested dispositions would seem to support the first, rather than the second, model posited above, suggesting that pretrial release tends to affect results. The model usually hypothesizes (1) that the effect derived either from hostility on the part of courts and jurors toward unreleased defendants; or (2) that the restraints on the defendant's mobility influence his and his attorney's ability to prepare adequately for trial; or (3) that both (1) and (2) apply. Since the judge determines the SOT result without much, or perhaps any, face-to-face contact with the defendant, and since the prosecuting and defense attorneys essentially determine the outcome of the guilty plea, we would expect the hostility factor to be minimal for SOTs and guilty pleas and greater for court and jury trials. Furthermore, since very little preparation is involved in an uncontested disposition, the defendant's participation is less important than in a court or jury trial. Our findings that custodial status affects the outcome of contested dispositions far more than the outcome of uncontested dispositions is consistent with both hypotheses and, therefore, would appear to support the first model.

The effect of custodial status on the level of sentence imposed on convicted defendants is analogous to what we have thus far observed. As Table 30 shows, theft defendants who were released before trial and subsequently convicted received slightly more than 10 percent fewer felony sentences than unreleased theft defendants.

Again, if we examine separately each type of attorney, we find the effect of custodial status to be about equal for all three types. It also holds across all four methods of disposition.

The composite picture this discussion produces is that defendants who are released while their case is pending receive somewhat more lenient treatment by the judicial system than those who are confined, and that these differences are not readily explained by reference to the defendants' personal attributes. Whether or not release is secured by bail or OR does not appear to affect significantly this pattern of treatment.

Table 30

DISTRIBUTION OF SENTENCE LEVELS FOR RELEASED AND
UNRELEASED DEFENDANTS WHILE CASE PENDING[a]

(In percent)

	Sentence Level		
Custodial Status	Felony	Misdemeanor	§17 PC
Released	41.0	53.2	5.8
Unreleased	51.6	46.8	1.6

[a]Sample of 2617 theft defendants in 1970 countywide felony defendant file.

THE EFFECTS OF TYPE OF ATTORNEY

The three types of attorneys apparently differ significantly in their ability to gain release for their clients while their cases are pending. As figures for our 1970 data in Table 31 show, over one-half of all indigent defendants—that is, those defended by the Public Defender or court-appointed attorneys—remain in jail during the disposition of their case; of private attorneys' clients, over two-thirds are released on bail and less than one-fifth spend the duration of their case in jail. In large measure this is because indigent defendants simply cannot afford bail while private attorneys' clients can.

Table 31

PRETRIAL CUSTODIAL STATUS OF DEFENDANTS DURING TRIAL,
BY TYPE OF ATTORNEY[a]

(In percent)

	Custodial Status		
Type of Attorney	Released on Bail	Released on OR	Remained in Jail
Public Defender	28.0	18.1	53.9
Court-appointed attorney	31.2	16.4	52.4
Private attorney	67.2	14.0	18.8
All defendants	38.3	16.9	44.9

[a]Sample of 2617 theft defendants in 1970 countywide felony defendant file.

We now examine whether or not there are differences between types of attorneys in the frequency with which they actively contest the charges against their clients and the methods of contest that they select. We have previously shown (Section III) that the method of disposition selected by the defense can have a significant effect on the final sentence received by the defendant if he is eventually convicted.

A priori, the only significant differences we would expect to find among types of attorneys is their inclination to seek a quick settlement. Each type of attorney is compensated in a different fashion. The private attorney is usually working on a retainer or fixed-fee basis. Under these circumstances, he has a strong financial incentive to handle each case as rapidly as possible so that he can increase his income. The court-appointed attorney, however, usually works on an hourly basis and therefore has some incentive to stretch out his case. Since generally accepted ground rules establish reasonable charges for each particular type of action, the only way a court-appointed attorney can increase his fee on a particular case is to go to trial. However, he cannot choose an adversary proceeding too often or the judges will not continue to appoint him.

The Public Defender is somewhere between the other two types. Of course, as a civil servant, he cannot increase his salary by handling more cases. In fact, if his office assigns an equal caseload to each man, his only method of reducing his workload is to seek quick dispositions in some cases. In reality, the Deputy Public Defender making a decision often escapes its eventual consequence because a different deputy may pick up the case at a later stage.

Table 32 displays the relationship between type of attorney and pattern of disposition. Although no great differences are shown among types of attorneys, their direction does tend to agree with the incentive pressures suggested above. Private attorneys are more likely to have their clients plead guilty, and court-appointed attorneys are more likely to go to trial. For some reason, the Public Defender appears to have less success than others in getting his cases dismissed.

Table 32

RELATIONSHIP BETWEEN TYPE OF ATTORNEY AND
METHOD OF DISPOSITION[a]

(In percent)

Type of Attorney	Disposition				
	Diverted	Dismissed	SOT	Trial	Guilty Plea
Public Defender	5	5	31	8	51
Court-appointed attorney	3	9	29	11	48
Private attorney	4	7	27	8	54

[a]Sample of 2617 theft defendants in 1970 countywide felony defendant file.

Observing the differences in the frequency with which the three kinds of attorneys resort to court or jury trials offers us another opportunity to check our model of lawyers' decisionmaking based on financial incentives. First, note that the use of either a court or a jury trial is extremely small relative to the total caseload. Only 11 percent of the cases are disposed of by trial. The court trial differs from the SOT in that all of its evidence is presented in Superior Court before a judge sitting without a jury. The transcript of the preliminary hearing may be used as evidence at the court trial, but most of the testimony will be given before the trial court.

It is far more time-consuming to prepare and conduct a jury trial than a court trial. Thus if we were to follow the predictions of our model of lawyers' decisionmaking based on financial incentives, we would expect court-appointed attorneys to use the jury trial most frequently, and private attorneys to use the jury trial least frequently. As we see in Table 33, this is precisely the case. Court-appointed attorneys use jury trials in roughly 44 percent of their vigorously contested cases, compared to only 27-percent use by private attorneys, and 32 percent by the Public Defender.

Given these observations, do the different types of attorneys vary in the success with which they represent their client's interests?

Table 33

RELATIONSHIP BETWEEN TYPE OF ATTORNEY AND
PREFERENCE FOR COURT OR JURY TRIAL[a]

(In percent)

Type of Attorney	Trial	
	Jury	Court
Public Defender	31.6	68.4
Court-appointed attorney	43.9	56.1
Private attorney	26.9	73.1
All defendants	34.1	65.9

[a]Sample of 2617 theft defendants in 1970 countywide felony defendant file.

Table 34 shows the acquittal rate by type of attorney for all defendants in the sample. As can be seen, acquittal rates for court-appointed attorneys are the highest, 21.9 percent, which is consistent with our understanding that they handle the least severe cases.

Table 35 shows the distribution of conviction levels among convicted defendants. We find that although the private attorney is more successful than the Public

Table 34

ACQUITTAL RATES BY TYPE OF ATTORNEY[a]

(In percent)

Type of Attorney	Result of Trial	
	Acquitted	Convicted
Public Defender	13.4	86.6
Court-appointed attorney	21.9	78.1
Private attorney	16.9	83.1

[a]Sample of 2617 theft defendants in 1970 countywide felony defendant file.

Table 35

DISTRIBUTION OF CONVICTION LEVELS BY TYPE OF ATTORNEY[a]

(In percent)

Type of Attorney	Conviction Level		
	Felony Charged	Lesser Felony	Misdemeanor
Public Defender	61.8	28.8	9.4
Court-appointed attorney	58.6	29.7	11.7
Private attorney	66.1	24.6	9.3

[a]Sample of 2617 theft defendants in 1970 countywide felony defendant file.

Defender in gaining an acquittal for his clients, the Public Defender has a distinctly better record of avoiding the original felony charge and gaining a lesser conviction. A private attorney's client has a 4.3 percent greater chance of being convicted of the original felony charge (given that he is not acquitted) than the Public Defender's client has. Again we observe that the court-appointed attorney has the most successful record of avoiding convictions at the maximum level.

Finally, Table 36 shows the corresponding data for the distributions of sentence levels. Here the difference is largest, with 6.3 percent more of the private attorneys' convicted clients receiving felony sentences than those of the Public Defender.

Table 36

DISTRIBUTION OF SENTENCE LEVELS BY TYPE OF ATTORNEY[a]

(In percent)

Type of Attorney	Sentence Level		
	Felony	Misdemeanor	§17 PC
Public Defender	44.0	52.2	3.8
Court-appointed attorney	49.4	47.2	3.4
Private attorney	50.3	45.9	3.8

[a]Sample of 2617 theft defendants in 1970 countywide felony defendant file.

RELATIONSHIP BETWEEN ETHNIC GROUP AND PATTERN OF TREATMENT

Within our sample, 48 percent of the defendants were Anglo-American, 40 percent black, and 12 percent Mexican-American. The blacks tended to have more extensive prior criminal records than the Anglo-Americans, and the Mexican-Americans more extensive than the blacks. A slightly greater percentage of the black and Mexican-American defendants were also minors as compared to Anglo-Americans; 11.5 percent of Anglo-Americans were minors whereas 14.0 percent of blacks and 14.9 percent of Mexican-Americans were minors.

Table 37 shows the acquittal rate of defendants in the three ethnic groups. The black acquittal rate is considerably higher than that of the Anglo-Americans and, to a somewhat lesser extent, higher than that of the Mexican-Americans. Table 38 shows that both blacks and Mexican-Americans tend to be convicted of the original felony charged about 9 percent less frequently than Anglo-Americans. Table 39 shows that convicted blacks receive felony sentences roughly 5 percent less frequently than Anglo-Americans, and Mexican-Americans roughly 4 percent less.

Table 37

ACQUITTAL RATE BY ETHNIC GROUP[a]

(In percent)

Race	Acquitted	Convicted
Anglo-American	12.7	87.3
Black	17.3	82.7
Mexican-American	13.5	86.5

[a]Sample of 2617 theft defendants in 1970 countywide felony defendant file.

Table 38

DISTRIBUTION OF CONVICTION LEVELS BY ETHNIC GROUP[a]

(In percent)

	Conviction Level		
Race	Felony Charged	Lesser Felony	Misdemeanor
Anglo-American	67.0	24.4	8.7
Black	58.5	31.3	10.2
Mexican-American	58.1	31.3	10.6

[a]Sample of 2617 theft defendants in 1970 countywide felony defendant file.

Table 39

DISTRIBUTION OF SENTENCE LEVELS BY ETHNIC GROUP[a]

(In percent)

	Sentence Level		
Race	Felony	Misdemeanor	§17 PC
Anglo-American	48.6	47.7	3.7
Black	43.9	52.3	3.8
Mexican-American	44.7	51.3	4.1

[a]Sample of 2617 theft defendants in 1970 countywide felony defendant file.

Ultimately, efforts to explain these differences can be classified into two hypotheses: either (1) these data demonstrate that the judicial system applies a double standard to minority groups, or (2) more innocent minority group members are being arrested and charged with felonies than innocent Anglo-Americans. Arguments for the first hypothesis are difficult to test with these data, since we have no way of measuring rates of over-arrest except by resorting to the acquittal rates that were the source of our hypotheses. In considering the possibility of over-arrest, however, one must remember that these data include only cases in which the District Attorney's screening has taken place and a Deputy District Attorney has decided a case is worthy of prosecution; and further, a Municipal Court judge has held the defendant to answer after a preliminary hearing to assess the merits of the case. Such screening does not exclude the possibility of over-prosecution of certain groups; in fact, if the over-arrest phenomenon is pronounced enough, we could simply be observing an inadequate correction mechanism that could be rejecting and dismissing more cases for the over-arrested groups than for the general population, but not frequently enough to compensate fully.

Table 40 shows that most of the differences between the black acquittal rate and that of other ethnic groups is concentrated in three Branches: Los Angeles (Central), Santa Monica, and Pomona. In the remaining five Branches, the differences are small and not statistically significant. Table 40 also shows the ethnic distribution of defendants tried in each of the eight Branches.

We note that there is no similarity between ethnic compositions of the three Branches in which we found acquittal rates related to the defendant's ethnic group. Los Angeles has the county's second largest minority population, Pomona has the second smallest minority population, and Santa Monica is right at the median. Santa Monica is the only Branch in which the Mexican-American acquittal rate is disproportionately high, and it has the county's second smallest Chicano population.

These facts at least suggest that differences in acquittal rates by ethnic group cannot be attributed to differences in either the group of defendants tried in each Branch or, by inference from the ethnic distribution of defendants, the ethnic composition of juries in these Branches. To some extent this tends to operate against the double standard explanation.

These disparities are almost equally pronounced among the Public Defender's clients. The black dismissal rate for Public Defender clients is 17.5 percent higher than we would expect, based on the average dismissal rate for all of the Public Defender's cases. On the basis of present data, we cannot say whether this suggests that blacks are more competently represented at trial by Public Defenders than are Anglo-Americans and Mexican-Americans, or that representation of blacks at the preliminary hearing by the Public Defender's office is inferior. But dismissal rates for blacks represented by court-appointed attorneys or private counsel are not different from those for Anglo-Americans.

Although black dismissal rates (5.7 percent) are slightly higher than those for Anglo-Americans (5.3 percent), the difference is not large enough to account for the

Table 40

BRANCH ACQUITTAL RATES BY ETHNIC GROUP[a]

(In percent)

Race	Los Angeles[b]	Long Beach	Santa Monica[b]	Van Nuys	Torrance	Norwalk	Pomona[b]	Pasadena
Acquittal Rates								
Anglo-American	15.9	10.5	16.2	9.2	13.7	7.1	10.6	17.3
Black	19.9	7.2	12.4	11.8	15.8	8.9	21.8	15.7
Mexican-American	19.6	6.3	25.5	6.8	13.7	6.1	11.5	17.5
Ethnic Distribution of Defendants Tried								
Anglo-American	35.1	63.9	63.1	77.2	34.1	57.1	68.7	52.5
Black	53.2	25.6	30.5	11.2	63.3	14.7	14.9	36.0
Mexican-American	11.7	10.5	6.4	11.6	2.7	28.2	16.3	11.5

[a]Sample of 2617 theft defendants in 1970 countywide felony defendant file.

[b]Statistically significant differences.

differences in acquittal rate. The most significant cause for the higher black acquittal rate can be found by looking at guilty plea rates. While 62.4 percent of the Anglo-American defendants and 56.7 percent of Mexican-American defendants plead guilty, only 39.9 percent of blacks do so. If we exclude all guilty pleas from the sample and base acquittal rate on this smaller group, we find a *reversal* in the disparities; the black acquittal rate of 28.7 percent is *lower* than either the Anglo-American acquittal rate of 33.7 percent or the Mexican-American rate of 31.2 percent. Of course, the salient question, which remains unanswered, is whether the lower rate of guilty pleas among black defendants reflects a distrust of the judicial system independent of the defendants' guilt, or a greater willingness to fight their cases because of a higher proportion of unwarranted prosecutions. If we believe that trials are accurate measures of true guilt, and if we further believe that no defendant pleads guilty who is not guilty, then in fact, the higher black acquittal rate is attributable to an over-prosecution of blacks. But it can also be argued that there is a positive probability that any prosecution, regardless of its merits, will result in an acquittal if contested; if this argument is true, then the higher black acquittal rate would not necessarily support the over-arrest explanation.

It is also reasonable to ask whether blacks more frequently contest prosecutions because they fare better at trials than Anglo-Americans or Mexican-Americans. An examination of the conviction rates by SOT, court trial, and jury trial shows that this is not the case. Blacks are convicted slightly more often than Anglo-Americans in a contested disposition, but are more likely to have the charge reduced or to receive a misdemeanor sentence.

In summary, there are moderate to small (but statistically significant) disparities in the treatment of defendants by ethnic group in the courts. The apparent greater frequency of acquittals for blacks over either Anglo-Americans or Mexican-Americans is probably attributable to a lesser likelihood that black defendants will plead guilty; 39.9 percent of blacks but 62.4 percent of Anglo-American defendants plead guilty. Both blacks and Mexican-Americans tend to be convicted of the original felony charged (robbery or burglary) about 9 percent less frequently than Anglo-Americans. Convicted blacks receive felony sentences roughly 5 percent less frequently than Anglo-Americans, and Mexican-Americans roughly 4 percent less. In contested dispositions, blacks are convicted slightly more often than Anglo-Americans, but are more likely to be convicted of a lesser charge and to receive a misdemeanor sentence. The most provocative question left unresolved is whether these disparities can be attributed to over-prosecution. The question of over-arrest is simply not amenable to analysis solely by use of the data at our disposal.

V. FILING AND TERMINATION OF FELONY CASES PRIOR TO SUPERIOR COURT

In this section we look at the actual outputs of the felony prosecution process, first at the complaint stage and then at the Municipal Court stage. We focus on those cases for which no further felony prosecution will take place, considering rejections at the complaint stage and dismissals and reductions to misdemeanors at the Municipal Court stage.

THE COMPLAINT PROCESS

We turn to a detailed examination of the Los Angeles District Attorney Office's handling of more than 78,000 complaints during the period January 1, 1971, to November 10, 1971.

During this period, the Office issued two policy directives dealing with the handling of felony complaints for which the Penal Code §17(b)(4) and (5) specifies a possible alternative felony or misdemeanor sentence. Basically, the directives set up criteria by which complaints for offenses carrying such alternative sentences can be rejected as a felony and either referred to the appropriate City Attorney or handled by the District Attorney's Office as a misdemeanor if the suspect involved has not had any prior conviction for an offense punishable as a felony.

Specific criteria are defined for six different offenses. The rejection criterion for possession of dangerous drugs (§11910 HS) is ten pills or less; for possession of marijuana (§11530 HS), five cigarettes or less; and for bookmaking (§337A PC), no suspicion of involvement in organized crime. For insufficient funds (§476A PC) and forgery (§470 PC), the criterion is whether or not the police indicate any reasons that would make a misdemeanor charge inappropriate. All complaints of unlawful sexual intercourse (statutory rape—§261.5 PC) are to be handled as misdemeanors if the suspect has not been previously convicted of an offense punishable as a felony.

According to the directives, the Complaint Deputy must secure permission of either the Head Deputy in charge (if in an Area Office) or the Head Deputy or his designated representative (if in a Branch Office) to reject these cases as felonies. In all other cases, permission to file misdemeanor charges can be given only by a Head Deputy or his designated representative.

To observe the impact of this policy change we confined our case sample to two time periods: January 1971 through May 1971 (prior to the change) and July 1971 through November 10, 1971 (after the change).

FELONY REJECTION RATES

Table 41 presents the felony rejection rates by offense for these two periods; included are all offenses for which complaints were made at least 100 times in both periods. Offenses carrying alternative felony misdemeanor sentences as defined by §17(b) PC are marked with asterisks. The data allow us to observe the variation in rejection rates across offenses, as well as between the two periods.

Code violations with the highest percentage of rejections are the following: §273D PC—wife or child beating, with 85 percent for the first period, 92 percent for the second; §245A PC—assault with a deadly weapon, 87 and 88; §242 PC—battery upon peace officers, 73 and 73; §261 PC—rape, 63 and 76; §20001 VC—hit and run with injury, 83 and 84; §23101 VC—drunk driving with injury, 77 and 74; §11530 HS—possession of marijuana, 41 and 61.

Code violations with the lowest percentage of rejections are the following: §337A PC—bookmaking, with 7 percent for the first period, 15 percent for the second; §484F.2 PC—credit card forgery, 13 and 18; §664/211 PC—attempted robbery, 10 and 11; §664/459 PC—attempted burglary, 17 and 10; §11501 HS—selling narcotics, 9 and 20; §11531 HS—transport of marijuana, 12 and 15; §11912 HS—sale of dangerous drugs, 7 and 14; §1550 WI—violation of false information obtained to aid perjury, 0 and 0. Of the Vehicle Code offenses listed, no rejection rate is less than 40 percent.

Comparison of the *overall* rejection rates for the two periods, i.e., 45 and 54 percent, indicates the effect of the directives. We observe increased rejection rates for each of the offenses for which specific criteria were provided in the directives. Rejection of complaints for possession of dangerous drugs increased from 34 to 53 percent; for possession of marijuana, from 41 to 61; bookmaking, from 7 to 15; insufficient funds, from 43 to 53; forgery from 26 to 30; unlawful sexual intercourse, from 59 to 69.

Other offenses carrying alternative sentences show either no change in rejection rate, or small increases, in the second period, except grand theft (person), which increased from 35 to 49 percent, and receiving stolen property, which increased from 32 to 47 percent. The general provision for handling as a misdemeanor those offenses carrying an alternative felony or misdemeanor sentence may well account for these shifts. Among the offenses not covered by the directive, the most notable changes in rejection rates occur for sex perversion, which rose from 20 to 39 percent, and for kidnapping, which fell from 73 to 56 percent. We also note the dramatic increase in rejection rates for conspiracy, from 10 to 40 percent.

In summary, rejection rates vary significantly across offenses in our data. In addition, rejection rates within some offense categories shift considerably from the first to the second period. The directives are the obvious explanation for many of the increased rejection rates observed.

Table 41

FELONY REJECTION RATES BY OFFENSE, 1971

Code	Offense	January-May 1971		July-November 10, 1971	
		Complaints	Rejection Rate (%)	Complaints	Rejection Rate (%)
Penal (PC)					
§182	*Conspiracy[a]	280	10	215	40
§187	Murder	329	33	286	27
§207	Kidnapping	177	73	186	56
§211	Robbery	1,999	45	1,905	47
§217	Assault with intent to murder	480	63	481	61
§220	Assault with intent to rape or rob	129	60	137	66
§242	*Battery upon peace officer	341	73	247	73
§245A	*Assault with deadly weapon	4,044	87	3,988	88
§245B	Assault with deadly weapon upon peace officer	120	50	101	50
§261	Rape	408	63	383	76
§261.5	*Unlawful sexual intercourse (formerly statutory rape)	126	59	105	69
§273D	*Wife or child beating	287	85	237	92
§288	Lewd and lascivious acts on child	294	51	291	51
§288A	Sex perversion	264	20	207	39
§337A	*Bookmaking	822	7	578	15
§459	*Burglary[b]	5,689	46	4,784	50
§470	*Forgery	1,130	26	905	30
§476A	*Insufficient funds	691	43	521	53
§484F.2	*Credit card forgery	364	13	201	18
§487.1	*Grand theft: over $200	1,340	52	1,097	55
§487.2	*Grand theft: person	227	35	245	49
§487.3	*Grand theft: auto	2,749	43	2,129	48
§496	*Receiving stolen property	513	32	509	47
§664/211	Attempted robbery	125	10	125	11
§664/459	*Attempted burglary[c]	198	17	140	10
§667	*Petty theft with prior record	163	59	146	59
§12020	*Prohibited weapons	369	50	298	69
§12021	*Excon or alien with weapon	123	33	128	29
Vehicle (VC)					
§10851	*Operating vehicle without owner's consent	163	54	104	54
§20001	*Hit and run with injury	331	83	327	84
§23101	*Drunk driving with injury	475	77	479	74
§23105	Driving under influence of narcotics	320	42	269	49
Health and Safety (HS)					
§11500	Possession of narcotics	855	43	830	49
§11500.5	Possession of narcotics for sale	408	20	266	30
§11501	Selling narcotics	253	9	206	20
§11530	*Possession of marijuana	6,474	41	4,067	61
§11530.1	*Cultivating marijuana	141	24	216	30
§11530.5	Possession of marijuana for sale	415	27	276	25
§11531	Transport of marijuana	293	12	190	15
§11910	*Possession of dangerous drugs	6,278	34	4,190	53
§11911	Possession of dangerous drugs for sale	558	27	327	32
§11912	Sale of dangerous drugs	424	7	235	14
Welfare and Institutions (WI)					
§1550	False information obtained to aid perjury	222	0	207	0
Overall[d]		43,564	45	34,695	54

NOTE: Asterisk (*). indicates offenses that carry alternative felony or misdemeanor sentences.

[a]This carries an alternative sentence if and only if the offense conspired to also does so.

[b]Only second-degree burglary carries an alternative sentence; first-degree does not.

[c]Only second-degree attempted burglary carries an alternative sentence; first-degree does not.

[d]All offenses, not simply those above, are included here.

REJECTIONS

Next we examine the rejections per se. A rejection constitutes one of the following four actions:

1. A recommendation that the case be referred to the City Attorney to be handled as a misdemeanor.
2. A decision to have the District Attorney's Office handle the case as a misdemeanor.[1]
3. A recommendation that further investigation be made.
4. An outright rejection with no recommendation for referral or further investigation.

In taking one of these actions, the deputy offers one or more reasons. Table 42 presents a self-explanatory categorization of these reasons, as made for our analysis.

We turn attention to the rejection actions and the given reasons for two offenses —burglary (§459 PC) and possession of dangerous drugs (§11910 HS)—as documented on the D.A. Rejection Form. All rejections of these two offenses occurring during the two periods were examined for each of the Branch Offices as well as two Area Offices, San Pedro and Whittier. In L.A. Central, we sampled only about 200 rejections from each period. Hence the following results, based on this sample, cannot be strictly considered as applying countywide, inasmuch as Los Angeles is underrepresented and all but two of the Area Offices are omitted from our sample.

Rejection Actions

Table 43 presents rejection actions for possession of dangerous drugs and burglary. In the January-May period 17 percent of the dangerous drug rejections were referred to the City Attorney to be handled as a misdemeanor, and 80 percent were fully rejected. In the second period, the referrals to the City Attorney increased to 51 percent, and the outright rejections dropped to 44 percent,[2] showing the effect of the directives' ten-or-less capsules rule. We noted earlier that the overall rejection rate for possession of dangerous drugs increased from 34 to 53 percent; of those rejections, we now see, the percentage referred to the City Attorney increased from 17 to 50.

Rejection actions for burglary for the two periods shown in Table 43 indicate a shift of preference from outright rejections to referrals, but the shift is much smaller than for possession. Referrals increase from 25 to 35 percent and outright rejections decrease from 66 to 55 percent.[3] Burglary, unlike dangerous drugs, was not specifically mentioned in the directives. In addition, only second-degree burglary carries an alternative felony/misdemeanor sentence, so complaints of first-degree burglary cannot be referred to the City Attorney. Hence, the shift here is much smaller.

---

[1] The distinction between (1) and (2) is simply one of jurisdiction.
[2] Two-tailed test significant at 0.01 level.
[3] Two-tailed test significant at 0.01 level.

64

Table 42

REASONS FOR REJECTIONS AND TERMINATIONS[a]

10. Insufficient Evidence (unspecified)
    12. Insufficient evidence of a felony, but there may be evidence
        of a misdemeanor.
    13. Insufficient evidence of the corpus of a crime.
    14. Evidence of a crime, but insufficient evidence to connect
        this suspect. This includes cases in which the victim
        cannot identify suspect.

20. No Corpus of a Crime (unspecified)
    22. No corpus of felony, but there exists corpus of misdemeanor.
    23. No corpus of any crime.
    24. There exists corpus, but not as to this suspect.

30. Discretionary Refusal to Prosecute Even Though There Exists
    Evidence to Convict (unspecified)
    31. Restitution to be made or already made.
    32. Trivial or insufficient quantity of contraband.
    33. Trivial nature of offense other than insufficient quantity.
    34. Suspect's personal history. (This includes no prior record
        and minimal prior record.)
    35. Officer requests rejection.
    36. Suspect is, or has agreed to be, an informer.
    37. Age of suspect.
    38. Other discretionary refusal to prosecute.

40. Indispensable Parties
    41. Victim. (This includes cases in which the victim will not
        cooperate in prosecution and those in which the victim is
        unavailable.)
    42. Witness. (This includes cases in which the witness will
        not cooperate in prosecution and those in which the witness
        is unavailable.)
    43. Defendant. (This includes cases in which the defendant is
        dead, incarcerated, on trial for more serious offenses, or
        cannot be found or extradited.)

50. Violation of Rights (unspecified)
    51. Search and seizure (§1538.5 PC).
    52. Evidence obtained by statements without proper advisement
        of constitutional rights.
    53. Unlawful detention or arrest.
    54. Other violation of rights.

60. Prosecution (unspecified)[b]
    61. Lack of prosecution, prosecution not ready.
    62. Prosecution error.

70. Other (unspecified)
    71. Transfer to another jurisdiction.
    72. Superseded by a new case.

[a]To facilitate cross-referencing in this study, numbers were
assigned to reasons.

[b]60 through 62 refer to terminations only.

Table 43

FELONY REJECTION ACTIONS FOR POSSESSION OF DANGEROUS DRUGS
AND FOR BURGLARY--TWO PERIODS, 1971

Offense	Cases (Rejections)		Felony Rejection Action							
			C.A. Misdemeanor (%)		D.A. Misdemeanor (%)		Further Investigation (%)		Outright Rejection (%)	
	Jan-May	July-Nov	Jan-May	July-Nov	Jan-May	July-Nov	Jan-May	July-Nov	Jan-May	July-Nov
Possession, dangerous drugs	1,134	956	17	51	1	2	2	2	80	44
Burglary	1,020	997	25	35	5	6	5	4	66	55

Rejection Reasons

The D.A. Rejection Forms often list more than one reason for rejecting a felony complaint. When we refer to *first* reasons in this discussion, we mean the *first* reason given on the form by the Deputy District Attorney; similarly for the *second* reason.

Table 44 gives the distribution in percent of the *first* reason for each rejection action for possession of dangerous drugs. The most frequent reasons given were insufficient evidence to connect the suspect (32 and 18 percent for the first and second periods, respectively), trivial quantity of contraband (31 and 50 percent), and search and seizure (16 and 10 percent). Of the reasons given in the first period for cases referred to the City Attorney, the most frequent are trivial quantity of contraband (42 percent), insufficient evidence to convict this suspect (35 percent), and insufficient evidence of felony, but possible evidence of misdemeanor (10 percent). In the second period, however, we observe a significant shift, undoubtedly the effect of the directives. Trivial or insufficient quantity constitutes the first reason given in 78 percent of the cases sent to the City Attorney. The apparent explanation is the ten-pills-or-less criterion provided by the directive.

Also, the reason of personal history, which typically indicates a defendant with no prior record or minimal prior record, constitutes 7 percent of the first reasons given for cases referred to the City Attorney in the second period, whereas in the first period personal history was given as the first reason in less than one-half of 1 percent[4] of these cases. This, too, may be a result of the directive.

Of the reasons given for outright rejections, the major contributors are insufficient evidence to connect the suspect (31 and 35 percent), trivial or insufficient quantity of contraband (29 and 20 percent), and search and seizure (19 and 22 percent). Little change is shown between the two periods because the directives do not concern outright rejections. Nevertheless, as will be shown in Section VII, outright rejections *were* affected at some D.A. Branches.

The contrasts between the two periods as to the reasons given for complete rejections of dangerous drug possession complaints become clearer if one compares in terms of both the first and second reasons given. Table 45 shows the frequency with which trivial or insufficient quantity and personal history appear either individually with no other reasons or in combination with another for felony rejections of dangerous drug possession complaints. In both periods, approximately 27 percent indicated "trivial or insufficient quantity" as the *only* reason and almost no one indicated "personal history" as the only reason. In the first period only about 1 percent indicated *both* of these as the first two reasons, whereas in the second period that percentage increased to about 22 percent.[5] In the second period, then, almost 25 percent of all rejections were made because of the trivial quantity involved and because the defendant had no prior record.

Table 46 presents the *first* reasons for felony rejection of burglary charges. Overall, in both periods, the three predominant reasons given are all types of insufficient evidence, the most frequent being insufficient evidence to connect the suspect (31 and 27 percent), the next being insufficient evidence of a felony but possibly evidence of a misdemeanor (23 and 21 percent), and the last, insufficient evidence

---

[4] Two-tailed test significant at 0.01 level.
[5] Two-tailed test significant at 0.01 level.

Table 44

REASONS FOR FELONY REJECTION ACTIONS, POSSESSION OF DANGEROUS DRUGS--TWO PERIODS, 1971

(In percent)

Reason for Rejection[a]	C.A. Misdemeanor		D.A. Misdemeanor		Further Investigation		Outright Rejection		Overall	
	Jan-May	July-Nov	Jan-May	July-Nov	Jan-May	July-Nov	Jan-May	July-Nov	Jan-May	July-Nov
Number of cases (rejections)	188	490	15	21	19	20	909	424	1131	955
0. No reason	--	1	--	10	21	--	--	--	--	1
10. Insufficient evidence (unspecified)	3	--	--	--	--	15	3	4	3	2
12. Insufficient evidence: felony	10	2	27	5	--	--	--	--	2	1
13. Insufficient evidence: corpus	1	--	7	--	21	40	3	3	3	2
14. Insufficient evidence: suspect	35	4	13	--	32	25	31	35	32	18
22. No corpus: felony	1	1	--	--	--	--	--	--	--	--
23. No corpus: any crime	1	--	--	--	5	--	6	6	5	3
24. No corpus: suspect	--	--	--	--	--	--	--	1	--	--
32. Trivial or insufficient quantity	42	78	53	71	16	--	29	20	31	50
33. Trivial nature of offense	--	1	--	--	--	--	--	--	--	--
34. Personal history	--	7	--	14	--	--	--	--	--	4
37. Age of suspect	--	5	--	--	--	--	--	--	--	3
38. Other discretion	--	1	--	--	--	--	--	--	--	1
42. Witness	--	--	--	--	--	5	--	2	--	1
50. Violation of rights (unspecified)	--	--	--	--	--	--	1	2	1	1
51. Search and seizure	6	1	--	--	--	10	19	22	16	10
52. Unlawfully obtained statements	--	--	--	--	--	--	--	--	--	--
53. Unlawful arrest	1	--	--	--	5	5	6	4	5	2
54. Other violation of rights	--	--	--	--	--	--	--	--	--	--

NOTE: All reasons for which no percentage, after rounding, for any action for any period is *greater than* 1 percent are omitted entirely, as are all individual percentages which are less than 1 percent, after rounding.

[a] To facilitate cross-referencing in this study, numbers were assigned to reasons (see Table 42).

of the corpus of a crime (11 and 10 percent). Scant differences between the two periods are evidenced.

By far the most frequent reason given in both periods for referring cases to the City Attorney and for referring cases to the District Attorney to be handled as misdemeanors is insufficient evidence of a felony but possibly evidence of a misdemeanor (66 and 44 percent for the City Attorney, and 74 and 76 percent for the District Attorney). A decrease in this percentage occurs between periods for those cases referred to the City Attorney, accompanied by an increase in use of the reason of trivial nature of offense.[6] Almost all cases rejected for further investigation were rejected for some reason of insufficient evidence, e.g., insufficient evidence of corpus of a crime (20 and 15 percent), insufficient evidence to convict the suspect (18 and 31 percent), or insufficient evidence with no additional explanation (20 and 13 percent). For those cases rejected outright, the most frequently used reason in both periods is insufficient evidence to connect the suspect (44 percent in both periods).

Table 45

PAIRS OF REASONS FOR REJECTION OF DANGEROUS DRUG
POSSESSION COMPLAINTS--TWO PERIODS, 1971

(In percent)

First Reason	Second Reason	Jan-May	July-Nov
Trivial or insufficient quantity	None	27.9	27.2
Personal history	None	0.0	0.5
Trivial or insufficient quantity	Personal history	0.3	19.7
Personal history	Trivial or insufficient quantity	0.4	2.7

TERMINATION PRIOR TO SUPERIOR COURT PROSECUTION

The period between issuance of a felony complaint by the District Attorney and prosecution in Superior Court (if case is not terminated) includes (1) filing the complaint, (2) arraignment in Municipal Court, and (3) preliminary hearing. In particular, we want to look at cases that are terminated during this time, that is, those for which felony complaints are issued, but which never reach Superior Court.

Such terminations are basically of two types: (1) outright dismissals or (2) reductions of the charge from a felony to a misdemeanor, often in conjunction with a guilty plea. The latter can occur only if the offense carries an alternative felony or

---

[6] Two-tailed test significant at 0.01 level.

Table 46

REASONS FOR FELONY REJECTION ACTIONS, BURGLARY COMPLAINTS--TWO PERIODS, 1971

(In percent)

Reason for Rejection[a]	Felony Rejection Action									
	C.A. Misdemeanor		D.A. Misdemeanor		Further Investigation		Outright Rejection		Overall	
	Jan-May	July-Nov	Jan-May	July-Nov	Jan-May	July-Nov	Jan-May	July-Nov	Jan-May	July-Nov
Number of cases (rejections)	250	346	46	63	49	39	672	547	1017	295
0. No reason	2	1	--	--	33	23	--	1	2	2
10. Insufficient evidence (unspecified)	1	1	11	--	20	13	8	7	7	5
12. Insufficient evidence: felony	66	44	74	76	--	--	5	2	23	21
13. Insufficient evidence: corpus	5	2	--	--	20	15	14	17	11	10
14. Insufficient evidence: suspect	4	4	2	--	18	31	44	44	31	27
22. No corpus: felony	8	13	4	10	--	--	1	--	3	5
23. No corpus: any crime	--	--	--	--	--	--	6	4	4	2
24. No corpus: suspect	--	--	--	--	4	--	3	2	2	1
31. Restitution made	2	2	--	2	--	--	1	3	1	2
33. Trivial nature of offense	8	20	6	11	--	--	2	1	4	8
34. Personal history	1	8	--	--	--	--	--	--	--	3
37. Age of suspect	--	2	--	2	--	--	--	--	--	1
38. Other discretion	--	1	--	--	--	--	--	--	--	1
41. Victim	--	1	2	--	2	15	9	13	6	8
42. Witness	--	--	--	--	--	--	1	1	1	1
43. Defendant	--	--	--	--	--	3	--	--	--	--
51. Search and seizure	--	--	--	--	--	--	1	2	1	1
53. Unlawful arrest	--	--	--	--	2	--	2	1	1	--

NOTE: All reasons for which no percentage, after rounding, for any action for any period is *greater than* 1 percent are omitted entirely, as are all individual percentages which are less than 1 percent, after rounding.

[a] To facilitate cross-referencing in this study, numbers were assigned to reasons (see Table 42).

misdemeanor sentence under §17(b)(4) and (5) PC, or if the actual charged offense is changed. In either case, if the termination occurs prior to preliminary hearing, a District Attorney Recommendation Form is completed, documenting whether the case is dismissed or reduced to a misdemeanor, and giving reasons for the decision. For a termination that occurs at the preliminary hearing, a Memorandum of Preliminary Examination records both the nature of and reasons for the termination.

We examined all terminations that occurred prior to Superior Court prosecution for felony filings of five different offenses[7] in Central and each Branch Office from January 1, 1971, to November 10, 1971. Terminations at Area Offices were not included. The five offenses included possession of dangerous drugs (§11910 HS), burglary (§459 PC), possession of marijuana (§11530 HS), grand theft auto (§487.3 PC), and robbery (§211 PC). Robbery and first-degree burglary do not carry alternative sentences, so they cannot by themselves be reduced to misdemeanors. Any reductions shown for robbery indicate either a dismissal of the robbery charge and a reduction to a misdemeanor of a second count, or a change in the original charge. Some of the burglary complaint reductions may be similarly explained, although undoubtedly the vast majority are simply reductions of second-degree burglary, which *does* carry an alternative sentence.

All results are presented individually for two periods because we anticipated that the Esteybar decision[8] and the District Attorney policy directives would affect the rates. The Esteybar decision handed down by the California Supreme Court on June 22, 1971, gave the Municipal Court magistrate the power to reduce any offense carrying an alternative felony or misdemeanor sentence to a misdemeanor, without the concurrence of the prosecutor as had previously been required. Thereafter, one might well expect an increase in the number of cases reduced to misdemeanors at preliminary hearings. The directives that the District Attorney issued were expected to affect terminations both directly, by their definition of a procedure for reducing to a misdemeanor a complaint filed as a felony, and indirectly, by virtue of the directives' effect on complaints filed, as discussed previously.

Types of Felony Termination

Terminations of felony complaints are basically either outright dismissals or reductions to misdemeanors (which can occur either in conjunction with a guilty plea or as a straight reduction). Table 47 displays the relative frequencies with which these occur both prior to and at the preliminary hearing. The guilty plea category includes cases in which some counts were dismissed on the condition that a guilty plea be made on at least one count.

More than 80 percent of terminations that occurred before the preliminary hearing were guilty pleas to misdemeanors. This is frequently the result of plea bargaining in the courtroom immediately before the preliminary hearing. For offenses that carry alternative felony/misdemeanor sentences, the prosecutor agrees to reduce the offense to a misdemeanor under §17(b)(4) PC if the defendant

---

[7] This is ambiguous to the extent that many cases include counts for more than one offense. The sample here consists of those cases for which the single offense on the Felony Index is one of the five listed. The intent of the Index is to list the "most serious" offense.

[8] *Esteybar v. Municipal Court*, 5 Cal. 3d 119 (1971).

Table 47

DISTRIBUTION OF FELONY TERMINATION TYPES--TWO PERIODS, 1971

(In percent)

Cases and Disposition	Prior to Preliminary Hearing		At Preliminary Hearing	
	Jan-May	July-Nov	Jan-May	July-Nov
Number of cases (terminations)	596	272	477	553
Dismissal	10	18	96	68
Guilty plea to misdemeanor	89	82	3	18
Reduction to misdemeanor	0	0	2	14

will enter a guilty plea. There are no straight reductions to a misdemeanor prior to the preliminary hearing. Screening of filed cases by the District Attorney appears never to have reversed the original decision to handle the case as a felony—unless there is the added inducement of a guilty plea. The 10- and 18-percent levels for dismissals, however, are undoubtedly the result of some type of post-filing screening.

At the preliminary hearing, most terminations result from a dismissal. However, Table 47 shows a substantial drop in this percentage—from 96 percent in the first period to 68 percent in the second.[9] This shift is discussed below when we examine the actual rates at which these terminations occur.

Felony Termination Rates

Table 48 presents felony termination rates as a percentage of filed cases, for dismissal and for reduction to a misdemeanor both prior to the preliminary hearing and at the preliminary hearing. The misdemeanor rate includes both the guilty plea to misdemeanor and the straight reduction to misdemeanor shown in Table 47.

Dismissals prior to preliminary hearings reflected rates ranging from just under 1 percent to just over 2 percent, regardless of the offense. Aside from an increase in the dismissal rate for possession of marijuana, from 8 to 21 percent,[10] little change occurred between the two periods.

The percentage of felony filings reduced to misdemeanors prior to the preliminary (each of which, as shown in Table 47, occurred in conjunction with a guilty plea) was much higher, however; the weighted averages were 10 and 8 percent, respectively, for the two periods. This rate varied considerably across offenses: 12 and 8 for dangerous drugs; 16 and 10 for marijuana; and 6 for both periods for grand theft, auto. Robbery rates were very low because, as mentioned earlier, robbery itself cannot be reduced; the rates were non-zero as a result of either the reduction of other

[9] Two-tailed test significant at 0.01 level.
[10] Two-tailed test significant at 0.02 level.

Table 48

FELONY TERMINATION RATES FOR FIVE OFFENSES PRIOR TO SUPERIOR COURT
PROSECUTION--TWO PERIODS, 1971

(In percent)

Offense	Number of Cases (filings)		Prior to Preliminary Hearing				At Preliminary Hearing				All Terminations	
			Dismissal		Misdemeanor		Dismissal		Misdemeanor			
	Jan-May	July-Nov	Jan-May	July-Nov	Jan-May	July-Nov	Jan-May	July-Nov	Jan-May	July-Nov	Jan-May	July-Nov
Possession, dangerous drugs (§11910 HS)	1476	678	1.4	2.1	12.0	8.0	9.0	15.0	0.5	9.0	23.0	35.0
Burglary (§459 PC)	1234	1033	1.3	1.0	6.0	7.0	6.0	8.0	0.2	3.6	14.0	19.0
Possession, marijuana (§11530 HS)	1537	613	0.8	2.1	16.0	10.0	12.0	19.0	0.5	10.9	28.0	42.0
Grand theft, auto (§487.3 PC)	543	420	1.7	1.4	6.0	6.0	7.0	8.0	0.4	2.6	15.0	18.0
Robbery (§211 PC)	419	431	1.2	1.6	1.0	2.0	8.0	9.0	0	0.7	11.0	13.0
Five offenses (weighted)[a]	5209	3175	1.2	1.6	10.0	8.0	9.0	13.0	0.4	6.4	20.0	28.0

[a]See Appendix E for an explanation of weighted averages as used in this study.

counts or a change in charge. From the first period to the second, drug offenses exhibited large decreases, with an absolute decrease of 4 percent for dangerous drugs and of 6 percent for marijuana.[11]

At the preliminary hearing terminations with all counts dismissed had weighted average rates of 9 percent for the first period and 13 percent for the second. This rate varied substantially across the offenses, being high for the drug violations; specifically, the rates for possession of marijuana (12 and 19) were twice as high, within each period, as those for burglary (6 and 8). Drug offense rates increased sharply between the two periods, with possession of dangerous drugs increasing in absolute terms by 6 percent and possession of marijuana by 7 percent.[12]

We would expect to see the effect of the Esteybar decision on the percentage of cases reduced to misdemeanors at the preliminary hearing. The increase is conspicuous, with the weighted average shifting from 0.4 to 6.4. The largest increases occur in drug offenses; possession of dangerous drugs and possession of marijuana both had rates of 0.5 in the first period, whereas in the second period, dangerous drug rates rise to 9 percent, and marijuana rates to 10.9. Large increases also occur in burglary (from 0.2 to 3.6) and grand theft (0.4 to 2.6).[13]

In summary, reductions to misdemeanors prior to preliminary hearing decrease and dismissals prior to preliminary hearing increase slightly in the second period. Both reductions and dismissals at preliminary hearing increase substantially.

The overall weighted averages for all terminations for the two periods are 20 and 28 percent. Between periods, all offenses have increased, but the large increases are in drug offenses, with an absolute increase of 12 percent for dangerous drugs and 14 percent for marijuana.[14]

Termination Reasons

For each of the four types of terminations shown in Table 48, Table 49 gives in percent the relative frequency with which each reason was cited as the first reason for that termination. These results are based on the same sample used in Table 48, but are aggregated across the five offenses.

The most frequent reasons given for dismissal prior to the preliminary hearing were no corpus of any crime (23 percent in the first period and 18 percent in the second) and insufficient evidence, suspect (8 and 28 percent). Reasons relating to unavailability of defendant and personal history of defendant also appeared frequently. The reasons of insufficient evidence to connect the suspect and personal history are more important in the second period than in the first.[15] For both periods the major reasons given for reductions to misdemeanors prior to preliminary hearings were, in descending order, personal history (46 and 41 percent), trivial or insufficient quantity (31 and 20 percent), and age of suspect (11 and 13 percent). Little change is evident between the two periods, except the drop in frequency of trivial or insufficient quantity.

---

[11] Two tailed test significant at 0.01 level.
[12] Two-tailed test significant at 0.01 level.
[13] Two-tailed test significant at 0.01 level.
[14] Two-tailed tests significant at 0.02 level.
[15] Two-tailed tests significant at 0.02 level.

Table 49

TYPE OF FELONY TERMINATION AND FIRST REASONS FOR TERMINATION PRIOR TO
SUPERIOR COURT PROSECUTION--TWO PERIODS, 1971

(In percent)

First Reason for Termination[a]	Prior to Preliminary Hearing				At Preliminary Hearing			
	Dismissal		Misdemeanor		Dismissal		Misdemeanor	
	Jan-May	July-Nov	Jan-May	July-Nov	Jan-May	July-Nov	Jan-May	July-Nov
Number of cases (filings)	62	50	534	222	456	374	21	179
0. No reason	--	2	1	1	1	2	10	17
12. Insufficient evidence: felony	2	--	3	2	1	--	5	2
13. Insufficient evidence: corpus	--	4	--	--	1	3	--	--
14. Insufficient evidence: suspect	8	28	1	1	17	22	--	2
22. No corpus: felony	--	--	--	1	--	--	--	1
23. No corpus: any crime	23	18	1	1	4	4	--	1
24. No corpus: suspect	6	6	--	1	--	--	--	--
30. Discretionary (unspecified)	2	--	--	--	--	--	--	--
31. Restitution made	--	--	2	4	--	--	--	3
32. Trivial or insufficient quantity	8	4	31	20	3	1	38	44
33. Trivial nature of offense	--	--	1	5	--	--	5	7
34. Personal history	3	16	46	41	1	--	24	15
35. Officer request	--	--	--	1	--	--	--	--
37. Age of suspect	3	2	11	13	--	--	--	3
38. Other discretionary	6	--	--	--	--	--	--	1
41. Victim	6	--	1	4	9	12	--	--
42. Witness	2	2	1	--	14	13	5	1
43. Defendant	16	6	--	2	1	1	5	3
50. Violation of rights (unspecified)	--	--	--	--	1	1	--	--
51. Search and seizure	2	--	1	2	25	23	5	1
52. Improper advisement of rights	--	--	--	--	--	1	--	--
53. Unlawful arrest	2	--	--	--	11	9	--	--
54. Other violation of rights	--	--	--	--	1	1	--	--
61. Lack of prosecution	--	--	--	1	3	2	5	--
62. Prosecution error	3	--	--	--	1	--	--	--
71. Transfer jurisdiction	3	--	--	--	5	2	--	--
72. Superseded	5	12	--	--	--	--	--	--

NOTE: All reasons for which no percentage, after rounding, for any action for any period is *greater than* 1 percent are omitted entirely, as are all individual percentages which are less than 1 percent, after rounding.

[a]To facilitate cross-referencing in this study, numbers have been assigned to reasons (see Table 42).

For terminations occurring at the preliminary hearing, the most frequent reasons given for dismissals were search and seizure (25 and 23 percent), insufficient evidence to connect the suspect (17 and 22 percent), and unavailability or noncooperability of a witness (14 and 13 percent), or the victim (9 and 12 percent). Little difference arose between the two periods. For reductions to misdemeanor at the preliminary, the two major reasons are trivial or insufficient quantity (38 and 44 percent) and personal history (24 and 15 percent). Again, we find little change between the two periods in the relative frequencies with which the various reasons are cited, except for personal history.

A comparison of reasons given for these four types of terminations shows similarity in reasons for reduction to misdemeanor prior to and at the preliminary. The two major reasons for both categories are trivial or insufficient quantity and personal history. In general, the reasons for reduction are of a discretionary nature, in marked contrast with dismissals, and in particular with the dismissals at the preliminary hearing. (Reasons given for dismissals were based more frequently on insufficient evidence or lack of corpus.) One distinction between the two dismissal rates is the infrequent occurrence of dismissals prior to the preliminary hearing based on search and seizure and unlawful arrest, contrasted with the frequent occurrence of dismissals based on such reasons at the preliminary hearing.

Table 50 presents the major first reasons for reduction to misdemeanor prior to the preliminary hearing, for possession of dangerous drugs and for burglary. Only reasons occurring at least 5 percent of the time for one offense for one period are included. Table 50 enables us to observe the differences in the reasons for reduction between these two offenses. For possession of dangerous drugs, trivial or insufficient quantity occurs frequently (39 and 38 percent); whereas for burglary, trivial nature of offense occurs much less frequently (5 and 16 percent). Personal history can be seen as the most frequent reason given for reduction with both of these offenses: 46 and 52 percent for dangerous drugs, and 39 and 31 percent for burglary. For burglary, age of suspect and insufficient evidence of felony are often given as reasons for reduction, whereas these are of little import for dangerous drugs.

Table 50

MAJOR REASONS FOR REDUCTION TO MISDEMEANOR PRIOR TO
PRELIMINARY HEARING FOR POSSESSION OF DANGEROUS
DRUGS AND FOR BURGLARY--TWO PERIODS, 1971

(In percent)

Major Reason for Reduction[a]	Possession, Dangerous Drugs (§11910 HS)		Burglary (§459 PC)	
	Jan-May	July-Nov	Jan-May	July-Nov
Number of cases	178	56	77	70
12. Insufficient evidence, felony	--	--	17	6
31. Restitution made	--	--	6	11
32. Trivial or insufficient quantity	39	38	--	--
33. Trivial nature of offense	--	--	5	16
34. Personal history	46	52	39	31
37. Age of suspect	8	--	22	24

NOTE: Only reasons accounting for at least 5 percent of the first reasons are included.

[a]To facilitate cross-referencing in this study, numbers have been assigned to reasons (see Table 42).

A more complete description is obtained by adding the second reason. Table 51 presents combinations of first and second reasons occurring at least 5 percent of the time. In possession of dangerous drugs, trivial or insufficient quantity and personal history occurred together as the first two reasons in the *majority* of all cases. It is also true, though not shown in Table 51, that one of these was included as one of the first two reasons in 97 percent of the reductions to misdemeanor prior to the

Table 51

FIRST TWO REASONS FOR REDUCTION TO MISDEMEANOR PRIOR TO
PRELIMINARY HEARING FOR POSSESSION OF DANGEROUS DRUGS
AND FOR BURGLARY--TWO PERIODS, 1971

(In percent)

First Two Reasons for Reduction	Possession, Dangerous Drugs (§11910 HS)		Burglary (§459 PC)	
	Jan–May	July–Nov	Jan–May	July–Nov
Number of cases	178	56	77	70
Trivial or insufficient quantity and personal history	61	50	--	--
Age of suspect and personal history	11	12	25	28
Restitution made and personal history	--	--	13	10
Trivial other and personal history	--	--	10	10

preliminary hearing during both periods. For burglary, age of suspect and personal history arose in combination approximately one-fourth of the time.

Table 52 compares dismissals at the preliminary hearing for two offenses: possession of dangerous drugs and burglary. The relative frequencies with which the various reasons were cited were quite disparate for these two offenses. As would be expected, illegal search and seizure, which occurs relatively infrequently for burglary, comprised almost 40 percent of all reasons for dismissal of possession of dangerous drug cases. Reasons associated with victims, which occurred quite frequently for burglary (18 and 23 percent), did not appear in possession of dangerous drugs, since the latter is a "victimless" offense. Insufficient evidence to connect the suspect and reasons associated with the witness each accounted for about one-fifth of the reasons cited for burglary and about one-tenth of those cited for possession of dangerous drugs. For neither offense did the distribution of the reasons cited change markedly between the two periods.

CONCLUDING REMARKS

The approach employed in this section can be used to measure the effects of changes such as those in internal policy as set forth in the directives and those resulting externally from the Esteybar decision. But inasmuch as these occurred almost concurrently, the effects are statistically confounded.

In the first part of this section, we observed increases, which we attributed to the directives, both in the overall rejection rate and in the proportion of rejections to be handled as misdemeanors. Next, we found a decrease in the rate of reduction

Table 52

MAJOR REASONS FOR DISMISSAL AT PRELIMINARY HEARING FOR POSSESSION
OF DANGEROUS DRUGS AND FOR BURGLARY--TWO PERIODS, 1971

(In percent)

Major Reason	Possession, Dangerous Drugs (§11910 HS)		Burglary (§459 PC)	
	Jan–May	July–Nov	Jan–May	July–Nov
Number of cases	132	104	74	82
12. Insufficient evidence, felony	--	--	7	--
14. Insufficient evidence, suspect	12	12	23	21
23. No corpus of any crime	10	9	--	--
41. Victim	--	--	18	23
42. Witness	8	12	22	21
51. Illegal search and seizure	40	36	--	11
53. Unlawful detention or arrest	17	12	--	9
71. Transfer jurisdiction	7	--	--	--

NOTE: Only reasons accounting for at least 5 percent of the first reasons cited are included.

to misdemeanors (with guilty pleas) prior to the preliminary hearing. It would appear that, because of the directives, some portion of cases carrying alternative sentences (which previously had been filed with the expectation of a reduction to a misdemeanor with a bargained guilty plea prior to the preliminary) are now reduced to a misdemeanor at the filing stage.

The increased rate of reduction to misdemeanor at the preliminary hearing, on the other hand, is likely the effect of the Esteybar decision, because the magistrates were able to reduce cases more frequently when the consent of the prosecutor was no longer needed. This reduction is the more striking because the population of cases reaching the magistrates in the second period should, on the average, be stronger, inasmuch as the District Attorney presumably winnowed more of the weaker cases by increased rejections at the filing stage.

VI. VARIATION IN OFFICE MANAGEMENT, PROCEDURES, AND WORKLOAD

In Section II we described the typical organization and procedures for processing cases in the Los Angeles County District Attorney's Office. In Section VII we examine differences in case outcomes *between* Offices. Here we describe variations in organization, procedures, workload, or community that may account for some of these differences.

ASSIGNMENT

Each Branch Office is assigned 18 to 23 Deputy District Attorneys with whom the Branch Head Deputy must cover the following: file felony complaints;[1] prosecute misdemeanors and conduct preliminary hearings in the Municipal Court; and perform all activities in the criminal departments of the Superior Court. Central Operations is unique in that because of its size, deputies are more likely to remain in separate units covering complaints, preliminary hearings, and trials, each run by a separate administrator.

Within the Branches, the most prevalent policy is to assign all deputies to one of three duties: Superior Court (each man is assigned to a specific department under the supervision of a Calendar Deputy), Municipal Court, or Complaints. The most senior grade IV's remain Calendar Deputies in a specific department. The more junior deputies alternate between assignments over an extended period (staying in one job for a month or more).

In some Branches a variation in this basic pattern emerges when the handling of complaints becomes the sole responsibility of one senior deputy, with others filling in on an exception basis. This practice occurs when the physical or emotional demands of the courtroom are too much for a particular deputy. Since the practice is to always have one senior man available for Complaints, this becomes the logical place to assign such a deputy. Pomona, Torrance, and Santa Monica currently follow this pattern.

A final variation in the basic assignment pattern occurs when only one senior

---

[1] In jurisdictions that have no City Attorney to prosecute misdemeanors, the District Attorney also files and prosecutes misdemeanors.

deputy is assigned to each Superior Court and the remaining deputies are held in an Office pool, to be assigned as necessary to specific cases, as is the current Long Beach practice. The justification offered for this policy is that it provides tighter control over individual workloads and performance, and allows the Office to concentrate its efforts on particularly tough cases.

WORKLOAD

There is no readily acceptable method for comparing workload across Branches. The authorized manpower for each Branch is basically justified on the basis of the number of courts it must serve. Yet this method of measurement ignores variations in the amount of time each court devotes to active consideration of criminal matters, the nature of the matters being considered, and the amount of consideration they require.

In an attempt to provide some measure of office workloads we devised the workload scale shown in Table 53. The processing of a single case through any of

Table 53

PROSECUTION WORKLOAD SCALE

Activity	Workload Units
Processing a complaint	1
Disposing of a misdemeanor	1
Preliminary hearing	1
Superior Court arraignment	1
Taking a plea	1
Submitting a case on the transcript	2
Court trial	10
Jury trial	50

the activities listed in the table increases the workload count for that Branch by the number of units indicated. The values assigned to each activity are the result of combining our observations about the amount of preparation required to perform each activity; more formal estimates of the actual court time required to complete each activity;[2] and our own study of times to process a complaint.[3]

[2] Caseload Relative Weight Study by Administrative Office of Los Angeles Superior Court (unpublished).

[3] The study was conducted by having the complaint receptionist at Central Operations log the elapsed time a police officer spent with a Complaint Deputy on a specific complaint; the charge; and the disposition. Of 624 cases for which data were recorded, 239 were referred to the City Attorney, 170 were filed, 162 were rejected, and for 53 no disposition was indicated. The average elapsed time in minutes for cases in each category was, respectively, as follows: referred to City Attorney, 9; filed, 31; rejected, 11; no disposition indicated, 21. The average processing time was 16 minutes.

To estimate Branch workloads we used both 1970 BCS data for Superior Court activities and D.A. records for the first 11 months of 1971, which we extended to one year by multiplying all numbers by 12/11. Table 54 shows the workload counts and weighted caseload for each Branch. If these estimates of the actual Branch workload are reasonably correct, they suggest that there are wide differences in the amount of time deputies have to prepare a case and in the resultant pressures to settle the matter without going to trial.

FILING STANDARDS

All Offices purport to follow the practice of filing only cases that they can reasonably expect to win; however, the procedures followed to ensure this practice vary considerably. In none of the Offices are the requirements for filing different types of offenses spelled out in written directives as is done by some other prosecutors.[4] Perhaps this is because the L.A. Civil Service System guarantees that there are enough deputies with trial experience in an Office, thus making it unnecessary to rely on formal standards, while other prosecutors must make do with less experienced deputies.

In the absence of written standards, the Offices that appear to have the most clearly articulated and monitored filing practices are Pomona and Long Beach, where deputies are questioned routinely if they deviate from accepted practices. In Long Beach (and sometimes in other Branches) this practice is carried even further and a deputy who files a weak case or "turkey" may be required to try it himself without recourse to plea bargaining.

The monitoring of filing standards on a routine basis appears to be weakest in Pasadena where the prevalent philosophy is that the deputies are well-qualified professionals and able to exercise the appropriate judgment without continual review. Filing standards may also be more informal in Central Operations since the Complaints Unit is organizationally distinct from the Trials Unit, and the deputies involved in filing can never carry through the cases they begin. In other Branches, deputies do see cases they originally filed through subsequent stages.

A similar effect occurs in some Branches where most of the cases to be tried are originally filed in one of the surrounding Area Offices. The variation can be seen by referring to Table 55, which shows the ratio of felony complaints filed to Superior Court dispositions for 1971.[5] Table 55 also shows that Norwalk files none of its cases, whereas Pomona and Torrance file very few.

One final factor in considering the filing standards employed is the extent to which Branch management discourages deputy-shopping on the part of the police. Although most Branch Head Deputies agreed that deputy-shopping was not a desirable practice, Long Beach and Pomona appeared to resist this practice most strenuously, whereas Pasadena and Van Nuys seem to be less concerned with it.

---

[4] The U.S. Attorney for the District of Columbia has a detailed filing manual which does list the evidentiary requirements for each type of case.

[5] These data are not entirely consistent since the D.A.'s records of complaints may show multiple filings on a single defendant which were eventually combined into one Superior Court case. Yet this inflation factor should be uniform across Branches.

Table 54

CASELOAD AND WORKLOAD BY BRANCH OFFICE, 1971[a]

Branch Office	Total Complaints	Misd Disp	Prelim	Superior Arraign	Plea	SOT	Court Trial	Jury Trial	Weighted Caseload	Deps Auth	Deps Asgd	Case-load per Asgd Dep
Central	39,312	---	26,926	12,241	4,984	3,870	1,114	556	130,143	109	100	1,301
Long Beach	3,574	498	1,801	2,283	1,329	416	214	114	18,157	23	18	1,009
Santa Monica	7,446	573	3,499	2,324	1,338	427	102	89	21,504	25	23	935
Van Nuys	13,878	1,321	5,705	3,152	2,106	487	107	89	32,656	28	23	1,420
Torrance	8,897	4,663	2,249	5,048	1,097	2,812	474	93	36,968	25	23	1,607
Norwalk	---	---	---	4,147	2,058	1,454	170	107	16,163	25	23	703
Pomona	6,857	5,085	1,069	2,515	1,303	556	189	46	22,131	22	19	1,165
Pasadena	11,031	6,702	2,336	1,432	778	174	148	47	26,457	20	14	1,896
Total	90,995	18,842	43,585	33,142	14,993	10,196	2,518	1,141	304,179	277	243	1,252
Weights	1	1	1	1	1	2	10	50				

[a]D.A. figures for first 11 months of 1971 adjusted to full year by multiplying them by 12/11.

Table 55

RATIO OF FELONY COMPLAINTS FILED TO
SUPERIOR COURT DISPOSITIONS, 1971

Branch Office	(1) Complaints Filed[a]	(2) Superior Court Arraignment[b]	Ratio (1)/(2)
Los Angeles	18,165	11,671	1.6
Long Beach	1,643	2,138	0.77
Santa Monica	3,245	2,415	1.34
Van Nuys	5,166	3,466	1.49
Torrance	2,243	5,325	0.42
Norwalk	0	5,352	0
Pomona	774	2,492	0.31
Pasadena	2,263	2,150	1.05

[a]D.A. figures for first 11 months of 1971 adjusted to full year by multiplying them by 12/11.

[b]Data obtained from California Bureau of Criminal Statistics, *Felony Defendants Disposed of in California Courts*, 1971.

MANAGEMENT REVIEW

In our observations of the various D.A. Offices, we identified four different styles of management control that we describe below. Since this was not an explicit objective at the time of our interviews, we probably missed some other styles or failed to categorize accurately those offices not specifically identified by name.

The Long Beach Office is characterized by the strictest control over filing, case assignment, and plea negotiation. Strict filing standards are observed and a senior deputy reviews each complaint for its appropriateness. Trial deputies operate from a central pool (their whereabouts must be known at all times) and are assigned cases by a senior deputy in accordance with their particular skill and experience level. The senior deputy monitors the progress of each case, after having first noted any special considerations it might entail.

In Pomona, as well as in the other Branch Offices, cases are assigned by the Calendar Deputies; however, the Pomona Branch Head reviews each case at the time a complaint is issued and flags about 25 percent for detailed monitoring, which he subsequently accomplishes by checking the Superior Court minutes. In addition, he flags some cases such as drug sales, etc., with red tape to indicate that the deputy trying it should not accept a deal or a continuance without checking with him first.

None of the other Offices appeared to routinely monitor cases. They ranged across a spectrum from active involvement by the Branch Head in many cases (Van Nuys and Torrance) to almost completely decentralized operations controlled by the Calendar Deputies (Pasadena). In Van Nuys, the Branch Head has a completely open-door policy (his office is also at a central traffic point), which encourages his deputies to enter and ask his advice on how a particular matter should be handled. He also makes it a point to visit each court to observe, and periodically substitutes for the Calendar Deputies.

In Pasadena, the presiding judge so dominates the flow of cases that the Branch Office appears to be completely decentralized to the courtroom level.

CALENDARING

The method of calendaring decided on by the court requires that cases involving defendants who are held to answer are assigned directly to one of the trial departments in the Superior Court by Municipal Court clerks. But only Long Beach, Norwalk, and Pomona have actually implemented this system. We learned of no actions taken in these three Branches to ensure that assignments are purely random, and the deputies concede that a persistent attorney often gets his case before the judge of his choice.

In other Branches, a master calendar department handles all arraignments, and often pleas and other short matters. Pasadena has an extreme version of this system in which no case is ever turned over directly to another department, but instead returns to the presiding judge after each step (motion, hearing, trial, etc.) is completed.

OTHER FACTORS THAT MIGHT INFLUENCE BRANCH PERFORMANCE

Since each Branch deals with different groups of arresting agencies, we asked each Head Deputy a number of questions about the performance of the police and his interaction with them. The only consistent patterns across all Branches were as follows:

- All District Attorneys thought that the police could improve their investigations, especially with the 48-hour arraignment rule in effect.
- None of the Branch Heads meet with the police regularly to discuss policy issues.

The relationship between the Branch Heads and the judges with whom they work remains quite formal in all Branches. Most deputies believe that their judges' performance is moderate to tough, except for Long Beach, where they are believed to be too lenient but are in fact the toughest in the county. All Branch Heads believe juries to be tough but fair.

VII. THE PATTERN OF DISPOSITIONS
ACROSS BRANCHES

We have examined the workings of the criminal justice system and the pattern of dispositions on a *countywide* basis. In this section we analyze the *within*-county pattern, focusing on (1) variations in the arrest process among the county's numerous law enforcement agencies, (2) variations in complaint issuance, terminations prior to and during the preliminary hearings, and Superior Court dispositions among D.A. Branch Offices, and (3) variations in sentencing practices of individual judges as well as in different Superior Court Branches. Where possible, our analysis and discussion aim at separating and explicating influences on outcome that are controllable by the District Attorney and ones that are uncontrollable.

ARREST AND COMPLAINT ISSUANCE

There are some 40 arresting agencies in Los Angeles County, of which eight made more than 1000 felony arrests in 1970. The Los Angeles Police Department (LAPD) accounted for about 51 percent of the 101,899 felony arrests in the county, and the Los Angeles Sheriff's Office (LASO) accounted for 23 percent. For the 292,943 adult misdemeanor arrests, the comparable figures were 56 percent for LAPD and 17 percent for LASO.

Table 56, which presents data for six arresting agencies, provides some insight into the differences existing among Los Angeles County police departments in making arrests, discriminating between felonies and misdemeanors, and securing complaints from the D.A.'s Office.

The first two indices of interest are the ratios of arrests to reported crimes for robbery and burglary. Variation among police departments may be attributable to differences in crime-solving competence, in criminals, in policies regarding grounds for arrest, or in crime reporting rate. There appears to be more variability in robbery arrest rates than in burglary arrest rates. And there appear to be greater differences among small police departments than among large ones. We know of no reason to believe that the high robbery arrest rates for Compton and Santa Monica and the high burglary arrest rate in Compton are due to a willingness to arrest without sufficient evidence. Unfortunately, this study could not include an explicit examination of differences in such "causal" variables among arresting agencies.

Table 56

ARREST DATA FOR SIX ARRESTING AGENCIES

Police Department or Jurisdiction	Arrest Ratio[a]		Felony/Misdemeanor Arrest Ratio			Felony Arrest Disposition[b]			
	Robbery	Burglary	All Arrests	Assault Arrests	Drug Arrests	Turned Over to Other Jurisdiction (%)	Released (%)	Mis-demeanors Filed (%)	Felonies Filed (%)
LAPD	0.030	0.088	0.32	2.48	4.78	4	27	23	46
LASO	0.024	0.100	0.48	1.06	10.43	11	30	13	46
Long Beach PD	0.030	0.102	0.22	1.73	0.66	5	36	15	44
Pasadena PD	0.021	0.085	0.74	2.56	35.50	3	43	13	41
Santa Monica PD	0.051	0.058	0.27	2.37	1.46	16	25	20	39
Compton PD	0.053	0.124	0.77	1.19	114.30	10	26	18	46
Countywide	0.029	0.088	0.35	1.67	4.42	7	28	18	47

SOURCE: California Bureau of Criminal Statistics, *Crime and Arrests*, 1970.

[a]For given felony offense, arrest rate is the ratio of number of arrests to total reported cases.

[b]Percent of total felony arrests.

The next measure of interest is the ratio of adult felony arrests to adult misdemeanor arrests. This ratio is shown for all offenses and for the restricted categories of assault and drugs. Variation in this measure among arresting agencies should reflect differences in composition of reported crime, in reluctance to make misdemeanor arrests (either due to explicit policy or because limited police resources are focused on felony crimes), or in charging standards of arresting officers. Notice that for all crimes and for drug offenses, an arrest by the Long Beach Police Department is least likely to be a felony, while the opposite is true in Compton. A LASO arrest is more likely to be for a felony than an LAPD arrest is. Again, except for the assault category, differences between the two large police departments are smaller than the differences among small police departments. Of the three "causal" factors in variability of this statistic, our guess is that differences in charging standards by arresting officers is most influential, although this study could not include explicit examination of these factors.

The final indices in Table 56 reflect the disposition of felony arrests in the charging process: the percentages turned over to other jurisdictions, released, charged with only a misdemeanor, and charged with a felony. The percentage of felony arrests for which felony complaints are filed is quite consistent across arresting agencies, except for the Santa Monica and Pasadena Police Departments—which exhibit lower figures. In Pasadena, this is due primarily to the very high fraction released. Table 56 does not make immediately clear to what extent the low felony filing rate may be due to differences in filing policies in the Pasadena Branch compared to other Offices and to what extent it is due to differences in charging standards between the Pasadena police and other police departments. The latter's charging standards probably contribute to the high percentage released because Table 56 also indicates very high felony/misdemeanor arrest ratios in Pasadena for all arrests and for drug arrests. In Santa Monica, the lower fraction of felony filings is probably due to the high fraction of arrestees turned over to other jurisdictions, since the fraction released and the fraction for which misdemeanors are filed are average.

A striking datum is the high fraction of rejects[1] that the LAPD turns into misdemeanor filings. Another significant observation, developed more fully below, is that the tough filing policy in the Long Beach Branch of the D.A.'s Office (as suggested by a high percentage released but a low percentage for which misdemeanors are filed) seems to have affected Long Beach PD's charging standards for arrest. Notice that the Long Beach PD's felony/misdemeanor arrest ratio for all arrests and for drug arrests is by far the lowest of all police departments shown.

FELONY REJECTION RATES

We now analyze felony rejection rates among D.A. Branch and Area Offices. A number of factors may influence rejection rates. Factors associated with arresting agencies include charging standards used by the agency and individual arresting

---

[1] Throughout the report the term felony rejection is used to denote the sum of felony arrests rejected outright (i.e., suspect is released) and felony arrests rejected but referred for filing as misdemeanors either to the District Attorney or to the appropriate city prosecutor.

officers, thoroughness and competence in building a case against the arrestee(s), how often cases turn on evidence that the court may declare inadmissible (e.g., illegal search and seizure), and so on. Factors associated with the prosecution include the competence of the individual Deputy District Attorney, the toughness or leniency of filing standards in the Branch or Area Office, the degree to which supervision and control over filing standards is actually exercised, whether or not arresting officers may "shop" for Deputy District Attorneys when attempting to secure a complaint, and the degree to which the D.A.'s Office influences the arresting agency's charging standards. In addition, filing standards may be influenced explicitly or implicitly by "second guessing" on the part of the Head Deputy or an individual deputy as to how individual judges (in Municipal or Superior Courts) or juries in that area will act.

Assuming that the variation in factors associated with arresting agencies is greater *among* agencies as opposed to *within* an agency, we first compare rejection rates among D.A. Branch or Area Offices for cases originating from a single arresting agency. Tables 57 and 58 display such results for five major offenses filed by the LAPD and the LASO from July through December of 1971. This comparison should help reveal the differences introduced by prosecution factors, since differences due to arresting agencies are reduced. Some will remain, of course, since one may expect differences among police divisions of a large police department.

It is fair to say that the data displayed in Tables 57 and 58 do in fact suggest that there *are* large differences in felony rejection rates attributable to prosecution factors. Except for auto theft, cases filed by LAPD in the Los Angeles Office of the District Attorney are less likely to be rejected than in the Van Nuys Branch Office. And in the San Pedro Area Office almost 75 percent of LAPD's cases are rejected. In fact, over 80 percent of all cases involving possession of marijuana, auto theft, and robbery filed by LAPD in San Pedro are rejected as felonies. The relative differences are even larger when we consider cases brought to the District Attorney by LASO.

Table 57

FELONY REJECTION RATES AMONG D.A. BRANCH OR AREA OFFICES FOR
FIVE MAJOR OFFENSES FILED BY LAPD, JULY-DECEMBER 1971

(In percent)

D.A. Branch or Area Office	Rejection Rate					
	Possession, Dangerous Drugs (§11910 HS)	Possession, Marijuana (§11530 HS)	Burglary (§459 PC)	Grand Theft, Auto (§487.3 PC)	Robbery (§211 PC)	Five Offenses (weighted)[a]
Branch Office						
L.A. (central)	58	59	54	58	50	56
Van Nuys	64	83	53	46	55	63
Santa Monica	56	62	61	41	64	58
Area Office						
San Pedro[b]	57	87	62	87	81	72

[a]See Appendix E for an explanation of weighted averages as used in this study.

[b]Felonies tried in Long Beach.

Table 58

FELONY REJECTION RATES AMONG D.A. BRANCH OR AREA OFFICES FOR
FIVE MAJOR OFFENSES FILED BY LASO, JULY-DECEMBER 1971[a]

(In percent)

D.A. Branch or Area Office	D.A. Branch Where Superior Court Trials Held	Rejection Rate					
		Possession, Dangerous Drugs (§11910 HS)	Possession, Marijuana (§11530 HS)	Burglary (§459 PC)	Grand Theft, Auto (§487.3 PC)	Robbery (§211 PC)	Five Offenses (weighted)[b]
Santa Monica	Santa Monica	48	44	51	44	17	44
Beverly Hills	Santa Monica	56	56	40	50	38	49
Torrance	Torrance	58	56	53	45	50[c]	54
Inglewood	Torrance	53	51	50	45	50	51
Bellflower	Norwalk	63	67	55	45	26	56
Downey	Norwalk	25	29	25	48	30[c]	29
East L.A.	Norwalk	48	43	56	74	30	50
Whittier	Norwalk	20	31	26	45	0[c]	25
Pomona	Pomona	64	52	58	0[c]	0[c]	46
El Monte	Pomona	46	50	49	40	43	47
West Covina	Pomona	62	71	24	0[c]	27	44
Pasadena	Pasadena	44	63	60	53	63	56
Glendale	L.A. (central)	60	71	76	75[c]	0[c]	63

[a]This table shows only a sample of Branch and Area Offices where LASO attempts to secure complaints. Some have been omitted because the number of cases brought in were small and rejection rate data were not statistically reliable. Others have been omitted for simplicity.

[b]See Appendix E for an explanation of weighted averages as used in this study.

[c]Based on small sample.

For example, the Glendale and Bellflower Area Offices and the Pasadena and Torrance Branch Offices reject between 54 and 63 percent of the felonies, whereas the Whittier and Downey Area Offices reject only 25 percent to 29 percent.

Before we make broader comparisons among D.A. Offices, it is useful to examine 1971 rejection rates by arresting agency and offense for the period prior to (January-May) and after (July-December) the issuance of the D.A.'s memo defining the conditions under which alternative felony/misdemeanors could be filed as misdemeanors. In general, this memo caused the proportion of offenses filed as misdemeanors to increase. As mentioned earlier, for example, possession of dangerous drug cases would be handled as misdemeanors if 10 capsules or pills or less were found in the defendant's possession, or possession of marijuana cases would be handled as misdemeanors if 5 cigarettes or less were found in the defendant's possession, when the defendant had no prior conviction for an offense punishable as a felony. The filing policy change also affected cases involving bookmaking; unlawful sexual intercourse; insufficient funds-checks; forgery; and, at the discretion of D.A. management officials, all other felony charges carrying an alternative misdemeanor sentence. In addition, for defendants *with* a prior conviction for an offense punishable as a felony, certain designated management personnel could, at their discretion, order the case processed as a misdemeanor.

Table 59 invites several observations. Prior to the D.A.'s filing policy change, the differences in rejection rates among arresting agencies generally were not large. Except for the Compton Police Department, which had a 21-percent rejection rate for the five weighted offenses, the rate varied between 32 and 46 percent, with a countywide average of 40 percent. After the filing policy change, however, the spread in rejection rates increased markedly; it varied between 29 percent for the Compton PD to 59 percent for LAPD. In fact, for dangerous drug and marijuana possession, rejection rates increased to more than 70 percent for some police departments. The countywide average increased to 53 percent. If one assumes that all Branch and Area Offices acted vigorously to implement the policy (an assumption examined subsequently), one can infer that some police departments' arrest policies responded more than others to the D.A.'s filing policy change. For example, it is reasonable to infer that, because LASO rejection rates increased less than did LAPD's and Long Beach PD's rejection rates, LASO was more responsive to the D.A.'s change; however, because Santa Monica, Whittier, and Compton PDs' rejection rates showed little or no upward change, it may be that filing practices in these Offices were relatively unaffected by the policy memo. This question is considered further below, when we examine rejection rate changes among D.A. Offices, taking into account filing for all arresting agencies seeking complaints in those Offices.

We consider next the level and variation of rejection rates, before and after the filing policy change, among all of the Branch Offices and two of the Area Offices (the Area Offices with the highest and lowest rejection rates). The data in Table 60 include all felony complaints sought by all arresting agencies served by each Office. The first issue we consider is the extent to which the various Branch and Area Offices responded to the filing policy change. On the average, countywide felony rejections rose from 40 to 53 percent for the five offenses, with much larger increases registered for drug charges. It would appear that the Central Office and the Long Beach, Van Nuys, and Pomona Branch Offices did in fact respond, particularly in drug cases. The Santa Monica, Torrance, and Pasadena Branches showed only small increases. The

Table 59

FELONY REJECTION RATES AMONG ARRESTING AGENCIES FOR FIVE MAJOR
OFFENSES--TWO PERIODS, 1971

(In percent)

Rejection Rate

Arresting Agency	Possession, Dangerous Drugs (§11910 HS)		Possession, Marijuana (§11530 HS)		Burglary (§459 PC)		Grand Theft, Auto (§487.3 PC)		Robbery (§211 PC)		Five Offenses (weighted)[a]	
	Jan-May	July-Nov	Jan-May	July-Nov	Jan-May	July-Nov	Jan-May	July-Nov	Jan-May	July-Nov	Jan-May	July-Nov
LAPD	31	59	42	66	50	55	47	56	47	52	42	59
LASO	33	47	38	51	46	51	43	45	46	53	40	49
Long Beach PD	31	69	33	78	32	44	36	49	37	30	33	59
Pasadena PD	53	64	48	71	45	30	41	58	31	25	46	52
Pomona PD	21	39	22	44[b]	49	38	47	39	22[b]	46	32	41
Santa Monica PD	31	47	48	50	47	43	36	10[b]	13[b]	21	38	40
Torrance PD	40	54	55	68	38	58	16	18	0[b]	10[b]	37	50
Whittier PD	44	26	50	29	17	26	31	33	42[b]	0[b]	37	25
Compton PD	38	47	31	41	4	19	4	3	13	6	21	29
Countywide (all arresting agencies)	34	53	41	61	46	50	43	48	45	47	40	53

[a]See Appendix E for an explanation of weighted averages as used in this study.

[b]Based on small sample.

Table 60

FELONY REJECTION RATES AMONG D.A. BRANCH OR AREA OFFICES FOR FIVE MAJOR
OFFENSES--TWO PERIODS, 1971

(In percent)

Rejection Rate

D.A. Branch or Area Office	Possession, Dangerous Drugs (§11910 HS)		Possession, Marijuana (§11530 HS)		Burglary (§459 PC)		Grand Theft, Auto (§487.3 PC)		Robbery (§211 PC)		Five Offenses (weighted)[a]	
	Jan-May	July-Nov	Jan-May	July-Nov	Jan-May	July-Nov	Jan-May	July-Nov	Jan-May	July-Nov	Jan-May	July-Nov
Branch Office												
L.A. (central)	25	57	35	58	49	54	46	58	45	50	38	56
Long Beach	30	68	38	76	34	44	37	48	38	30	35	58
Santa Monica	44	52	47	58	50	57	47	40	49	49	47	53
Van Nuys	34	63	52	82	50	52	49	46	51	56	46	62
Torrance	41	46	51	60	40	45	21	33	38	34	41	47
Pomona	29	50	26	50	44	40	43	37	18	35	33	44
Pasadena	45	45	45	63	42	42	41	50	34	27	43	48
Area Office												
San Pedro	56	57	61	87	65	62	58	87	65	81	61	72
Whittier	25	22	28	30	18	26	17	38	30	0	23	25
Countywide	34	53	41	61	46	50	43	48	45	47	40	53

[a]See Appendix E for an explanation of weighted averages as used in this study.

San Pedro Area Office showed a modest increase in rejections, whereas the Whittier Area Office showed essentially no change.

Generally speaking, these observations are consistent with the pictures of the various Branch Offices that emerged from interviews with Branch Office Head Deputies. Offices such as Long Beach, Pomona, and, to some extent, Van Nuys, which have moderately strict to strict filing standards and tight supervision and control of Complaint Deputies, tended to be more responsive to the filing policy change. Offices with less supervision and more permissive filing standards, such as Pasadena, and to some extent, Santa Monica, tended to be less responsive. The small increase in rejection rates for the Torrance Office, however, tended to be inconsistent with the tough filing standards, close supervision image of the Office. Since we did not conduct interviews at Area Offices, we cannot comment on the consistency among rejection rates, filing standards, and characteristics of these Offices. An alternative hypothesis for these findings could be that the Offices showing little change had already adopted the more lenient charging practices before the memo was issued and therefore large increases in rejection rates would not be expected.

The next issue is related to the variation in rejection rate level among Offices over a given period. Is there "overfiling" in some and "underfiling" in others? Is prosecutorial discretion exercised evenhandedly? We have already seen that, after fixing upon a single arresting agency, LASO rejection rates vary dramatically from location to location, particularly among Area Offices (Table 58), so one cannot attribute most of the variation among Branch and Area Offices to arresting agency differences. Table 60 confirms such observations. Why did marijuana possession rejection rates from July through December 1971 vary from 30 percent in the Whittier Office to 87 percent in the San Pedro Office? And why did auto theft rejection rates vary from 38 percent to 87 percent in these Offices? (The variation in rejection rates over the earlier period prior to the filing policy change was also considerable.) We can only raise such questions at this point, since we need to examine the reasons for rejection and the subsequent disposition of felony filings in the Municipal and Superior Courts before we can begin to answer them. But to anticipate—the administration of criminal justice within Los Angeles County, as measured by the criteria discussed earlier—does *not* appear to be evenhanded.

REJECTION ACTIONS

We now examine Branch disparities in rejection more thoroughly by comparing the rates for each of the various rejection actions. Table 61 displays these data for burglary[2] and dangerous drugs. All table entries are given as percentages of complaints made.

First we compare the misdemeanor rates for the Branches in the first period, before the issuance of the directives. For burglary, the rates range from a high of 24 percent of all complaints in Van Nuys and of 16 percent in Santa Monica to a low of 1 percent in Long Beach. The same pattern holds for dangerous drugs, with Van Nuys and Santa Monica at 13 percent each and Long Beach at 0 percent.

---

[2] Sample described in Section IV.

Table 61

FREQUENCY OF REJECTION ACTIONS BY BRANCH OFFICES OF ATTEMPTED FILINGS FOR BURGLARY AND POSSESSION OF DANGEROUS DRUGS--TWO PERIODS, 1971

(In percent)

Branch Office	No. of Cases (complaints)		Felony Filing		Felony Rejections					
					C.A. or D.A. Misdemeanor		Further Investigation		Outright Rejection	
	Jan-May	July-Nov	Jan-May	July-Nov	Jan-May	July-Nov	Jan-May	July-Nov	Jan-May	July-Nov
A. Burglary										
L.A. (central)	2048[a]	1778[b]	51	46	13	17	2	0	34	36
Long Beach	159	111	66	56	1	24	0	1	33	19
Pasadena	235	245	58	58	8	18	0	2	34	22
Pomona	118	81	56	60	7	19	4	0	33	21
Santa Monica	366	365	50	43	16	27	7	4	26	26
Torrance	216	190	60	55	10	16	3	6	26	23
Van Nuys	662	511	50	48	24	26	1	1	26	25
B. Possession, Dangerous Drugs										
L.A. (central)	1266[c]	1035[d]	75	43	2	31	0	0	23	26
Long Beach	318	142	70	32	0	55	2	0	28	13
Pasadena	325	143	55	55	1	11	1	3	43	32
Pomona	70	64	71	50	3	0	0	3	26	47
Santa Monica	314	244	56	48	13	26	1	3	31	22
Torrance	340	219	59	54	8	9	1	3	32	34
Van Nuys	655	450	66	37	13	48	0	1	21	14

[a] of these, 996 were rejections, of which only 230 were sampled to estimate the distribution among the various rejection categories.

[b] Similarly here, of 958 rejections, only 213 were sampled.

[c] Of these, 316 were rejections, of which only 222 were sampled to estimate the distribution among the various rejection categories.

[d] Similarly here, of 595 rejections, only 223 were sampled.

A comparison of the rates before and after the directive reveals substantial Branch differences in terms of both the location and magnitude of the effect. In Central, for example, for both offenses, a shift from felony filings to misdemeanors occurs, with outright rejection remaining quite constant. The change is, as would be expected, more marked for the drug offense. In contrast, for both offenses, Pasadena has no change in filing rate but has a shift from outright rejections to misdemeanors. Long Beach combines these with substantial decreases in *both* filings and outright rejections, and marked increases in misdemeanors. Pomona, however, moves from outright rejections to misdemeanors for burglary, but for possession of dangerous drugs the shift is apparently from filings to outright rejections. Torrance seems almost unaffected.

Next we compare the absolute rates for misdemeanors in the second period. Disparities in burglary rates in the second period have become very small. For possession of dangerous drugs, however, the dispersion has greatly increased, with rates ranging from 0 percent for Pomona and about 10 percent for both Pasadena and Torrance, to rates of about 50 percent for both Long Beach and Van Nuys. Long Beach, which previously had had the lowest misdemeanor rates for both offenses, now has among the highest.

REASONS FOR REJECTION

Table 62 summarizes *reasons for rejection* for *burglary* cases before and after the policy change. Each entry shows the percentage rejected and the percentage breakdown between those referred to the District Attorney or City Attorney for misdemeanor filing and those rejected outright. Where the sum of the two percentages is less than 100, the remaining rejects usually required further investigation. Table 62 thus provides an overview of reasons for rejection, by Branch and by D.A. action, and insight into the effects of the filing policy change. Only reasons accounting for 5 percent or more of the rejections in any Branch are included.

Prior to the filing policy change, four categories of insufficiency of evidence accounted for more than two-thirds of the rejections in all Branches, fairly uniformly across Branches. Most cases were rejected outright due to insufficient evidence of the corpus of a crime or insufficient evidence to prosecute the suspect. In cases rejected on grounds of insufficient evidence of a felony, but where there was evidence of a misdemeanor, only Long Beach, and to some extent Pomona, rejected the cases outright. The other Branches referred such rejections for misdemeanor filing in almost all of these cases. This pattern is consistent with the strict filing standards in Long Beach and Pomona and the more permissive standards in the other Branches. No other reason alone accounted for more than 10 percent of the rejections, with the exception of "victim won't cooperate" in the Central Office.

After the change in filing policy, insufficiency of evidence in general played a lesser role in Long Beach and Central rejections; otherwise there was little change in the other Offices. The data show that Long Beach responded by increasing the proportion of rejects referred for misdemeanor filing on three grounds: (1) evidence of misdemeanor but not a felony, (2) "triviality," and (3) defendant's personal history —particularly when the defendant lacked a prior record. Pomona responded

Table 62

MAJOR REASONS FOR BURGLARY REJECTIONS, BY BRANCH OFFICE--TWO PERIODS, 1971

(In percent)

| | Branch Office | | | | | | | | | | | | | | | |
| | L.A. (central) | | Long Beach | | Santa Monica | | Van Nuys | | Torrance | | Pomona | | Pasadena | | Countywide | |
Reason[a]	Jan-May	July-Nov	Jan-May	July-Nov	Jan-May	July-Nov	Jan-May	July-Nov	Jan-May	July-Nov	Jan-May	July-Nov	Jan-May	July-Nov	Jan-May	July-Nov
0. No reason	---	---	---	---	7(8/0)[b]	5(45/18)	5(9/91)	---	5(25/0)	---	---	---	---	---	---	---
10. Insufficient evidence	---	---	---	---	15(11/57)	13(15/81)	---	---	12(10/90)	5(0/50)	15(25/75)	---	16(0/94)	5(0/100)	7(11/76)	5(9/81)
12. Insufficient evidence: felony	16(86/14)	14(97/3)	20(9/91)	10(60/40)[c]	24(93/7)	22(98/2)	34(96/4)	24(98/2)	28(75/25)	28(100/0)	15(37/63)	44(100/0)	18(94/6)	27(96/4)	23(85/15)	21(96/4)
13. Insufficient evidence: corpus	15(18/65)	9(0/100)	18(0/100)	---	10(6/83)	9(5/74)	9(26/69)	12(20/80)	---	6(0/80)	10(0/80)	19(0/100)	13(0/100)	13(0/92)	11(10/81)	11(6/89)
14. Insufficient evidence: suspect	37(0/99)	31(3/97)	31(0/100)	20(10/90)	21(8/90)	20(10/83)	28(10/87)	28(7/90)	29(0/88)	33(0/79)	40(0/90)	22(0/100)	33(3/97)	23(0/100)	31(4/93)	27(5/91)
22. No corpus: felony	---	9(100/0)	---	---	---	7(100/0)	5(75/25)	6(100/0)	---	---	6(0/100)	---	---	---	---	---
23. No corpus: any crime	---	---	7(0/100)	---	---	---	---	---	8(0/100)	---	---	6(0/100)	---	---	---	---
31. Restitution made	---	---	---	---	---	---	---	---	---	---	---	---	---	---	---	---
33. Trivial nature of offense	---	5(91/9)	9(0/100)	20(100/0)	6(70/30)	10(100/0)	---	11(100/0)	---	8(86/14)	---	---	---	8(75/25)	---	8(95/5)
34. Personal history	---	---	---	16(100/0)	---	---	---	---	---	---	---	---	---	6(100/0)	---	---
38. Other discretionary	---	---	---	6(100/0)	---	---	---	---	---	---	---	---	---	---	---	---
41. Victim	12(0/100)	20(2/98)	---	6(0/67)	6(9/82)	6(0/83)	---	---	---	---	---	---	---	5(0/40)	7(3/96)	8(3/90)
42. Witness	7(0/100)	7(0/100)	---	---	---	---	---	---	---	---	---	---	---	---	---	---
51. Search and seizure	---	---	---	---	---	---	---	---	---	5(0/100)	---	---	---	---	---	---
53. Unlawful arrest	---	---	---	---	---	---	---	---	6(0/80)	---	---	---	---	---	---	---

[a] For cross-referencing purposes, numbers have been assigned to reasons in this study (see Table 42). Only those reasons that account for ≥ 5 percent of the rejections in any Branch are included in this table.

[b] The first entry in each column indicates the percentage of rejections rejected for the reason shown (for example, 7 percent for *no reason* in Santa Monica. The first entry in parentheses shows the percentage of those rejections for which misdemeanors were filed; the second entry shows the percentage rejected outright. For example, in Santa Monica, 8 percent of rejections for *no reason* were filed as misdemeanors and 0 percent were rejected outright. The remaining 92 percent required further investigation.

[c] Boxed entries show large changes in rejection percentages resulting from filing policy change.

primarily by increasing the number of rejects referred for misdemeanor filing which had been rejected on grounds that there was evidence of a misdemeanor but not a felony; on the other hand, there were fewer outright rejections on grounds of insufficient evidence to prosecute the suspect. Several Branches increased the proportion of rejects in which the District Attorney asked for further investigation. The Branches and grounds for this action were: Long Beach and Pasadena on the grounds that the victim would not cooperate; Santa Monica on general grounds of insufficient evidence and of insufficient evidence of the corpus of a crime; and Torrance on the same grounds as Santa Monica, plus insufficient evidence to prosecute the suspect. Other than these effects, there were no startling changes in the distribution of reasons for rejection and rejection actions across Branches that could be linked to the filing policy change in burglary cases. Of course, as we showed in Table 60, the increase in overall burglary rejection rate was not large in any Branch, particularly when compared to the rejection rate increases for drug crimes attributable to the new filing policy.

Table 63 presents a similar breakdown of reasons for rejection for dangerous drug possession cases before and after the filing policy change. Table 64 best summarizes the reaction of each Branch to the filing policy, since the sole objective of the policy change in drug possession offenses was to convert cases involving minor amounts of contraband (which the District Attorney was filing as felonies) to misdemeanors and to the jurisdiction of the City Attorney and the Municipal Courts. A comparison of overall rejection rates for this offense in each Branch shows that all but Pasadena responded as expected, with Long Beach, Central, and Van Nuys showing the greatest change.

In Long Beach, Central, and Van Nuys, changes in the percentage of all dangerous drug cases that were referred to the City Attorney for misdemeanor prosecution because there was an insufficient quantity of drugs to warrant a felony are even more dramatic than changes in rejection rates. Santa Monica also appears responsive. The results for Pomona are probably explained by the fact that the City of Pomona has no prosecutor of its own, so misdemeanors are filed by the District Attorney himself without the need to refer them—making it appear that they are outright rejections.

A decrease in percentage of cases rejected outright for insufficient quantity of drugs is shown for most Branches after the filing policy change and appears to reflect a greater reliance on the City Attorney to screen such cases for misdemeanors.

Since the other reason for shifting to misdemeanors cited in the policy change —prior record of the defendant—is exercised significantly only in Long Beach, the percentage of total cases rejected for reasons *other* than insufficient quantity ought not to have changed. Central, Long Beach, and Pomona began rejecting more cases for reasons other than those cited in the policy—or listed the reason incorrectly on the rejection forms.

TERMINATION PRIOR TO SUPERIOR COURT PROSECUTION

Here again we examine cases that are filed as felonies but that are terminated before reaching Superior Court. Again within this category we distinguish those

Table 63

MAJOR REASONS FOR REJECTION FOR POSSESSION OF DANGEROUS DRUGS, BY BRANCH OFFICE--TWO PERIODS, 1971

(In percent)

Reason[a]	Branch Office															
	L.A. (central)		Long Beach		Santa Monica		Van Nuys		Torrance		Pomona		Pasadena		Countywide	
	Jan-May	July-Nov	Jan-May	July-Nov	Jan-May	July-Nov	Jan-May	July-Nov	Jan-May	July-Nov	Jan-May	July-Nov	Jan-May	July-Nov	Jan-May	July-Nov
10. Insufficient evidence	---	---	---	---	13(22/78)[b]	---	---	---	---	---	---	6(0/0)	6(0/100)	20(0/100)	---	---
12. Insufficient evidence: felony	---	---	---	---	---	---	6(100/0)	---	---	---	---	---	---	---	---	---
13. Insufficient evidence: corpus	---	---	7(0/86)	---	---	7(11/33)	5(18/82)	---	---	---	5(0/100)	---	---	5(0/33)	---	---
14. Insufficient evidence: suspect	23(6/94)	22(15/85)	17(0/81)	10(0/100)	23(16/84)	13(0/94)	39(36/64)	15(34/66)[c]	34(21/79)	36(0/89)	10(0/100)	19(0/100)	31(0/100)	11(0/100)	32(19/80)	18(11/86)
23. No corpus: any crime	5(0/100)	---	12(0/100)	---	7(22/67)	---	---	---	---	5(20/80)	21(0/100)	12(0/100)	5(0/100)	---	5(3/95)	---
32. Trivial or insufficient quantity	42(13/87)	60(83/17)	36(0/94)	48(96/4)	29(49/51)	60(80/20)	27(54/46)	60(98/2)	23(25/74)	25(56/74)	42(25/75)	41(0/100)	33(6/92)	34(59/41)	31(25/74)	50(82/18)
34. Personal History	---	---	---	12(100/0)	---	---	---	9(100/0)	---	---	---	---	---	---	---	---
37. Age of suspect	---	---	---	12(100/0)	---	---	---	---	---	---	---	---	---	---	---	---
38. Other discretionary	---	---	---	5(100/0)	---	---	---	---	---	---	---	---	---	---	---	---
51. Search and seizure	22(0/100)	11(0/100)	18(0/100)	---	8(0/100)	5(0/100)	12(19/81)	5(9/91)	27(16/84)	22(0/100)	21(0/100)	16(0/100)	14(0/100)	17(0/82)	16(6/94)	10(3/95)
53. Unlawful arrest	---	---	8(0/100)	---	5(0/100)	---	---	---	6(0/89)	---	---	---	5(0/100)	---	5(4/95)	---

[a] For cross-referencing purposes, numbers have been assigned to reasons in this study (see Table 42). Only those reasons that account for ≥ 5 percent of the rejections in any Branch are included in this table.

[b] The first entry in each column indicates the percentage of rejections rejected for the reason shown (for example, 13 percent for *insufficient evidence* in Santa Monica). The first entry in parentheses shows the percentage of those rejections for which misdemeanors were filed; the second entry shows the percentage rejected outright. For example, in Santa Monica, 22 percent of rejections for insufficient evidence were filed as misdemeanors and 78 percent rejected outright. Where numbers in parentheses do *not* total 100 percent, the remaining percentage required further investigation.

[c] Boxed entries show large changes in rejection percentages resulting from filing policy change.

Table 64

POSSESSION OF DANGEROUS DRUG CASES: EFFECT OF FILING POLICY CHANGE
ON BRANCH OFFICE REJECTIONS FOR INSUFFICIENT QUANTITY
AND OTHER REASONS

(In percent)

Branch Office	Rejection Rate		D.A. Cases Referred to City Attorney		D.A. Cases Rejected Outright		Rejected for Other Reasons	
	Jan-May	July-Nov	Jan-May	July-Nov	Jan-May	July-Nov	Jan-May	July-Nov
L.A. (central)	25	57	1.4	28.3	9.1	5.8	14.5	22.9
Long Beach	30	68	0.6	31.3	10.2	1.3	19.2	35.4
Santa Monica	44	52	6.3	25.0	6.5	6.0	31.2	21.0
Van Nuys	34	63	5.0	37.0	4.2	0.8	24.8	25.2
Torrance	41	46	2.4	6.4	7.1	5.1	31.5	34.5
Pomona	29	50	3.0	0	9.0	20.5	16.9	29.5
Pasadena	45	45	0.9	9.0	13.7	6.3	30.4	29.7
Countywide	34	53	---	---	---	---	---	---

terminated prior to the preliminary hearing from those terminated during the actual hearing. Also, as before, the types of terminations are aggregated into two categories: cases for which all counts are dismissed, and those for which at least one count is reduced to a misdemeanor. The latter category includes cases for which the reduction occurred in conjunction with a guilty plea as well as straight reduction without a plea. It also includes cases in which some counts were dismissed, provided at least one count was reduced to a misdemeanor. Our interest now, however, is to determine the extent to which the Branch Offices differ as to the frequency with which these terminations occur and the effect on these frequencies of the issuance of the directives.

The sample of cases here is identical to that used in the analyses of terminations in Section V.[3] For the reductions to misdemeanor prior to the preliminary and the dismissals at the preliminary, the results are presented individually for each of the five offenses; for the dismissals prior to the preliminary and the reduction to misdemeanor at the preliminary, only the weighted averages are presented.

First, Table 65 presents only the weighted rates for dismissals prior to the preliminary hearing, because the rates vary only from 0 to less than 4 percent. Within this range, Long Beach is on the low side and Santa Monica on the high. Only two significant changes from one period to the next appear: the first is Santa Monica, which doubled its rate from 1.5 to 3.6; the second is Pomona whose rate decreased from 2.1 to 0.

Consider next the reduction to misdemeanor prior to the preliminary hearing, as shown in Table 66. As described in Section V, these reductions always occur in conjunction with a guilty plea, probably as a result of plea bargaining which occurs immediately prior to the preliminary. In terms of variation among the Branch Offices, there is considerable consistency across offenses. Almost without exception, Central, Torrance, and Long Beach appear on the low side, with weighted averages of about 5 percent for both periods, as compared with Van Nuys which is consistently

[3] The sample sizes corresponding to each entry in Tables 65-69 are given in Appendix B.

Table 65

WEIGHTED RATES FOR DISMISSALS PRIOR TO
PRELIMINARY HEARING--TWO PERIODS, 1971

(In percent)

Branch Office	Five Offenses (weighted)[a]	
	Jan–May	July–Nov
L.A. (central)	1.4	1.3
Long Beach	0.4	0.9
Santa Monica	1.5	3.6
Van Nuys	1.5	1.6
Torrance	0.7	0.9
Pomona	2.1	0
Pasadena	0.8	1.6
Overall	1.2	1.6

[a]See Appendix E for an explanation of
weighted averages as used in this study.

high with weighted averages of 15 and 13 percent for the two periods. One anomaly is the rates in Van Nuys of 5 and 8 for robbery, as compared with other branches with rates of 0, inasmuch as robbery itself does not carry an alternative misdemeanor sentence. This is likely due to bargained guilty pleas to counts against other offenses with the robbery charge being dismissed. Whatever the reason, the fact remains that this is unique to Van Nuys. It may well be too that whatever accounts for this may explain the high reduction rates for each offense in Van Nuys.[4] As noted previously, and as the weighted averages in Table 66 show, shifts following the directives can be seen for the two drug offenses. Pomona, Santa Monica, and Van Nuys show large decreases for these offenses; Central, Long Beach, Torrance, and Pasadena changed little.

Turning attention next to terminations occurring at the preliminary hearing, as shown in Table 67, first consider dismissals. The rate of dismissals serves as an apt measure of the Branches' screening ability. Presumably, Branches that screen cases "well" should show low dismissal rates. In terms of the weighted average rate, Long Beach maintained a consistently low level of 4 percent for both periods. Santa Monica and Pomona, too, maintained low dismissal rates, around the 8-percent level. In the first period Pasadena possessed the lowest weighted average rate (1 percent) of any Branch, but the rate then increased to a moderate level (10). By contrast, Central's rates are twice as high as any other Branch and five times as high as Long Beach. About one-fifth of all cases filed by Central are dismissed at the

---

[4] It would be worthwhile to determine the cause. To do so with the current data system requires the reading of the narratives on individual District Attorney Recommendation forms. Even then it is frequently impossible to determine what happened with each count. An automated system which tracks all counts in each case would ease the difficulties.

Table 66

REDUCTION TO MISDEMEANOR RATE PRIOR TO PRELIMINARY HEARING FOR
TWO PERIODS, BY OFFENSE AND BRANCH OFFICE

(In percent)

Branch Office	Possession, Dangerous Drugs (§11910 HS)		Possession, Marijuana (§11530 HS)		Burglary (§459 PC)		Grand Theft, Auto (§487.3 PC)		Robbery (§211 PC)		Five Offenses (weighted)[a]	
	Jan-May	July-Nov	Jan-May	July-Nov	Jan-May	July-Nov	Jan-May	July-Nov	Jan-May	July-Nov	Jan-May	July-Nov
L.A. (central)	4	4	7	5	3	5	3	7	0	1	4	5
Long Beach	10	7	12	10	1	2	3	0	0	0	6	5
Santa Monica	18	9	19	12	10	7	10	8	0	0	13	8
Van Nuys	19	11	27	20	7	11	9	11	5	8	15	13
Torrance	4	7	6	6	5	1	7	0	0	0	5	4
Pomona	18	0	12	6	8	2	8	0	0	0	11	2
Pasadena	11	16	16	14	12	11	7	0	0	0	11	11
Overall	12	8	16	10	6	7	6	6	1	2	10	8

[a]See Appendix E for an explanation of weighted averages as used in this study.

Table 67

DISMISSAL RATE AT PRELIMINARY HEARING FOR TWO PERIODS,
BY OFFENSE AND BRANCH OFFICE

(In percent)

Branch Office	Possession, Dangerous Drugs (§11910 HS)		Possession, Marijuana (§11530 HS)		Burglary (§459 PC)		Grand Theft, Auto (§487.3 PC)		Robbery (§211 PC)		Five offenses (weighted) [a]	
	Jan-May	July-Nov	Jan-May	July-Nov	Jan-May	July-Nov	Jan-May	July-Nov	Jan-May	July-Nov	Jan-May	July-Nov
L.A. (central)	22	34	26	30	12	11	15	13	19	16	19	23
Long Beach	4	2	6	10	3	2	5	4	0	3	4	4
Santa Monica	10	14	10	16	4	6	2	0	0	3	7	10
Van Nuys	8	10	12	14	5	5	4	4	6	4	8	8
Torrance	7	18	8	14	2	6	6	6	0	3	5	11
Pomona	10	6	11	6	9	20	0	0	0	0	8	8
Pasadena	1	8	0.5	13	1	8	3	16	2	9	1	10
Overall	9	15	12	19	6	8	7	8	8	9	9	13

[a]See Appendix E for an explanation of weighted averages as used in this study.

preliminary hearing. The rates for the individual offenses are consistent with the weighted average rates. Long Beach is invariably low and Central is high.

From Table 68 we can make two observations about the rates of reduction to misdemeanor at the preliminary hearing. First, the rates for each Branch change markedly from the first period to the second, typically on the order of from about 0.5 percent to about 4 percent. This shift at every Branch undoubtedly reflects the Esteybar decision. Second, Pomona's rates for both periods are extraordinary. A fuller comparison of Pomona with the overall Branch sample for each of the individual offenses as shown in Table 69 reveals that for each of the four offenses carrying an alternative felony/misdemeanor sentence, Pomona has an anomalously higher reduction rate. The rate for three of the five offenses is above 50 percent. Precisely what accounts for this cannot be ascertained here. It may be that more cases should be rejected as a felony at the filing stage and handled as misdemeanors. Pomona's rejection rates are low, an average of 44 percent for the second period as compared with a countywide average of 53 percent; however, this difference obviously could not in itself account for the much larger disparity in the rates of reduction to misdemeanor at the preliminary. The explanation may more likely be found in a comparison of the Municipal Courts in Pomona with the rest of the county.

In summary, *prior* to the preliminary hearing there was only minor Branch variation in dismissal rates but major variation in reduction rates. *At* the preliminary, pronounced Branch variation occurred in dismissal rates, but, with one notable exception, scant variation in reduction rates among Branches. Dismissal rates before the preliminary hearing tended to change little between the two periods at any of the Branches; reduction rates for drug offenses in some Branches exhibited

Table 68

WEIGHTED RATES FOR REDUCTION TO MISDEMEANOR
AT PRELIMINARY HEARING--TWO PERIODS, 1971

(In percent)

Branch Office	Five Offenses (weighted) [a]	
	Jan-May	July-Nov
L.A. (central)	0	5.2
Long Beach	0	5.6
Santa Monica	0.4	2.1
Van Nuys	0.3	3.7
Torrance	0.1	8.9
Pomona	3.9	48.8
Pasadena	1.0	3.5
Overall	0.4	6.4

[a]See Appendix E for an explanation of weighted averages as used in this study.

Table 69

REDUCTION TO MISDEMEANOR RATE AT PRELIMINARY HEARING: POMONA RATE
COMPARED WITH OVERALL SAMPLE, JULY-NOVEMBER 1971

(In percent)

Branch Office	Possession, Dangerous Drugs (§11910 HS)	Possession, Marijuana (§11530 HS)	Burglary (§459 PC)	Grand Theft, Auto (§487.3 PC)	Robbery (§211 PC)	Five Offenses (weighted)[a]
Pomona	53	67	41	58	0	49
Overall	9	11	4	3	1	6

[a]See Appendix E for an explanation of weighted averages as used in this study.

nontrivial decreases from the first period to the second. At the preliminary hearing, some Branches showed significant increases between periods in dismissal rates for the drug offenses, but all Branches showed very substantial increases in reduction rates.

DISPOSITIONS IN SUPERIOR COURT

The pattern of dispositions for all felonies in each Superior Court Branch in 1970 is shown in Table 70.[5] Although these data do not suffice for judgments about the individual performance of the D.A. Offices, still they are helpful in assessing the effects of differences in policy among the Offices.

Consider first the three dismissal-rate categories: Interests of Justice (IOJ), §1538.5 PC, and §995 PC. We would expect rigorous complaint screening or strict Municipal Court screening to result in low dismissal rates in Superior Court. Notice that Long Beach, Norwalk, and Torrance generally have the lowest rates. It is not surprising to find Long Beach in this category, since it does appear to employ the most rigorous complaint screening practices in the county, but the other two are unexpected. Norwalk files none of its own complaints, and Torrance files only 30 percent. Our discussions with D.A. personnel led us to believe that the separation of authority between filing and trials would lead to filing of many poor cases. In fact, this is the reason usually suggested for the high dismissal rates and poor conviction rates in the Los Angeles Central Office.

Table 71, which gives the dismissal rates by Branch for a number of offenses, shows that this measure of Office performance is generally consistent across all offense categories. The high dismissal rates in Pasadena are consistent with its reputation for permissive filing standards. The deputies in Pasadena ascribe this phenomenon to vagaries of the presiding judge.

From the data shown in Table 70, we see that Central Los Angeles, Torrance, and Norwalk are particularly active in the use of SOT. Since our previous data

[5] Disposition data for specific crime categories (1970 and 1971) are given in Appendix C.

Table 70

DISPOSITIONS FOR ALL FELONIES BY SUPERIOR COURT BRANCH OFFICES, 1970
(In percent)

Disposition	Branch Office								County-wide
	Los Angeles	Long Beach	Santa Monica	Van Nuys	Torrance	Norwalk	Pomona	Pasadena	
No. cases disposed	12,241	2,283	2,324	3,152	5,048	4,147	2,515	1,432	33,142
% of countywide	36.9	6.9	7.0	9.5	15.2	12.5	7.6	4.3	100.0
Dismissed (diverted)	5.0	3.9	5.0	4.4	3.7	4.9	7.5	5.0	4.8
Dismissed (Int of Jus)	4.3	3.2	6.2	3.3	3.2	1.7	3.8	7.3	3.9
Dismissed (§1538.5 PC)	1.3	1.4	1.4	0.6	1.9	0.9	1.7	1.8	1.3
Dismissed (§995 PC)	3.4	0.7	3.2	3.3	2.6	1.4	3.8	5.9	3.0
SOT rate	31.6	18.2	18.4	15.5	55.7	35.1	22.1	12.2	30.8
SOT conviction rate	77.4	90.6	71.9	77.0	86.9	85.4	74.5	60.3	81.0
Jury trial rate	4.5	5.0	3.8	2.8	1.8	2.6	1.8	3.3	3.4
Jury trial conviction rate	63.3	73.7	83.2	79.8	75.3	72.0	76.1	70.2	69.8
Court trial rate	9.1	9.4	4.4	3.4	9.4	4.1	7.5	10.3	7.6
Court trial conviction rate	61.0	80.8	47.1	64.5	57.8	70.6	57.1	63.5	62.2
Plea (orig charge)	2.9	17.1	10.6	18.3	6.1	9.5	14.1	19.1	8.7
Plea (change NG to G)	37.8	41.1	46.9	48.5	15.7	40.2	37.7	35.3	36.5
Guilty plea rate	42.9	60.6	60.6	69.9	22.6	52.1	56.0	57.2	47.5
Overall conviction rate	77.5	89.5	80.1	86.9	79.9	88.4	80.0	74.3	81.2

SOURCE: California Bureau of Criminal Statistics computer tapes.

indicated that SOT was being used as a substitute for a plea of guilty, and that SOT defendants were obtaining more lenient treatment in sentencing than other defendants, reducing the percentage of SOTs in these branches would have the effect of increasing the severity of sentencing.[6]

Those Branches with low SOT rates generally have high guilty plea rates, so the two are compensating. The percentage of cases that actually go to trial varies from 6.2 percent in Van Nuys to 14.4 percent in Long Beach. There does not appear to be any direct relationship between jury or court conviction rates and the frequency with which cases go to trial.

Summarizing the 1970 data in Table 70 by Branch,[7] we see the following:

- Long Beach's performance was characterized by low dismissal rates, above-average guilty plea rates (particularly original pleas), high trial conviction rates, and a high overall conviction rate.
- Norwalk's performance approached Long Beach's except for its higher SOT rate and lower trial conviction rates.

[6] The 1971 data in Appendix C show that this has, in fact, occurred.

[7] Many of these findings are different for 1971 (see Table C-9); thus these statements are primarily of historical interest.

Table 71

SUPERIOR COURT DISMISSAL RATES, 1970

(In percent)

Superior Court	All Felonies			Robbery			Burglary			Possession, Marijuana			Possession, Dangerous Drugs		
	Int of Jus	§995 PC	§1538.5 PC	Int of Jus	§995 PC	§1538.5 PC	Int of Jus	§995 PC	§1538.5 PC	Int of Jus	§995 PC	§1538.5 PC	Int of Jus	§995 PC	§1538.5 PC
Los Angeles	4.32	3.43	1.27	4.69	1.87	0.13	2.41	2.69	0.46	6.20	5.46	3.78	4.50	2.96	2.40
Long Beach	3.20	0.66	1.40	2.83	0.94	0	2.78	0	0	3.56	0.67	4.01	2.54	1.76	1.56
Santa Monica	6.15	3.23	1.42	13.41	1.22	0	5.16	3.44	0	6.12	5.16	3.63	6.18	2.35	2.65
Van Nuys	3.30	3.33	0.57	2.03	1.35	0	3.11	1.36	0.39	3.77	9.08	0.86	2.08	1.56	1.22
Torrance	3.17	2.56	1.88	4.71	0.34	0	2.64	2.36	0.55	3.29	4.87	6.06	2.98	2.88	3.29
Norwalk	1.66	1.35	0.94	1.09	1.09	0	0.57	0.57	0	2.97	1.75	2.44	1.77	1.31	1.23
Pomona	3.78	3.78	1.67	2.06	4.12	0	1.96	1.40	0	6.44	7.88	3.34	3.73	3.55	3.20
Pasadena	7.26	5.87	1.75	4.00	1.33	0	3.94	2.96	0.99	11.11	12.70	4.76	6.57	9.49	3.65
Average	3.85	2.96	1.32	4.21	1.50	0.06	2.57	2.06	0.34	5.14	5.47	3.65	3.41	2.68	2.26

- Van Nuys maintained the highest guilty plea rate, although court conviction rates were only average.
- Santa Monica and Pomona had above-average dismissal rates, low court conviction rates, and above-average jury conviction rates.
- Torrance had low guilty plea rates and low court conviction rates.
- Central Los Angeles had high dismissal rates, low guilty plea rates, and low conviction rates.
- Pasadena had high dismissal rates and low conviction rates, especially for SOT. This probably indicates that some of the SOTs are really slow dismissals.

In addition, for all felonies taken together, jury conviction rates exceed court conviction rates in all Branches except Long Beach. The tables in Appendix C show that this is also true for many individual offense categories.

SENTENCING

Sentencing data at the D.A. Branch, or Superior Court Division level, are summarized in Table 72 for eight felony offense categories, using two sentencing measures: the felony sentence rate and the state prison rate. Also included are county-wide data for each offense category and weighted quantities for all offense categories. (For the weighted quantities, all eight offense categories were included in the felony sentence rate, but only six offense categories were included for the prison rate, for few defendants convicted of possession of dangerous drugs or possession of marijuana received state prison sentences.)

Observations based on these data are the following:

- For any offense, the felony sentence rate and the prison rate vary considerably across Branches; often the rates for the highest Branch are twice those for the lowest.
- Long Beach has consistently the highest felony sentence rate for all offense categories. Norwalk is next highest, except for sale of narcotics. Pasadena and Pomona are generally above average for most offenses. Santa Monica and Van Nuys, and to some extent, Torrance, are well below average.
- Long Beach has the highest prison rates, except for assault; Pasadena is high except for possession or sale of narcotics, and Pomona is generally above average except for assault. With some exceptions, Torrance, Norwalk, and Los Angeles are generally below average.
- Generally speaking, the two sentencing measures are positively correlated. Courts in Long Beach, Pasadena, and Pomona impose both above-average felony sentence rates and above-average prison rates. In Torrance, both measures are below average. However, there are some exceptions. In Norwalk, the felony sentence rate is high, but the prison rate is low. In Santa Monica and Van Nuys, the felony sentence rate is very low, but the prison rate is above average.

Table 72

VARIATIONS IN SENTENCING, BY OFFENSE AND BRANCH OFFICE, 1970

(In percent)

Branch Office or Superior Court Division	Possession, Dangerous Drugs		Burglary		Possession, Marijuana		Robbery		Forgery		Possession, Narcotics		Assault		Sale, Narcotics		All Offenses (weighted)[a]	
	Felony Rate	Prison Rate	Felony Rate	Prison Rate	Felony Rate	Prison Rate	Felony Rate	Prison Rate	Felony Rate	Prison Rate	Felony Rate	Prison Rate	Felony Rate	Prison Rate	Felony Rate	Prison Rate	Felony Rate	Prison Rate
Los Angeles	28	(b)	37	5	19	(b)	70	24	42	6	73	7	35	8	73	8	39	9
Long Beach	48	(b)	69	13	36	(b)	90	30	69	10	98	17	48	3	86	13	61	14
Santa Monica	26	(b)	37	9	13	(b)	66	23	41	12	56	9	22	5	76	9	36	11
Van Nuys	22	(b)	45	6	14	(b)	74	31	48	9	72	7	27	6	68	12	38	11
Torrance	22	(b)	47	4	13	(b)	81	27	39	4	68	0	30	6	73	12	39	9
Norwalk	34	(b)	50	6	26	(b)	82	21	66	4	92	10	40	11	73	9	48	9
Pomona	22	(b)	47	6	22	(b)	88	33	53	7	83	21	29	1	77	10	43	11
Pasadena	30	(b)	43	9	26	(b)	59	27	54	17	63	0	38	9	74	8	42	12
Countywide	29	(b)	44	6	20	(b)	75	26	47	7	76	9	33	7	74	10	42	10

[a]See Appendix E for an explanation of weighted averages as used in this study.

[b]Few defendants are sentenced to state prison for conviction of dangerous drugs or possession of marijuana.

- In terms of judicial sentencing practices as perceived by D.A. officials in the Branches, there is generally fair consistency between the objective data in Table 72 and subjective evaluations of how "tough" or "lenient" the judges as a group are perceived. For example, the Long Beach and Pomona courts are perceived as tough and the sentencing measures bear this out. The Santa Monica, Van Nuys, and Torrance courts are perceived as average, or somewhat lenient, and the sentencing measures are fairly consistent with these perceptions. In Norwalk, the judges are perceived as average in sentencing severity, and one sentencing measure is high but the other is low; that is, although more defendants receive felony sentences, more are given probation rather than state prison sentences. Pasadena has a significant *inconsistency* between perceptions and fact. Sentencing practices of judges there are perceived as lenient, yet both sentencing measures are generally above average in severity.

All the sentencing data, by Branch and offense, shown in Table 72 are weighted uniformly by prior record; i.e., each sentencing measure for each offense is weighted in proportion to the *countywide* incidence of each of the four major prior record categories (none, minor, major, prison).[8] Tables 73, 74, and 75 display the data, disaggregated by prior record category, for three offenses: possession of dangerous drugs, burglary, and robbery.

A number of observations follow from these data:

- For most Branches, sentencing severity (felony sentence rate and prison rate) increases with increasingly serious prior record. This is to be expected. There are, however, several *anomalies,* as follows:
  - (a) For possession of dangerous drugs, defendants with prior prison records receive fewer felony sentences than those with prior major records in five of the eight Branch Offices. Only in Van Nuys and Norwalk is the converse true.
  - (b) Although robbery felony sentence rates in Long Beach are very high for all prior record categories, the rate is identical for defendants with minor prior records or none at all, and is actually higher for defendants with major prior records compared to those with prior prison records.
  - (c) In Santa Monica, robbery prison sentence rates for defendants with prior minor records are much lower than for defendants with no prior record at all. Long Beach is similar.
  - (d) In Pomona, prison rates for robbery are much lower for defendants with major prior records than for those with minor priors.
  - (e) In Pasadena, burglary felony sentence rates are much lower for defendants with minor prior records compared to defendants with no priors at all.
- In some Branches, the effects of prior record are quite pronounced on one or both sentencing measures; in others, the effects are minimal. For example, in Los Angeles, felony sentence rates for robbery are quite constant and almost independent of prior record category. In Norwalk, burglary

---

[8] The weighting scheme and the weights themselves are found in Appendix E.

Table 73

FELONY SENTENCE RATE FOR POSSESSION OF DANGEROUS DRUGS,
BY PRIOR RECORD AND BRANCH OFFICE, 1970

(In percent)

Branch Office	Prior Record				
	None	Minor	Major	Prison	All Categories (weighted)[a]
Los Angeles	21	24	37	30	28
Long Beach	33	56	57	38	48
Santa Monica	14	24	37	30	26
Van Nuys	9	20	28	39	22
Torrance	13	15	33	34	22
Norwalk	21	27	44	54	34
Pomona	16	20	31	17	22
Pasadena	28	27	36	20	30
Countywide	19	26	39	36	29

[a]See Appendix E for an explanation of weighted averages as used in this study.

Table 74

VARIATIONS IN SENTENCING RATES FOR BURGLARY,
BY PRIOR RECORD AND BRANCH OFFICE, 1970

(In percent)

Branch Office	Prior Record									
	None		Minor		Major		Prison		All Categories (weighted)[a]	
	Felony Rate	Prison Rate	Felony Rate	Prison Rate	Felony Rate	Prison Rate	Felony Rate	Prison Rate	Felony Rate	Prison Rate
Los Angeles	23	1	33	2	43	6	47	12	37	5
Long Beach	65	0	65	2	73	13	71	36	69	13
Santa Monica	22	4	31	5	45	8	48	17	37	9
Van Nuys	34	1	37	3	50	5	55	14	45	6
Torrance	21	1	45	1	55	5	61	14	47	6
Norwalk	32	0	33	0	62	6	65	18	50	6
Pomona	17	1	41	1	57	4	67	20	47	5
Pasadena	39	3	21	3	57	11	45	18	43	9
Countywide	28	1	38	2	52	6	54	15	44	6

[a]See Appendix E for an explanation of weighted averages as used in this study.

Table 75

VARIATIONS IN SENTENCING RATES FOR ROBBERY,
BY PRIOR RECORD AND BRANCH OFFICE, 1970

(In percent)

Branch Office	Prior Record								All Categories (weighted)[a]	
	None		Minor		Major		Prison			
	Felony Rate	Prison Rate	Felony Rate	Prison Rate	Felony Rate	Prison Rate	Felony Rate	Prison Rate	Felony Rate	Prison Rate
Los Angeles	67	9	71	16	72	29	68	37	70	24
Long Beach	87	10	78	6	100	29	89	74	90	30
Santa Monica	47	21	70	10	68	21	75	42	66	23
Van Nuys	54	4	70	20	82	32	84	64	74	31
Torrance	83	10	71	10	80	27	89	62	81	27
Norwalk	68	11	76	9	85	18	96	49	82	21
Pomona	71	12	87	35	92	20	100	71	88	33
Pasadena	39	11	55	18	70	30	67	44	59	27
Countywide	67	10	73	15	78	27	80	50	75	26

[a]See Appendix E for an explanation of weighted averages as used in this study.

felony sentence rates increase sharply for defendants with major, compared to minor, prior records, and prison rates increase sharply for defendants with prior prison records compared to prior major records. In Long Beach, robbery prison rates rise from 29 to 74 percent for defendants with prior major compared to prison records; yet, felony sentence rates actually decrease from 100 to 89 percent.

- For a specific offense and sentencing measure, a Branch may rank quite differently in sentencing severity, depending on the prior record category. For example, although Pasadena's felony sentence rate for burglary is third lowest on the average, it is second highest for the no prior record category but lowest for the prior prison record category.

- These observations merely confirm the fact that *defendants convicted of similar offenses, with similar prior records, receive inconsistent treatment in sentencing* in the various courts within Los Angeles County.

Clearly, sentencing inequities reflect disparities in the sentencing practices of individual judges, as shown in Table 76, which gives the high and low value of each of the two sentencing measures, together with an identification number for the judge responsible, for three offenses: possession of dangerous drugs, burglary, and robbery. These data are drawn from the fuller set of tables in Appendix D, which displays felony sentence rates and prison rates by judge for several offenses.[9]

[9] Judges who sentenced only a few defendants for any offense category are excluded from these tables. The tables include only judges who sentenced 300 or more defendants (for all offenses) during calendar year 1970. In practical terms, each judge included in these tables sentenced between 10 and 200 defendants for any given offense category.

Table 76

JUDGES' SENTENCING VARIATIONS, BY BRANCH OFFICE AND OFFENSE, 1970

(In percent)

Branch Office	Number of Judges	Possession, Dangerous Drugs				Burglary				Robbery			
		Felony Rate		Prison Rate		Felony Rate		Prison Rate		Felony Rate		Prison Rate	
		High	Low	High	Low	High	Low	High	Low	High	Low	High	Low
Los Angeles	14	54(#11)[a]	8(#6)	---	---	52(#1)	9(#4)	11(#14)	0(#4)	86(#7)	44(#14)	57(#11)	7(#10)
Long Beach	3	62(#3)	7(#1)	---	---	82(#2)	60(#1)	20(#2)	6(#1)	97(#1)	76(#2)	27(#1)	11(#2)
Santa Monica	3	36(#3)	13(#1)	---	---	47(#3)	24(#1)	12(#2)	0(#3)	75(#3)	48(#1)	38(#1)	20(#2)
Van Nuys	3	27(#1)	6(#3)	---	---	45(#1)	33(#3)	7(#2)	4(#1)	80(#1)	68(#2)	37(#1)	22(#2)
Torrance	5	48(#4)	17(#3)	---	---	65(#4)	37(#5)	16(#2)	2(#5)	96(#4)	80(#3)	51(#4)	17(#5)
Norwalk	4	42(#2)	25(#4)	---	---	57(#2)	36(#1)	12(#4)	2(#1)	90(#3)	66(#4)	38(#3)	13(#1)
Pomona	2	27(#2)	18(#1)	---	---	50(#2)	49(#1)	7(#1)	5(#2)	90(#2)	79(#1)	33(#2)	28(#1)
Pasadena	1	NA[b]	NA	---	---	NA	NA	NA	NA	NA	NA	NA	NA
Countywide	35	62	6	---	---	82	9	20	0	97	44	57	7

[a]Each entry shows the value of the sentencing measure followed by the judge responsible in parentheses. In this case Judge #11 has the highest felony sentence rate (54 percent) for possession of dangerous drugs in Los Angeles.

[b]Not applicable because most sentencing decisions in Pasadena are attributed to one judge (due to the court division's master calendaring system).

Notice that, in general, *consistency in sentencing practices is mixed.* For example, Judge #1 in Van Nuys and Judge #2 in Pomona tend to sentence severely. Judge #1 in Pomona and Judges #1 and #4 in Norwalk tend to sentence leniently. In some cases, however, a judge tends to sentence severely for one offense and leniently for another. For example, in Long Beach, Judge #2's felony sentence rate and prison rate for burglary are the highest, whereas Judge #1's are the lowest; for robbery the converse is true. In still other cases, a judge may impose felony sentences frequently for a particular offense, but rarely impose prison sentences. For example, in Santa Monica, Judge #3 imposed felony sentences for burglary most frequently (47 percent of the time), but imposed *no* prison sentences at all. On the other hand, Judge #1 imposed felony sentences for robbery least frequently (48 percent of the time), but imposed prison sentences most frequently (38 percent of the time).

The data in Table 76 attest to large disparities among judges in sentencing severity. One judge imposed felony sentences in only 6 percent of dangerous drug possession convictions and another in 62 percent of the cases; one in only 9 percent of burglary convictions and another in 82 percent of the cases; one in only 44 percent of robbery convictions and another in 97 percent of the cases. And, among the several judges, the prison sentence rate for burglary varied from zero to 20 percent; and for robbery, from 7 percent to 57 percent. One cannot attribute such judicial inconsistency to differences in individual cases because, as mentioned earlier, the sentencing results for each judge in each offense category are based on between 10 to 200 cases, where no judge sentenced fewer than 300 defendants across all offense categories.

PROSECUTORIAL MANAGEMENT MODELS—AN OVERVIEW

We have seen that large and significant differences exist across Branches in the arrest process, in complaint issuance and rejection, in termination rates in Municipal Court, in Superior Court dismissal rates, in method of disposition and conviction rates in Superior Court, and, finally, in sentencing severity. But to what degree do these differences reflect underlying patterns or models of police, prosecutorial, and judicial decisionmaking? At least one clear prosecutorial model—the *Rigorous Model*—seems to be supported by the data. Others are not as clear.

The Rigorous Model may be characterized as an independent, strict, closely managed, prosecutorial office. In terms of management style, procedures, and philosophy, it is characterized by the following:

- Close management supervision over complaint issuance, preliminary hearings, plea bargaining, and trials.
- Well-articulated (formal or informal), strict filing standards and guidelines.
- Resistance to police pressure to file marginal cases.
- Discouragement of complaint deputy-shopping by police officers who seek to secure complaints.
- Positive efforts to influence and affect police arrest and charging standards and to upgrade the quality of police investigations.

- A strong inclination to adversary proceedings (court and jury trials) rather than to bargaining (pleas and SOT), especially if caseload per deputy is not excessive, notwithstanding the high cost of such proceedings.
- Little influence by the courts over prosecutorial procedures and personnel assignments to individual courts.
- Positive efforts to make the prosecutor's views known at probation and sentencing hearings.

Now, which Branch Offices are consistent with these characteristics and how would these characteristics manifest themselves in the various outcome measures? Of all the Branches, the Long Beach Branch most closely approximates this Model. In terms of complaint rejection rates, the Model suggests that rejection rates should not be particularly high if police investigations are of high quality and if police arrest and charging standards are similar to the prosecutor's standards. (On the other hand, the Model suggests that rejection rates *should* be high, if police investigation quality is low and police arrest and charging standards are more permissive than those of the prosecutor's.) Long Beach's rejection rates are somewhat below average, evidencing that this Branch Office substantially influences at least the Long Beach Police Department's arrest and investigation standards. In terms of dismissal and reduction rates in Municipal Court, high filing standards should result in better initial screening; hence, dismissals and reductions before or at the preliminary hearing should be below average, *ceteris paribus*. The Long Beach Branch's termination rates in Municipal Court are consistently low and fit the Model quite well.

All other things being equal, the Rigorous Model suggests that Superior Court dismissal rates, especially on §995 PC and §1538.5 PC motions, also should be somewhat below average, given strict filing standards. The Long Beach Branch Office fits the Model in this respect too; §995 PC dismissal rates are well below average and §1538.5 PC dismissal rates are about average for all felonies.

In terms of disposition method and conviction rates in Superior Court, the careful initial screening of complaints embodied in the Rigorous Model should create a decided inclination to adversary proceedings rather than to plea bargaining and SOT, provided court calendars are not unduly crowded and case load per deputy is not excessive. Court and jury trial rates ought then to be above average, whereas SOT plus overall plea bargaining rates should be below average. Furthermore, original guilty plea rate ought to be above average whereas plea change rate (from not quilty to guilty) ought to be below average, since the prosecutor's stance is likely to be more "hardnosed." Finally, the Rigorous Model suggests that, with careful screening, an inclination to go to trial, and a management style that insists on careful trial preparation, jury and court conviction rates ought to be well above average, and overall conviction rates should also be well above average.

The Long Beach Branch statistics fit this Model quite well. Caseload per deputy is below average. Jury and court trial rates are very high; SOT rate is below average; original guilty plea rates are well above average for most felonies (all felonies taken together, possession of marijuana and dangerous drugs, burglary, forgery) and somewhat above average for others (robbery, assault, possession and sale of narcotics); plea change rates are somewhat above average for some felonies, average for others, and below average for still others; jury and court conviction rates are very high for many felonies and well above average for others; SOT conviction rates are very high for almost all felonies; and finally, overall conviction rates are extremely high for six offense categories and above average for the other three.

Sentencing severity mainly reflects the practices of individual judges, as we noted above. But when the prosecutor is willing to participate actively and make his views known in probation and sentencing hearings, it is reasonable to assume that sentence severity would be higher than if, as occurs in many prosecutorial offices, he stands mute. Our Rigorous Model hypothesizes such a prosecutorial interaction. The Long Beach Branch conforms to this aspect of the Model since it actively participates in probation and sentencing hearings. Moreover, in Long Beach, felony sentence rates are quite high for all felony categories, and prison rates are also very high for most felonies and above average for the remainder. But also such *statistical* evidence is, of course, not conclusive that the Long Beach Branch Office did, in fact, affect the severity of judicial sentencing there.

Other Branch Offices of the Los Angeles County District Attorney fit the Rigorous Model in some respects, in terms of some outcome statistics, but none fit as well as the Long Beach Branch. But management style is generally quite different in other Branches. For example, although overall conviction rates are very high in the Norwalk Branch, jury and court conviction rates are not well above average; SOT and plea rates are somewhat above average; although caseload is about average, there is no strong inclination to engage in adversary proceedings; jury trial rates are below average and court trial rates are well below average. Moreover, the management style is not consistent with the Model. Plea bargaining and other prosecutorial functions are not closely supervised at the highest levels. Because the Norwalk Branch does not file complaints, but merely prosecutes complaints filed in several Area Offices, complaint issuance standards and the stance taken toward deputy-shopping and police arrest and investigatory standards are irrelevant here.

In Torrance, management style is more consistent with the Rigorous Model than in Norwalk, but statistical outcome measures are less consistent with this Model. Supervision is fairly close, filing standards are moderately strict (but the Office files fewer than half of all cases it prosecutes), and deputy-shopping by police is discouraged. Influence over police arrest and investigatory standards is slight. The courts do exert some influence over deputy personnel assignments to individual courts. There is no strong inclination to engage in adversary proceedings, even though caseload per deputy is the lowest in the county. But felony rejection rates are about average (drug possession cases are above average, whereas other felonies are below average)—not entirely consistent with relatively strict filing standards and little or no influence over police arrest and investigatory standards. By contrast, generally low dismissal and reduction rates in Municipal Court are more consistent with its management style and moderately strict filing standards. Also, Superior Court dismissal rates on §995 PC motions are about average, whereas §1538.5 PC dismissals are well above average. These measures are fairly consistent with moderately strict filing standards. Jury trial rates are considerably below average and court trial rates are about average. Torrance uses SOT extensively, so plea rates are very low. Overall conviction rates are somewhat below average, SOT conviction rates are considerably above average, court conviction rates are above average, but jury conviction rates are about average.

To lesser degrees, the other Branches fit the Rigorous Model in terms of management style and outcome measures. But to some degree they also fit the contrasting *Laissez-Faire Model.* For example, the management style in Pasadena seems to better fit the Laissez-Faire Model: relatively permissive filing standards, scant influence over police arrest and investigatory standards,[10] no resistance to deputy-shopping by police, and considerable court control over deputy personnel assignments in the courts. Despite this resemblance in management style, outcome statistics for Pasadena support this Model unevenly. Felony rejection rates are average overall (high for drug offenses, low for others), and termination rates in Municipal Court are also average. This is fairly consistent with more permissive filing standards and little attempt to influence police charging policies. Superior Court dismissal rates are very high for almost all felonies, and this is also consistent with permissive filing standards. Jury trial rates are average, however, and court trial rates are very high, whereas SOT is rarely used, and plea rates are somewhat above average—characteristics more consistent with the Rigorous Model than the Laissez-Faire Model. Consistency of Pasadena's conviction rates with the Laissez-Faire Model is also mixed: overall and SOT conviction rates are very low, but jury and court trials are about average.

In summary, then, large differences exist in Los Angeles County in the exercise of prosecutorial discretion and in the disposition of felonies. These differences may be only partially "explained" by appealing to different prosecutorial management styles. But the large differences themselves should be cause for concern on the part of police chiefs, the District Attorney, and the judiciary, because it means that criminal justice lacks evenhandedness in the county.

---

[10] The Deputy District Attorneys in Pasadena are viewed by Branch management as professionals who are expected to use good judgment in their exercise of prosecutorial discretion, therefore needing little supervision.

VIII. CONCLUSIONS AND RECOMMENDATIONS

This report has described a range of phenomena spanning many phases of the criminal justice process in Los Angeles County. In numerous instances the data have raised more questions than they have answered about why the system behaves the way it does. Since this report is the first of its kind to explore the variations existing within a particular system, the reader may feel that the *only* logical course of action is to pursue the unanswered questions through additional research efforts until the process can be better understood. We favor such continuing action. But we offer additional recommendations based on the conclusions that emerge from this work. These recommendations are directed primarily toward the District Attorney since our work was performed largely for his agency.

1. *Conclusion: No reasonable set of performance standards currently exists for criminal justice agencies.* Unlike other areas of endeavor in which the performance of managers can be gauged by historical performance standards such as sales, profits, reading achievement, or cure rate, criminal justice officials are judged mainly on the basis of *individual actions,* administrative competence, and priorities for prosecuting various crime types, rather than on the *total performance* of their agencies. Until some standards are established, there will be no consistent basis on which to judge the performance of new programs or management policies.

Recommendation: Large criminal justice agencies, such as the Los Angeles District Attorney's Office, should develop performance measures for judging the work of their employees. Once constructed, these measures could also be used to explain the prosecutor's performance to the general public. In this report we have suggested a variety of measures that might be used.

2. *Conclusion: The performance of criminal justice agencies in Los Angeles County varies considerably from those in the rest of the state.*

- An arrest in Los Angeles County is more likely to be based on felony than misdemeanor charges by the police than elsewhere in the state.
- The Los Angeles District Attorney is much less likely to file felony charges, given a felony arrest.
- A felony charge is less likely to be reduced to a misdemeanor in the Los Angeles Municipal Courts.
- Many more cases in Los Angeles County are submitted for judgment on the transcript of the preliminary hearing.

116

- A felony defendant in the Los Angeles Superior Courts is less likely to be convicted.
- If he is convicted, he is much less likely to receive a felony sentence.

Recommendation: Research should be conducted to determine the basis for these differences and whether or not any change in practice is in order.

3. *Conclusion: The disparity between felony arrests and felony convictions is much greater in Los Angeles County than elsewhere in the state.* This disparity leads to several undesirable effects:

- Many suspects who are subsequently found not guilty of behavior deserving felony punishment are unnecessarily subjected to the anxiety, costs, and loss of freedom associated with a felony arrest as opposed to the much more limited costs associated with a misdemeanor arrest.
- Habitual offenders are encouraged to believe they can consistently escape with much lighter sentences than those prescribed for their arrest charge.
- The criminal justice system must bear the wasted costs of processing huge numbers of felony cases which could have been settled much less expensively in the lower courts with the same results.

Whether this disparity is due primarily to excessive arrest charges by the police or to more lenient findings by the court cannot be ascertained solely from the data available to us.

Recommendation: The standards used by the police departments, the District Attorney, and the courts to control their discretion should be periodically monitored and publicized, using, for example, the rejection, dismissal, and sentencing rates as illustrated in this report. These agencies should use such indices to identify and analyze major discrepancies that continue to exist.

4. *Conclusion: Wide variations exist among local police departments, Offices of the District Attorney, and the courts, in the way they process similar offenses.* The result is undesirable inconsistency in the outcome of individual cases. Defendants arrested for a particular offense in one particular jurisdiction are likely to suffer more severe or more lenient treatment solely because of the location of their arrest or of their adjudication. A skillful defense attorney may also secure more lenient treatment for his client by appropriately maneuvering his case.

Recommendations:

- As in the previous recommendation, the arrest, filing, and sentencing actions of individual police departments, District Attorney units, and the courts should be periodically reviewed so that discrepancies in the administration of justice do not arise simply out of ignorance.
- The District Attorney might work with the police to develop a more consistent set of guidelines for making arrests than those now in effect.
- The District Attorney should monitor the output from each of his Offices to ensure that consistent practices are being followed. Special attention should be devoted to the initial screening of cases for filing and the position taken in negotiated settlements.

- Supervising judges should monitor sentencing practices within the courts. Statistical summaries of the type described in this report, as well as periodic seminars or conferences, should be helpful. Consideration should be given to formulating specific standards for various categories of offense and defendant background. Appellate review of sentences, such as has been incorporated in the proposed new Federal Criminal Code, now before Congress, could be a helpful, albeit controversial, measure.
- Where differences in sentencing practices continue, calendaring practices should be carefully monitored to discourage maneuvering by defense attorneys.

5. *Conclusion: The system offers strong incentives to settle cases without a trial.* Defendants who plead guilty or choose SOT tend to receive lighter sentences than those who demand a court or jury trial. This can be interpreted either as a bonus to those defendants who cooperate in lessening the burden on the criminal justice system or as a penalty to those defendants who insist on the full panoply of their Constitutional rights. Still another view is that the system gives a defendant an opportunity of trial acquittal only if he is willing to chance a heavier sentence if convicted.

Recommendation: The District Attorney should develop a priority scheme similar to that utilized in PROMIS, which will identify the cases in which he is unwilling to negotiate.

6. *Conclusion: Defendants who have secured some form of pretrial release are more likely to be acquitted and less likely to receive a felony sentence if convicted than defendants who have not been released. Defendants who are black, and to a lesser extent those who are Mexican-American, are more likely to be acquitted, less likely to plead guilty and less likely to receive a felony sentence if convicted than Anglo-American defendants.*

Recommendation: Further reserach should be conducted to determine whether these differences are in fact, attributable to unequal treatment within the system. For instance, the disparities in treatment of defendants by ethnic group in the courts might be due to the initiation of more numerous weak cases against minority group defendants by the police or the prosecutor.

7. *Conclusion: No information sources currently exist that would allow the responsible agencies to systematically monitor or diagnose the problem defined in Conclusions 3 and 4.*

Recommendation: An information system should be developed to make timely performance data of the type used in this report available to the management of each criminal justice agency. These data would provide the basis for communication and coordination among agencies at policymaking levels. As suggested in Appendix B, a further refinement in recordkeeping procedures would be to compute moving averages of these data from the most recent quarter as a basis for counting activities.

8. *Conclusion: It is now unnecessarily difficult for D.A. top management to monitor the performance of the District Attorney's Branch and Area Offices.* Since there are wide policy variations in issuing complaints, plea bargaining, and uses of

manpower, the development of an information system would make it much more feasible for management to review and improve the consistency of performance in these decentralized Offices.

Recommendation: The District Attorney should develop an information system that allows him to review and improve the consistency of filing and settlement of cases by individual deputies and by Branch and Area Office. Where the data show disparities in performance by an individual or an Office, every effort should be made to determine whether the cause is within the control of that individual or Office or due to some outside factors. For example, the filing standards employed by each deputy might be tested by having each one screen a special sample of standardized cases. Special attention should be given to reviewing the performance of the Long Beach Branch Office to determine whether the management practices in effect there are appropriate to other Offices.

IX. EPILOGUE:
IMPACTS OF THE RESEARCH STUDY

Our research study was released publicly in early spring of 1973 and received substantial coverage by the Los Angeles newspapers and the electronic media.[1] In the aftermath of its release and in response to the study's findings and recommendations, the District Attorney introduced several policy and management changes over the next two years. His actions also received wide coverage in the local media.[2]

In this chapter we briefly describe these policy changes and trace their subsequent effects on the functioning of the criminal justice process throughout Los Angeles County, in general, and of the District Attorney's Office, in particular.[3]

THE POLICY CHANGES

The policy and management changes introduced by the District Attorney after the study's release concerned: (1) the policy governing the filing of alternate felony/misdemeanors; (2) plea bargaining policies; (3) the use of the SOT procedure; (4) planning for, and first steps in implementing a PROMIS-like, computer-based information system designed to enable the District Attorney and other Office officials to better manage and evaluate the performance of in-

---

[1] See, for example, "L.A. County Scored for Uneven Justice" (Page 1, Part I), "Busch Calls Report a Myth-Shattering Milestone" (Page 1, Part II), "Felon's Chance of Leniency Greater in L.A. Courts, Rand Survey Shows" (Page 1, Part II), Los Angeles Times, April 25, 1973; "The Cynicism of Unequal Justice," Editorial, Los Angeles Times, April 27, 1973; and "Justice? It's Where You Get Arrested" (Page A-1), Los Angeles Herald Examiner, April 24, 1975.

[2] See for example, "Results of Two Programs to Aid Justice Released" (Page 8, Part II), Los Angeles Times, December 18, 1973; and "Uneven Justice, District Attorney Ends Sentence Bargaining," Long Beach, California, Press Telegram, February 17, 1974.

[3] The quantitative changes in the functioning of the criminal justice process we present below are based solely on data contained in a recently released study of the Office of the District Attorney. See *The Principal Law Enforcement Agencies of Los Angeles County Government: Part II, The Office of the District Attorney*, Public Commission on County Government, February 5, 1976.

dividual prosecutors, sub-units within the Office and the Office as a whole. Some Officewide policy innovations were preceded by pilot programs. For example, the new plea bargaining and SOT policies were tested in felony proceedings in the Pomona and Van Nuys Courts as well as in five Courts of the Central Branch (downtown Los Angeles) during the seven-month period from April to October in 1973.

An innovation designed to make the complaint filing decision more uniform was the preparation of two documents—a Uniform Crime Charging Standards and Uniform Crime Charging Manual—by the California District Attorneys Association.[4] The Los Angeles District Attorney, then president of the Association, played a pivotal role in their preparation. But they were not introduced until early 1975—too recent for their impact to be assessed in this book.

Alternate Felony/Misdemeanor Filing Policy

Our research study examined the effects of a June 1971 policy change defining the conditions under which alternate felony/misdemeanors could be considered for prosecution as misdemeanors. For possession-of-dangerous-drug cases, the condition was ten or fewer capsules or pills found in the defendant's possession; for maijuana-possession cases, the condition was five or fewer cigarettes found in the defendant's possession.

Since our study analyzed data from 1970 and 1971, it did not reflect that in December of 1972 the condition for marijuana possession was changed to one ounce or less found in the defendant's possession.

A major change of policy, superceding the 1971 and 1972 conditions, occurred in July 1974. Policy guidance was then set forth that alternate felony/misdemeanors should be considered for prosecution as misdemeanors:

- *unless* the prosecutor believes a felony sentence is warranted or
- if the interests of justice would best be served.

The District Attorney specified that several factors be considered in the exercise of this prosecutorial discretion including severity of the crime, probability of continued criminal conduct, and prior criminal record.

When the facts and circumstances surrounding the offense were sufficiently serious or aggravated, the case was to be filed as a felony under the new policy. Illustrative situations described by the District Attorney included: serious assault; property crimes where the value of property exceeded $1000; burglaries (and attempts) of a home; weapon control law violations involving a sawed-off shotgun; narcotic possession cases involving hashish, LSD, or methamphetamine powder; auto thefts in which the vehicle was not recovered or, if recovered, was substantially altered; and fraudulent obtaining of aid to needy children where the amount obtained exceeded $200. A partial list of situations in which a misdemeanor filing might be appropriate under the new policy included: non-major, non-organized-crime-associated bookmaking; petty theft with a prior; violations

---

[4]See the two documents (entitled as above) published by the California District Attorneys Association, December 1974.

of certain sections of the Vehicle Code in which there were no severe injuries; property crimes involving a small amount of property; auto-theft cases in which the vehicle was quickly recovered locally in unaltered condition; and so on.

A case was to be filed as a felony if the defendant was a professional criminal (as evidenced by modus operandi, tools used, criminal associations, etc.) or if the crime was related to gang activities or organized crime. A felony filing was also appropriate if the defendant had a state prison commitment within the past ten years; a prior felony conviction within the past five years; a prior conviction arising out of the same type of criminal conduct within the past five years; a juvenile court record of felony commission within the past two years; and a record of arrests or convictions demonstrating the likelihood of excessive criminality within the past three years.

Plea Bargaining Policy

Responding to our study's findings that large disparities in sentencing were found across various Branch Offices, the District Attorney in early 1974 changed the Officewide policy concerning pretrial determination of guilt. Henceforth, no deputy district attorney was to agree to a plea bargain which included any *sentence commitment or representation.* Deputies were instructed to object to any plea bargaining effort seeking to include a sentence commitment or representation by the District Attorney's Office. However, with prior written approval of his Head Deputy in an appropriate case, a deputy could agree to a felony sentence commitment of no state prison time, but nothing else. In extraordinary cases, when the interests of justice required, a deputy could, with prior written approval of his Head Deputy, his Director, and the Assistant District Attorney, agree to other sentence commitments.

Use of the SOT

Our finding that the SOT was being used largely as a substitute for a plea of guilty and that SOT defendants were obtaining more lenient treatment in sentencing prompted the District Attorney in early 1974 to change his Officewide policy regarding the use and proper role of the SOT. Noting that, in addition, the use of SOT without adequate standards and safeguards, might also contribute to inordinate appellate reversals, he redefined the policy as follows:

- A deputy could use SOT for any felony case, provided calendar deputy approval was obtained.
- A calendar deputy would approve use of SOT only if he felt it was the most effective way to present the People's case.
- The SOT would be used neither to expedite a finding of not guilty nor to have the defendant found guilty of an offense less serious than a charged offense.
- SOT could not be used unless *all* charges were to be determined by the Court.
- SOT could not be used in a court other than where the case was originally set for trial. That is, "forum shopping" was absolutely prohibited in the use of SOT.

- A calendar deputy was required to submit separate weekly reports on all SOT dispositions to his Head Deputy; moreover, any conviction on a less serious charge than a charged offense and any not guilty finding would require an explanatory report.
- A Head Deputy, in turn, was required to submit similar reports to his superiors.
- A monthly report of sentences imposed on SOT cases was required from each calendar deputy indicating the original charge, the nature of the conviction, and the identity of the judge.
- Finally, in unusual cases, when the interests of justice required, a deputy could deviate from the foregoing policies in using the SOT with prior approval of his Head Deputy, his Director, and the Assistant District Attorney.

The PROMIS System

In mid-1973 the District Attorney's Office received an LEAA planning grant to examine whether a PROMIS-like system would be a useful tool for his office. (PROMIS—*Prosecutor's Management Information System*—is a computer-based management information system for public prosecution agencies developed under an LEAA grant and first implemented several years ago in Washington, D.C. Since then, it has been implemented, or is planned to be implemented, in some sixteen prosecution agencies.) A follow-up grant was received for the following year. All told, LEAA funds plus direct and indirect county funds expended during the two years totaled some $600,000. Some Officewide version of PROMIS is likely to eventuate in the District Attorney's Office. It should enable the District Attorney and other Office officials to better manage and gauge the performance of individual deputies, sub-units within the Office and the entire Office itself.

IMPACTS OF THE POLICY CHANGES

Given these policy changes, what impacts resulted? Below we compare changes in the functioning of the District Attorney's Office and in felony proceedings between the 1970-71 period and the 1973-74 period (after the changes had opportunity to take effect). We first examine Countywide (or Officewide) effects and then turn to the variation among Branch Offices (i.e., geographical evenhandedness).

Countywide Impacts

Table 77 compares the prosecutor's filing actions taken on the adult felony arrests made in Los Angeles County in 1970 and 1974. The 1970 entries are reproduced from Table 6, Chapter II.

It is apparent that between 1970 and 1974 there were only minor shifts in the proportion of felony arrests that were rejected outright or that resulted in rerouting to another jurisdiction. But by 1974 it was much less likely for the District Attorney to file felony charges and much more likely that felony ar-

Table 77

ADULT FELONY ARRESTS AND PROSECUTORIAL FILING
ACTIONS IN LOS ANGELES COUNTY

YEAR	1970	1974
Total number of felony arrests	101,899	112,876
Released without charge (rejected outright) (%)	28	24
Rerouted to another jurisdiction (%)	7	6
Referred for misdemeanor prosecution (%)	18	41
Charged with felony (%)	47	29

restees would be referred for misdemeanor prosecution. In fact, the rise in the latter is almost completely explained by the fall in the former—strongly suggesting that the new policy implemented in 1974 defining conditions under which alternate felony/misdemeanors could be considered for prosecution as misdemeanors was largely responsible.

The fact that the outright rejection rate changed so little between 1970 and 1974 supports the hypothesis that charging standards for felonies in general (excepting those governing alternative felony/misdemeanors) have not changed substantially during that time span. On the other hand, the same data also support an hypothesis that a relatively constant outright rejection rate may be the joint product of *both* stricter prosecutorial screening standards and better arrests by the police (i.e., fewer "bad" arrests having evidentiary, witness, or other problems). But we have no other evidence to support the latter hypothesis.

Table 78 compares felony dispositions in the Superior Court during 1970, 1971, 1973, and 1974. The 1970 and 1971 data are reproduced from Table 70 and Table C-9. Notice that the absolute number of felony dispositions fell considerably in the later years as a consequence of the new policy guidance governing filing of alternate felony/misdemeanors. Notice, too, that the rate of dismissals in Superior Court remained fairly constant over the four years—a further indication that general charging standards and quality of screening did not change materially over that time span. (Dismissals and terminations in lower court—another indicator of screening quality—could not be compared because the California Bureau of Criminal Statistics changed their method of compiling these data in 1973 and the 1974 data were not yet available when the Public Commission on County Government report was written.)

It is very clear that the new policy limiting the use of SOT was successfully implemented and that the new procedures took hold. From a high of 30 percent in 1970, the use of SOT dropped to 15 percent in 1973, and it was further reduced to 2.4 percent in 1974. The question then arises as to what extent cases

Table 78

FELONY DISPOSITIONS IN SUPERIOR COURT IN LOS ANGELES COUNTY,
1970, 1971, 1973, AND 1974
(In percent)

Year	1970	1971	1973	1974
Total cases disposed (100%)	33,142	35,009	20,956	19,834
Dismissed (diverted)	4.8	4.3	1.0	1.1
Dismissed (Interests of Justice)	3.9	2.8	5.4	
Dismissed (§1538.5 PC)	1.3	1.7	3.5	13.7
Dismissed (§995 PC)	3.0	2.6	1.3	
Total dismissed & diverted	13.0	11.4	11.2	14.8
SOT rate	30.8	25.0	15.0	2.4
Jury trial rate	3.4	2.9	6.9	7.5
Court trial rate	7.6	5.3	5.8	8.2
(Jury + court trial rate)	(11.0)	(8.2)	(12.7)	(15.7)
Guilty Pleas				
Plea (original charge)	8.7	16.2	9.4	67.0
Plea (change NG to G)	36.5	39.1	52.6	
Guilty plea rate	47.5	57.8	62.6	67.8
Conviction Rates				
SOT	81.0	79.0	76.9	75.0
Jury Trial	69.8	64.9	70.1	71.0
Court Trial	62.2	55.0	48.7	67.0
Overall conviction rate (includes pleas)	81.2	83.4	81.3	80.5

which were formerly submitted as SOT were disposed of by guilty pleas or trials. The data clearly show that most of the displacement was to pleas of guilty, lending credence to the characterization by numerous critics of the SOT as a "slow plea of guilty." Overall guilty plea rates rose steadily from 47.5 percent in 1970 to 62.6 percent in 1973, and rose further to 67.8 percent in 1974. And almost all of the increase in 1973 was in plea changes rather than pleas to the original charge; in 1974, data were not available to differentiate between plea types.

On the other hand, jury plus court trial rates also rose—from 8.2 percent in 1971 to 15.7 percent in 1974. The overall rise reflected a sharper increase in jury trials than in court trials. This effect also lends credence to an alternative characterization by some of the SOT as a "mini-trial."

The SOT conviction rate declined slowly and modestly over time, but inexplicably the court trial conviction rate dipped below the 1970 value in 1971 and 1973 but rose dramatically in 1974. The jury trial conviction rate was relatively constant in 1970, 1973, and 1974, but declined somewhat in 1971. The net effect of declining SOT rates and increasing guilty plea rates, together with the changes in SOT and trial conviction rates was a relatively constant overall conviction rate. In effect, then, *the change in the SOT policy changed the process but not the results*—at least in terms of overall conviction probability of persons charged with felonies. However, one purpose of the District Attorney's SOT policy change was to influence sentences, since our study demonstrated that SOT defendants were being sentenced more leniently. We could not trace the effects of the SOT policy change in sentencing because the Public Commission on County Government report did not examine sentencing during 1973 and 1974. Since the change in the misdemeanor filing policy (regarding alternate felony/misdemeanors) resulted in a lower felony charging rate and a higher misdemeanor filing rate, the felony conviction rate per felony arrest dropped significantly.

Unfortunately, we cannot trace here the effects of the new policy that discouraged sentence bargaining, since the Public Commission on County Government report did not examine changes in sentencing during 1973 and 1974.

Evenhandedness Impacts

Table 79 compares the variation in felony filing and rejection (outright rejections plus misdemeanor filings) rates for all felonies among the Branch Offices in 1971 and 1974. The 1971 entries are computed from data showing total complaints (Table 54) and complaints filed (Table 55). The data show that 1974 felony rejection and filing rates are more consistent in general than in 1971—one indication that the new filing policy on alternate felony/misdemeanors was being applied more uniformly.

In Table 80 we compare Branch Office variations in felony dispositions in Superior Court for 1971 and 1974. Although we noted previously that the Countywide dismissal rates in Superior Court remained relatively constant between 1970 and 1974 (see Table 78), we see (in Table 80) large variations among Branch Offices for *both* 1971 and 1974. Furthermore, in most Branch Offices dismissal rates did not fall. These two observations suggest that charging standards did not seem to be discernibly higher, nor were they more uniformly applied in 1974 than they were in 1971.

However, the new SOT policy did take hold evenly among the Branch Offices, and SOT's were virtually eliminated. It was used in almost every Office, but never to settle more than 4.3 percent of the cases (Central Office). In Torrance and Norwalk, its use dropped from abut 30 percent of the time in 1971 to one or two percent in 1974.

There was a consistent increase in the use of jury trials in all Offices, and, for all Offices except Long Beach, there was a rise in the use of court trials. The use of the guilty plea increased consistently across Offices, and, because SOT rates decreased consistently, there was less variation in plea rates across Offices in 1974. The net effect of increased plea rates, lower SOT rates, and changed

Table 79

BRANCH OFFICE VARIATIONS IN FELONY
FILING AND REJECTION RATES
IN 1971 AND 1974
(ALL FELONIES)

Branch Office / Year	Filing Rate (%)		Rejection Rate (%)	
	1971	1974	1971	1974
Los Angeles	46.2	35.7	53.8	64.3
Long Beach	45.9	24.9	54.1	75.1
Santa Monica	43.5	33.4	56.5	66.6
Van Nuys	37.3	46.2	63.7	53.8
Torrance	25.2	27.8	74.8	72.2
Norwalk	---	---	---	---
Pomona	11.2	22.2	88.8	77.8
Pasadena	20.5	35.1	79.5	64.9

trial conviction rates was that overall conviction rates changed only slightly within each Office over time, but there was still considerable variation across Offices.

If one constructs a qualitative summary table for 1974 (Table 81) and compares it with its early period counterpart shown on page xii of the Summary, we see that there has been *some* movement toward the mean—that is, performance became more uniform across Offices in 1974. However, differences still remained. Pomona and Pasadena were most like the Countywide averages. Long Beach was least like the County, but its deviation from the mean represents performance that is much closer to the Rigorous Model.

In sum, the evidence indicates that the District Attorney took our study's findings and recommendations seriously, acted on some of them, and was able to produce some movement in his organization toward greater evenhandedness of outcomes across Offices.

Table 80

SUPERIOR COURT DISPOSITIONS FOR ALL FELONIES BY BRANCH OFFICE IN 1971 AND 1974
(In percent)

Disposition	Los Angeles 1971	Los Angeles 1974	Long Beach 1971	Long Beach 1974	Santa Monica 1971	Santa Monica 1974	Van Nuys 1971	Van Nuys 1974	Torrance 1971	Torrance 1974	Norwalk 1971	Norwalk 1974	Pomona 1971	Pomona 1974	Pasadena 1971	Pasadena 1974	Countywide 1971	Countywide 1974
Total cases disposed (100%)	11,671	8,888	2,133	1,003	2,415	1,520	3,466	2,161	5,325	1,631	5,352	1,944	2,492	1,201	2,150	1,262	35,009	19,610
Dismissed (diverted)	4.9	17.0	3.2	3.9	5.4	15.9	3.7	12.5	3.6	11.3	4.0	8.4	4.6	12.9	3.9	11.4	4.3	1.1
Dismissed (Int. of Justice)	2.9		2.0		4.6		3.2		2.7		1.2		3.1		4.9		2.8	13.7
Dismissed (§1538.5 PC)	1.7		1.5		1.8		1.2		2.0		1.2		2.9		3.1		1.7	
Dismissed (§995 PC)	3.3		1.0		2.8		1.9		1.8		1.2		3.3		5.7		2.6	
Total dismissed and diverted	12.8	17.0	7.7	3.9	14.6	15.9	10.0	12.5	10.1	11.3	7.6	8.4	13.9	12.9	17.6	11.4	11.4	14.8
SOT rate	29.2	4.3	15.9	-	18.1	.6	11.6	1.1	33.6	1.0	29.8	2.0	18.6	-	14.4	1.3	25.0	2.4
Jury trial rate	3.7	8.2	6.1	13.1	2.9	7.8	2.3	4.2	1.8	6.4	2.2	6.2	2.5	9.0	2.0	6.5	2.9	7.5
Court trial rate	5.9	9.4	8.1	7.4	2.9	5.7	2.1	2.7	8.8	12.3	2.9	7.2	5.3	9.8	4.7	9.1	5.3	8.2
(Jury & court trial rate)	(9.6)	(17.6)	(14.2)	(20.5)	(5.8)	(13.5)	(4.4)	(6.9)	(10.6)	(18.7)	(5.1)	(13.4)	(7.8)	(18.8)	(6.7)	(15.6)	(8.2)	(15.7)
Guilty Pleas																		
Plea (original charge)	7.0	61.0	22.3	75.7	17.3	69.9	26.7	79.5	20.3	68.9	15.4	76.2	25.7	68.3	23.9	71.7	16.2	67.0
Plea (change NG to G)	41.4		39.9		44.1		47.4		25.6		42.3		34.0		37.4		39.1	
Guilty plea rate	50.9		64.3		65.0		77.0		47.6		60.1		62.6		63.9		57.8	67.8
Conviction rates																		
SOT	77.5	75.5	88.2	-	71.7	60.0	68.4	73.9	85.2	82.3	82.4	69.2	71.1	-	68.9	81.2	79.0	75.0
Jury trial	48.6	65.1	83.1	80.1	77.5	73.7	76.9	74.4	77.1	79.0	69.8	83.3	67.2	72.2	86.1	70.7	64.9	71.0
Court trial	47.2	62.3	72.8	89.2	69.0	59.8	48.7	81.3	54.8	64.0	57.1	71.6	63.9	69.5	58.4	82.6	55.0	67.0
Overall conviction rate (includes pleas)	79.5	75.5	90.1	92.7	83.2	79.5	88.0	79.5	83.7	82.7	88.9	87.9	81.7	81.6	78.8	84.9	83.4	80.5

Branch Office

Table 81

BRANCH OFFICE VARIATIONS IN FELONY
DISPOSITIONS: A QUALITATIVE SUMMARY FOR 1974

DISPOSITION MEASURES	Los Angeles	Long Beach	Santa Monica	Van Nuys	Torrance	Norwalk	Pomona	Pasadena
D.A. Felony Rejection Rate	Avg	H	Avg	VL	H	–	VH	Avg
Superior Court Dismissal Rate	VH	VL	H	Avg	Avg	L	Avg	Avg
Method of Disposition								
SOT	VH	–	VL	L	L	Avg	–	L
Plea of Guilty	L	H	Avg	VH	Avg	H	Avg	Avg
Court Trial	Avg	Avg	L	VL	VH	Avg	Avg	Avg
Jury Trial	Avg	VH	Avg	L	Avg	Avg	Avg	Avg
Conviction Rate								
SOT	Avg	–	L	Avg	H	L	–	H
Court	Avg	VH	L	H	Avg	Avg	Avg	H
Jury	L	VH	Avg	Avg	VH	VH	Avg	Avg
Overall Conviction	L	VH	Avg	Avg	Avg	H	Avg	Avg

NOTE: VH = very high, H = high, Avg = average, L = low, VL = very low

Appendix A

DATA SOURCES

The principal data source for our Los Angeles District Attorney Study was the California Bureau of Criminal Statistics (BCS). Secondary sources were the District Attorney's own Felony Filing and Felony Rejection Indexes, as well as figures published by the Judicial Council. Other sources were the various divisions of the Los Angeles County Clerk's Office. Each source is discussed in some detail.

BCS

The BCS operates within California's State Department of Justice. Each year it publishes a series of reports and monographs that detail crimes committed, the number of arrests, felonies adjudicated in the State's Superior Courts, and probation activities, as well as a number of related materials. We used the data from the BCS Superior Court Disposition File for 1970 and 1971. These data described cases disposed of in 1970 and 1971 (even if they were initiated during an earlier year). These files enabled us to examine the following variables:

- District Attorney Branch Office
- Charged offense
- Convicted offense
- Data filed, date of disposition, and total time
- Type of proceeding
- Insanity plea
- Disposition
- Reason for dismissal or off-calendar
- Level of conviction
- Sentence
- Length of probation
- Length of jail term
- Amount of fine
- Defendant's race and sex
- Type of defense counsel

- Defendant's prior record
- Defendant's existent criminal status
- Defendant's bail status
- The sentencing judge

The BCS records are based on *one crime per defendant per year,* using a priority system if that one defendant commits *multiple* crimes. That is, a defendant could conceivably be tried and convicted for more than one crime during a given year. BCS would consolidate these offenses and only enter the defendant once in the Felony Disposition File on the most serious offense he was convicted of. They do this because they believe that the defendant is the primary unit of analysis; if he is in prison for one offense, BCS does not count him being sentenced with a fine for an earlier conviction if the two convictions are, time-wise, in relatively close proximity.

In their publication *Felony Defendants Disposed of in California Courts, 1970,* BCS uses a base figure of 31,571 defendants who had felony charges filed against them in the Superior Courts for Los Angeles County. We employed a base number of 33,142 for many of our 1970 calculations since we included 1600 defendants whose charges were originally filed in Los Angeles County but whose cases were diverted or remanded to other Superior Court Districts.[1] We included the diverted/remanded defendants in the base figure because they were originally filed in Los Angeles and were part of the process workload, if only for a brief period; they were excluded in calculating conviction rates.

The BCS Felony Disposition File is compiled from forms the County Clerk's Office sends to the Bureau. The Criminal Division of the County Clerk's Office prepares these forms for all the Superior Court Districts in the county. To ensure quality and consistency, the Central Office sends its personnel to the various courts on a regular schedule to fill out these forms, which are based on the Superior Court dockets for completed cases. The forms are then sent to the BCS in Sacramento where they are edited, keypunched, and entered into the Felony Disposition File.

DISTRICT ATTORNEY INDEXES

The District Attorney's Office prepares the Felony and Rejection Indexes, both of which are machine-readable. For every police request for the issuance of a felony complaint, the Complaint Deputy prepares forms stating whether or not a felony complaint was issued. If the complaint is issued, it is recorded in the Felony Index. If it is not issued, it is recorded in the Rejection Index. Even if the defendant has a misdemeanor complaint filed against him, because the felony complaint was rejected but referred for misdemeanor filing, it will still be recorded in the Rejection Index. In brief, all cases are either filed as felonies or rejections. The sum of these two files should equal the number of police felony arrests (not subsequently released by the police) for the county for identical time periods.

---

[1] The two base numbers are essentially the same. If 1600 is added to the BCS base figure of 31,571, the sum is 33,171; the two base numbers are thus reconciled to within 29 defendants, a difference of less than one-tenth of 1 percent. The number of defendants found guilty is even closer: ours is 25,641 versus 25,642 for BCS.

The Felony and Rejection forms are completed by the Branch or Area Complaint Deputies, but they are all encoded and keypunched by the Records section in the Los Angeles Central Office of the District Attorney. The cards are then sent to the Justice Data Center, which is part of the County's Data Processing Department; the Justice Data Center, in turn, creates and maintains the Felony Index and Rejection Index on magnetic tape.

The Felony Index contains the following information:

- Defendant's name
- Defendant's CII number[2]
- Charged offense
- Date of filing
- Custody code
- Filing District Attorney's Office
- Arraigning Municipal Court

The Rejection Index contains the following data elements:

- Defendant's name
- Defendant's CII number
- Multiple defendant code
- Rejection number
- Date of rejection
- District Attorney's Office
- Arresting agency
- Charge

For the first ten months in 1971, the Felony and Rejection Indexes contained 43,064 and 50,547 records, respectively.

In addition to these machine-readable records, the District Attorney provided over 5,000 case records, rejection forms, memoranda of preliminary hearings, and District Attorney Recommendation forms. These were sampled to study Municipal Court dismissal rates and to study reasons for felony rejections and terminations in Municipal Court.

JUDICIAL COUNCIL FIGURES

The Judicial Council gathers and aggregates court workload and cost figures for all the courts in California. Besides reporting the number of cases, these data are used to allocate judicial manpower throughout the state. Except for some work on estimating caseloads and court costs, we did not avail ourselves of these data, as discussed below.

---

[2] A unique identification number assigned by the Bureau of Criminal Identification and Investigation (CI&I).

COUNTY CLERK FIGURES

A final data source is the County Clerk. The various divisions of the County Clerk service both the Municipal Court Districts and the Superior Courts. The Administrative Services section of the County Clerk's Superior Court Division prepares caseload analyses to assist in court management; the Statistical Section of the same Division prepares the material for the Judicial Council from Minute Orders, the record of court transactions. The County Clerk's Criminal Division gathers the BCS data from the court dockets.

It is essential to be aware that these data are not identical, even though they are basically measuring the same processes. The Judicial Council is concerned with caseloads. Given this emphasis, it records the *total* number of defendants who go through Superior Court criminal proceedings. In other words, if a person is convicted of two crimes within the year, the Judicial Council data have two entries for that defendant. (Recall that BCS data show the defendant convicted only once—for the most serious offense.) These differing emphases are almost certain to provide larger numbers in the Judicial Council data than in the BCS data. For example, the County Clerk's 1970 data for the Judicial Council were 2,059 defendants higher than the BCS number of defendants.

Appendix B

USING STATISTICAL MEASURES OF PROSECUTION EFFECTIVENESS

In this report we have introduced, and argued for, the use of a number of statistical measures of prosecution performance. The purpose of this Appendix is to discuss in greater depth the definition of these measures, the relationships among them, and how they might be used to measure the effectiveness of a prosecution program.

We contend that the measures we shall discuss can be used for a variety of evaluative purposes. They might be used to compare two or more Offices operating in similar environments—much as we did with the Branch Offices of the District Attorney. They might be used to evaluate the impact of a particular program or policy change by observing performance both before and after a change, as we did in Section VII. Finally, these measures can be used to indicate whether or not different classes of defendants, within the same Office, are being treated equitably.

We suggest that there are six essential performance measures that must be examined to assess the *effectiveness* of a prosecutor's office. Each has its unique meaning that cannot be obtained from the others. Taken together they present a fairly complete picture of felony prosecution effectiveness.

1. *Rejection Rate.* That percentage of cases presented by the police for prosecution in which the District Attorney refuses to file (includes those which police themselves characterize as rejections, as well as those which the District Attorney rejects but police feel should be filed).
2. *Dismissal Rate.* That percentage of the defendants whom the court releases prior to adjudication. The dismissal may occur in Municipal Court before or at the preliminary hearing. It may result from a failure of the Grand Jury to indict, or it may result from a motion by the defense or prosecution in Superior Court.
3. *Straight Plea Rate.* That percentage of the defendants who plead guilty as charged or to the most serious charge.
4. *Gross Plea Rate.* That percentage of the defendants who plead guilty to any charge or are found guilty absent an affirmative defense (includes all pleas and SOTs).

5. *Trial Conviction Rate.* That percentage of cases that go to trial and result in a conviction in Superior Court.
6. *Overall Conviction Rate.* That percentage of cases filed in Superior Court which result in either a guilty plea or a conviction.

It should come as no surprise to those familiar with court statistics that these definitions raise a host of semantic and procedural questions about their application in specific cases. Here we outline a few general guidelines about how they should be applied and then discuss each in detail, elaborating on the definition, explaining its value, and describing how it relates to the other effectiveness measures.

The period for which these measures are to be calculated is problematical. If the period is too short, the sample sizes are small and the measures will reflect a large degree of fluctuation due simply to chance. If the data are collected on a yearly basis, the delay encountered in taking corrective actions vitiates their use as a management tool. A resolution of this dilemma would be to compute a moving average in which data from the most recent quarter, six months, or year, are used to compute the measures on a monthly basis. Each month, the oldest month's data are dropped and the most recent month's data are added to the data pool from which the measures are calculated. This procedure would not represent much extra effort even in manual record systems. Further refinements would involve discounting each month's data so that the measures would be more heavily weighted toward recent months; or grouping the data elements, as is done in statistical quality control methods, to make them more responsive to sudden shifts in performance levels.

Another difficulty concerns the links between prosecutorial events. In many offices it is a common practice to compute statistics similar to those we have described on a weekly or monthly basis, but to compute these statistics simply from the total number of events that occur in a period. That is, "independent" numbers of dismissals, pleas, acquittals, and convictions in a single period are computed with the dependencies denominator between the events in individual cases being discarded. Our approach requires that such links be retained. For example, instead of calculating the number of convictions achieved in month X, one calculates successively in months X, X + 1, X + 2, ... the cumulative number of convictions achieved for cases filed in month X.

This suggested refinement in recordkeeping procedures does impose slightly more effort, but it also provides a possibility for cross-checking the data for accuracy, which is absent in the current procedures.

In using this procedure it is probably preferable to remove pending cases from both the numerator and denominator for all the ratios. Otherwise, the data would not be meaningful until most of the cases were complete. Table B-1 illustrates how the overall conviction rate might behave over time for a given month.

In our definitions we have used the terms *case* and *defendant* interchangeably. We assume that each individual defendant and set of charges for which he is to be tried represent a single case. Two defendants for a single crime represent two cases. One defendant with multiple charges represents a single case, unless multiple cases are filed and separate adjudication procedures are employed. These definitions need not be considered sacred as long as all data are recorded consistently. We assume that these definitions apply in the remainder of our discussion.

Table B-1

OVERALL CONVICTION RATE FOR CASES FILED IN MAY 1972 (ILLUSTRATION)

Item	As of June 30, 1972	Completed During July	As of July 31, 1972
Filings in May	100		100
Pleas	54	4	58
Convictions	10	7	17
	64		75
Dismissals	10	1	11
Acquittals	6	3	9
	16		20
Completed	80		95
Overall conviction rate	64/80 = 80%		75/95 = 79%

In our discussion of effectiveness measures, we presume that any case filed is in one, and only one, of the following categories. Of course its category may shift over time.

- *Diverted.* Cases that are no longer in the system being studied, such as those shifted to another court, combined with another case, the defendant has died, etc. Once diverted, a case does not return to another category. Diverted cases will never be counted in the numerator or denominator of any measures.
- *Straight Plea.* The defendant has pleaded guilty to the charges as stated or to the most serious count.
- *Reduced Plea.* The defendant has pleaded guilty to some reduced charge or has been found guilty without offering any defense (includes straight SOT).
- *Dismissed.* The court has dismissed the case against the defendant. If the District Attorney refiles, it is treated as another case.
- *Convicted.* A jury or the court has found the defendant guilty of some charge after adjudicating the case.
- *Acquitted.* A jury or the court has found the defendant not guilty.
- *Pending.* None of the above.

Rejection Rate

The rejection rate represents cases the police present to the prosecutor that he elects not to file as felonies. In Los Angeles County, a felony arrest that results in the filing of any felony charge is *not* a rejection. A felony arrest that results only in the filing of misdemeanor charges *is* a rejection.

A key assumption underlying the following discussion is that the rejection decision is not arbitrary—that, in general, the probability of dismissal is greater on the average for those cases rejected than for those filed. There is no sound way of statistically verifying this assumption without taking a sample of rejected cases, filing them, and observing the results, an experiment that hardly seems justified, considering the burden it might place on the defendants and the criminal justice system. Most people familiar with court practices would be convinced of the validity of this assumption by simply comparing the characteristics of a sample of rejected and filed cases.

The standards used to screen cases for filing are discussed elsewhere in this report (see Section II). It suffices here to note that the screening is not a strictly mechanical, factual process, but involves a subjective assessment both of the seriousness of the case and of the probability that it would result in a conviction. These latter factors are not unrelated, for defendants may be dismissed or acquitted because the judge or a jury does not believe the offense is serious enough to warrant conviction, even though the defendant is technically guilty.

A useful test for consistency that could be applied to the screening process would be to submit a test sample of cases to a number of prosecutors to solicit their filing decisions on each. The extent of agreement or correlation among their decisions would be a measure of consistency in filing standards. To our knowledge this has never been done in a systematic fashion.

If our assumption about the quality of screening holds, then the results of the filing practices should show up in the dismissal and conviction rates. All other things being equal (police arrest policy, judges, juries, quality of prosecution presentation), raising the rejection rate should lower dismissal rates and raise conviction rates. All other things being equal, an Office with a lower rejection rate must be doing a better job of screening (i.e., of discriminating convictable cases from losers), or of presenting cases, than an Office with a higher rejection rate.

The more usual circumstance is shown in Table B-2. Office B has more permissive filing standards than Office A. The difference in their conviction rates has nothing to do with their level of performance, but results instead from the difference in their screening policies. The result is that B only achieves a 50-percent conviction rate on the additional 10 cases it filed and A rejected. This brings down its total

Table B-2

EXPECTED RESULTS FROM ALTERNATIVE
FILING PRACTICE

| | Office | | Marginal |
Item	A	B	Filed by B
Arrests	100	100	
Rejects	50	40	
Filings	50	60	10
Convictions	40	45	5
Conviction rate	80%	75%	50%

conviction rate. Whether or not the additional five convictions achieved are worth the time or effort expended, and how unconvicted defendants may be affected, is a matter for some policy consideration.

Rejections can and sometimes do influence police behavior. The written rejection can be partly addressed to the police and contain an explanation valuable and educational to them. This may modify their conduct. In at least one Branch Office in Los Angeles County, the written rejections are studied by the investigating officer, his supervisors, and the arresting officers (who frequently cause the rejection).

Dismissal Rate

The dismissal rate is one measure of prefiling screening success. For jurisdictions in which the prosecutor files most cases brought in by the police, a large percentage are usually dismissed in Municipal Court or before trial in Superior Court. This dismissal may often be based on the prosecutor's decision not to press the case. However, a high dismissal rate may also reflect a degree of independence in the judge who grants dismissals, or it may reflect the prosecutor's refusal to accept a court's policy in not pressing some particular type of case. Other things being equal, a low dismissal rate is usually a preferred posture for a prosecutor.

Straight Plea Rate and Gross Plea Rate

High plea rates reflect the ability of the prosecutor to convince the defendant that there is a high probability of his conviction (risk) or at least that there is a high-gravity x risk factor (i.e., expected punishment), even if risk is not very high. High plea rates may also reflect the defendant's desire to avoid a longer stay in custody, if pleading guilty early means earlier release from custody. Pleas certainly save taxpayer expense, but a system with a guilty plea rate of 100 percent would be unhealthy, if not suspect. A system with some percentage of adversary trials is necessary—because it produces respect from the public, it produces an indispensable guide to filing decisions, and it provides the environment for plea bargaining.

Our primary purpose in distinguishing between straight plea rates and gross plea rates is that the former is much less susceptible to plea bargaining. Although in many instances a plea to some lesser offense is preferable to a lengthy trial, for both the State and the defendant, presumably an unscrupulous District Attorney could ensure an arbitrarily high gross plea rate by increasing the discrepancy in severity between the more lenient sentences received by those who plead guilty and the more severe sentences that are received by those who do not plead guilty and who are tried and found guilty.

Trial Conviction Rate

The probability that a defendant will be found guilty by trial is an apt measure of the prosecutor's case preparation and presentation. Of course, it also reflects on earlier screening decisions. A high probability of conviction, to the extent that it measures expected punishment, is a good argument for convincing guilty defendants to plead. A low conviction rate and a high gross plea rate together would suggest that defendants are being induced to plead guilty to lesser offenses or fewer charges by offers of a more lenient bargain, rather than through anticipation that they would be convicted of a more serious charge if they went to trial.

Overall Conviction Rate

This measure is the one most usually quoted in reference to a prosecutor's performance and does reflect the most comprehensive picture. Yet, we hope to have shown that, taken by itself, it can distort. Skimming off only the best cases or offering overly lenient bargains can easily inflate the overall conviction rate of a particular Office. It is also difficult to compare published overall conviction rates among prosecutors of various counties since they use different conventions to determine the total number of cases being considered. The only cases we drop are those diverted or pending. Some District Attorney Offices might also drop some dismissals in Superior Court, especially if they are on the prosecutor's motion.

Appendix C

SUPERIOR COURT DISPOSITIONS FOR 1970 AND 1971

Table C-1

SUPERIOR COURT FELONY DISPOSITIONS BY BRANCH OFFICE, 1970: POSSESSION OF MARIJUANA

(In percent)

Disposition	Los Angeles	Long Beach	Santa Monica	Van Nuys	Torrance	Norwalk	Pomona	Pasadena	County-wide
No. cases disposed	1483	449	523	584	759	573	419	252	5042
% of countywide	29.4	8.9	10.4	11.6	15.0	11.4	8.3	5.0	100.0
Dismissed (diverted)	6.2	4.9	6.3	4.6	3.6	8.4	8.8	2.8	5.8
Dismissed (Int of Jus)	6.2	3.6	6.1	3.8	3.3	3.0	6.4	11.1	5.1
Dismissed (§1538.5 PC)	3.8	4.0	3.6	0.9	6.1	2.4	3.3	4.8	3.7
Dismissed (§995 PC)	5.5	0.7	5.2	9.1	4.9	1.8	7.9	12.7	5.5
SOT rate	38.0	20.7	24.5	17.6	54.2	40.1	27.5	12.3	33.2
SOT conviction rate	66.1	92.5	67.2	68.0	84.9	76.5	59.1	51.6	73.1
Jury trial rate	2.0	1.8	1.3	1.2	0.3	1.2	0.7	0.8	1.3
Jury trial conviction rate	40.0	75.0	57.1	57.1	100.0	57.1	33.3	0.0	50.0
Court trial rate	7.3	5.8	3.4	2.7	8.3	3.1	7.2	9.9	6.0
Court trial conviction rate	47.2	80.8	50.0	62.5	54.0	50.0	36.7	40.0	51.0
Plea (orig charge)	2.5	16.9	11.5	23.5	6.5	11.0	8.4	15.5	9.8
Plea (change NG to G)	28.5	41.7	38.1	36.6	13.0	29.0	29.8	30.2	29.5
Guilty plea rate	33.1	61.6	52.9	63.0	20.2	43.6	41.9	46.9	41.8
Overall conviction rate	64.4	88.1	73.1	78.1	72.8	79.6	62.8	57.6	71.5

SOURCE: California Bureau of Criminal Statistics computer tapes.

Table C-2

SUPERIOR COURT FELONY DISPOSITIONS BY BRANCH OFFICE, 1970: POSSESSION OF DANGEROUS DRUGS

(In percent)

Disposition	Los Angeles	Long Beach	Santa Monica	Van Nuys	Torrance	Norwalk	Pomona	Pasadena	County-wide
				Branch Office					
No. cases disposed % of countywide	1624 26.4	512 8.3	340 5.5	576 9.4	973 15.8	1300 21.1	563 9.1	274 4.5	6162 100.0
Dismissed (diverted)	5.6	3.3	7.9	4.2	3.7	5.9	8.4	3.6	5.3
Dismissed (Int of Jus)	4.5	2.5	6.2	2.1	3.0	1.8	3.7	6.6	3.4
Dismissed ($1538.5 PC)	2.4	1.6	2.7	1.2	3.3	1.2	3.2	3.7	2.3
Dismissed ($995 PC)	3.0	1.8	2.4	1.6	2.9	1.3	3.6	9.5	2.7
SOT rate	36.3	17.8	16.5	17.4	61.6	33.9	21.0	12.0	32.9
SOT conviction rate	76.1	86.8	66.1	78.0	86.1	84.3	71.2	63.6	80.7
Jury trial rate	2.1	1.8	2.1	0.4	0.6	1.2	0.2	0.0	1.2
Jury trial conviction rate	58.8	100.0	100.0	100.0	83.3	81.3	100.0	0.0	76.0
Court trial rate	7.0	9.6	3.2	2.1	6.7	3.5	6.6	8.0	5.8
Court trial conviction rate	64.0	79.6	45.5	50.0	56.9	71.1	59.5	50.0	63.4
Plea (orig charge)	2.7	19.1	12.1	26.0	5.8	14.2	13.0	17.2	11.2
Plea (change NG to G)	36.5	42.6	47.1	45.1	12.5	37.1	40.5	39.4	35.2
Guilty plea rate	41.5	63.8	64.2	74.3	19.0	54.5	58.3	58.7	49.1
Overall conviction rate	76.8	89.5	79.9	89.9	78.6	88.5	79.1	70.8	81.9

SOURCE: California Bureau of Criminal Statistics computer tapes.

Table C-3

SUPERIOR COURT FELONY DISPOSITIONS BY BRANCH OFFICE, 1970: BURGLARY

(In percent)

Disposition	Los Angeles	Long Beach	Santa Monica	Van Nuys	Torrance	Norwalk	Pomona	Pasadena	County-wide
No. cases disposed	1746	288	349	514	721	524	358	203	4703
% of countywide	37.1	6.1	7.4	10.9	15.3	11.1	7.6	4.3	100.0
Dismissed (diverted)	4.4	5.9	5.2	4.1	4.2	3.6	7.8	4.9	4.7
Dismissed (Int of Jus)	2.4	2.8	5.2	3.1	2.6	0.6	2.0	3.9	2.6
Dismissed (§1538.5 PC)	0.5	0.0	0.0	0.4	0.6	0.0	0.0	1.0	0.3
Dismissed (§995 PC)	2.7	0.0	3.4	1.4	2.4	0.6	1.4	3.0	2.1
SOT rate	31.27	16.3	13.8	10.5	60.3	34.0	17.9	11.8	29.7
SOT conviction rate	84.3	93.6	77.1	85.2	94.3	92.7	71.9	75.0	87.8
Jury trial rate	4.70	6.3	4.0	4.5	1.7	2.3	2.5	2.5	3.7
Jury trial conviction rate	69.5	66.7	78.6	69.6	66.7	75.0	66.7	60.0	69.7
Court trial rate	9.05	8.7	2.0	2.5	6.7	3.1	4.5	8.4	6.4
Court trial conviction rate	69.6	76.0	57.1	76.9	70.8	68.8	56.3	94.1	71.0
Plea (orig charge)	2.4	20.8	9.2	15.0	5.1	8.0	24.6	22.2	9.0
Plea (change NG to G)	42.7	39.2	57.3	58.6	16.5	47.9	39.4	42.4	41.6
Guilty plea rate	47.1	63.8	70.1	76.7	22.6	58.0	69.4	67.9	53.1
Overall conviction rate	84.7	91.5	85.8	91.3	88.0	94.7	87.9	87.1	87.9

SOURCE: California Bureau of Criminal Statistics computer tapes.

144

Table C-4

SUPERIOR COURT FELONY DISPOSITIONS BY BRANCH OFFICE, 1970: ROBBERY

(In percent)

Disposition	Los Angeles	Long Beach	Santa Monica	Van Nuys	Torrance	Norwalk	Pomona	Pasadena	County-wide
No. cases disposed	747	106	82	148	297	184	97	75	1736
% of countywide	43.0	6.1	4.7	8.5	17.1	10.6	5.6	4.3	100.0
Dismissed (diverted)	3.4	0.9	3.7	5.4	2.0	1.6	5.2	4.0	3.1
Dismissed (Int of Jus)	4.7	2.8	13.4	2.0	4.7	1.1	2.1	4.0	4.2
Dismissed (§1538.5 PC)	0.1	0.0	0.0	0.0	0.0	0.0	0.0	0.0	0.1
Dismissed (§995 PC)	1.9	0.9	1.2	1.4	0.3	1.1	4.1	1.3	1.5
SOT rate	21.2	9.4	9.8	10.8	48.5	22.3	14.4	8.0	22.9
SOT conviction rate	85.4	100.0	50.0	87.5	86.1	92.7	92.9	100.0	86.7
Jury trial rate	13.0	9.4	12.2	6.8	6.4	4.9	7.2	17.3	10.1
Jury trial conviction rate	69.1	70.0	90.0	100.0	73.7	88.9	71.4	53.9	72.6
Court trial rate	14.9	13.2	2.4	2.0	12.8	6.5	9.3	10.7	11.4
Court trial conviction rate	65.8	78.6	50.0	100.0	55.3	91.7	66.7	87.5	67.5
Plea (orig charge)	0.7	8.5	2.4	4.1	3.0	4.9	11.3	18.7	3.7
Plea (change NG to G)	40.3	54.7	54.9	67.6	22.2	57.6	46.4	36.0	43.1
Guilty plea rate	42.4	63.8	59.5	75.7	25.8	63.5	60.9	56.9	48.3
Overall conviction rate	80.5	90.5	77.2	95.0	80.4	95.0	87.0	84.7	84.2

SOURCE: California Bureau of Criminal Statistics computer tapes.

Table C-5

SUPERIOR COURT FELONY DISPOSITIONS BY BRANCH OFFICE, 1970: ASSAULT

(In percent)

Disposition	Branch Office								County-wide
	Los Angeles	Long Beach	Santa Monica	Van Nuys	Torrance	Norwalk	Pomona	Pasadena	
No. cases disposed % of countywide	622 39.7	64 4.1	104 6.6	146 9.3	236 15.1	210 13.4	117 7.5	67 4.3	1566 100.0
Dismissed (diverted)	6.3	6.3	2.9	4.8	5.9	3.3	5.1	9.0	5.5
Dismissed (Int of Jus)	5.1	1.6	10.6	4.1	4.2	1.9	6.0	11.9	5.0
Dismissed (§1538.5 PC)	0.0	0.0	0.0	0.0	0.0	0.0	0.9	0.0	0.1
Dismissed (§995 PC)	1.6	0.0	1.0	5.5	0.4	0.5	4.3	3.0	1.8
SOT rate	30.4	17.2	14.4	12.3	47.9	35.7	19.7	16.4	29.1
SOT conviction rate	78.3	100.0	73.3	88.9	89.4	90.7	65.2	18.2	81.8
Jury trial rate	9.2	15.6	8.7	5.5	2.5	8.6	0.9	0.0	7.0
Jury trial conviction rate	50.9	20.0	66.7	87.5	50.0	61.1	0.0	0.0	53.2
Court trial rate	14.5	10.9	7.7	7.5	20.8	9.1	9.4	25.4	13.5
Court trial conviction rate	65.6	85.7	62.5	54.6	53.1	63.2	36.4	47.1	59.4
Plea (orig charge)	0.0	1.6	3.9	2.7	2.1	0.5	8.6	3.0	1.7
Plea (change NG to G)	33.0	46.9	51.0	57.5	16.1	40.5	45.3	31.3	36.3
Guilty plea rate	35.2	51.7	56.4	63.3	19.4	42.4	56.8	37.7	40.3
Overall conviction rate	75.7	83.3	78.2	84.2	77.9	87.2	73.9	54.1	77.8

SOURCE: California Bureau of Criminal Statistics computer tapes.

Table C-6

SUPERIOR COURT FELONY DISPOSITIONS BY BRANCH OFFICE, 1970:   FORGERY

(In percent)

Disposition	Branch Office								County-wide
	Los Angeles	Long Beach	Santa Monica	Van Nuys	Torrance	Norwalk	Pomona	Pasadena	
No. cases disposed	682	94	87	135	244	142	125	52	1561
% of countywide	43.7	6.0	5.6	8.7	15.6	9.1	8.0	3.3	100.0
Dismissed (diverted)	6.2	3.2	0.0	3.7	6.2	5.6	12.8	0.0	5.7
Dismissed (Int of Jus)	1.5	3.2	4.6	2.2	0.4	0.0	0.8	7.6	1.7
Dismissed (§1538.5 PC)	0.3	0.0	0.0	0.0	0.0	0.0	0.0	0.0	0.1
Dismissed (§995 PC)	1.6	0.0	0.0	0.7	0.8	0.7	0.8	1.9	1.1
SOT rate	23.6	16.0	14.9	8.9	59.0	19.7	11.2	5.8	24.9
SOT conviction rate	78.3	80.0	61.5	50.0	88.9	89.3	78.6	66.7	81.5
Jury trial rate	1.9	2.1	1.2	1.5	1.6	0.7	2.4	1.9	1.7
Jury trial conviction rate	76.9	50.0	100.0	100.0	100.0	100.0	100.0	100.0	85.2
Court trial rate	5.0	2.1	2.3	4.4	4.9	0.7	7.2	0.0	4.2
Court trial conviction rate	61.8	50.0	50.0	66.7	91.7	100.0	66.7	0.0	68.2
Plea (orig charge)	7.6	34.0	19.5	28.2	9.8	14.1	31.2	46.2	15.8
Plea (change NG to G)	52.4	39.4	57.5	50.4	17.2	58.5	33.6	36.5	44.7
Guilty plea rate	63.9	75.8	77.0	81.5	28.8	76.9	74.3	82.7	64.1
Overall conviction rate	88.4	91.2	88.5	90.8	91.3	97.0	92.7	88.5	90.4

SOURCE: California Bureau of Criminal Statistics computer tapes.

Table C-7

SUPERIOR COURT FELONY DISPOSITIONS BY BRANCH OFFICE, 1970: POSSESSION OF NARCOTICS

(In percent)

Disposition	Los Angeles	Long Beach	Santa Monica	Van Nuys	Torrance	Norwalk	Pomona	Pasadena	County-wide
No. cases disposed	309	42	54	84	77	95	36	12	709
% of countywide	43.6	5.9	7.6	11.9	10.9	13.4	5.1	1.7	100.0
Dismissed (diverted)	3.9	2.4	5.6	1.2	2.6	0.0	0.0	8.3	2.8
Dismissed (Int of Jus)	8.4	2.4	1.9	2.4	15.6	2.1	19.4	0.0	7.2
Dismissed ($1538.5 PC)	3.9	2.4	0.0	0.0	3.9	3.2	2.8	0.0	2.8
Dismissed (§995 PC)	3.9	0.0	0.0	2.4	6.5	2.1	2.8	0.0	3.1
SOT rate	35.6	14.3	22.2	21.4	27.3	41.1	30.6	25.0	31.0
SOT conviction rate	80.0	83.3	58.3	88.9	85.7	82.1	72.7	66.7	80.0
Jury trial rate	2.3	7.1	3.7	1.2	0.0	6.3	2.8	0.0	2.8
Jury trial conviction rate	57.1	100.0	100.0	100.0	0.0	100.0	100.0	0.0	85.0
Court trial rate	9.1	16.7	5.6	6.0	16.9	5.3	11.1	25.0	10.0
Court trial conviction rate	71.4	71.4	33.3	80.0	15.4	80.0	75.0	100.0	61.8
Plea (orig charge)	2.9	4.8	0.0	14.3	3.9	4.2	0.0	16.7	4.5
Plea (change NG to G)	30.1	50.0	61.1	51.2	23.4	35.8	30.6	25.0	36.1
Guilty plea rate	34.3	56.1	64.7	66.3	28.0	40.0	30.6	45.5	41.8
Overall conviction rate	72.1	87.0	84.3	91.6	54.7	84.2	63.9	90.9	75.9

SOURCE: California Bureau of Criminal Statistics computer tapes.

Table C-8

SUPERIOR COURT FELONY DISPOSITIONS BY BRANCH OFFICE, 1970:   SALE OF NARCOTICS

(In percent)

Disposition	Branch Office								County-wide
	Los Angeles	Long Beach	Santa Monica	Van Nuys	Torrance	Norwalk	Pomona	Pasadena	
No. cases disposed	839	155	231	202	319	326	216	135	2423
% of countywide	34.6	6.4	9.5	8.3	13.2	13.5	8.9	5.6	100.0
Dismissed (diverted)	5.2	1.3	4.8	3.5	1.3	3.1	4.2	5.2	3.9
Dismissed (Int of Jus)	5.7	4.5	4.3	4.5	3.1	1.5	2.8	3.0	4.1
Dismissed (§1538.5 PC)	2.2	0.7	0.9	0.5	1.9	0.9	3.7	0.7	1.7
Dismissed (§995 PC)	3.7	0.7	2.6	5.9	3.1	1.5	3.7	2.2	3.2
SOT rate	33.5	24.5	23.8	25.3	57.7	58.3	36.1	19.3	37.3
SOT conviction rate	89.3	97.4	94.6	82.4	91.3	93.7	91.0	69.2	90.5
Jury trial rate	4.5	7.7	6.5	2.0	3.1	2.5	2.3	6.7	4.2
Jury trial conviction rate	81.6	83.3	86.7	100.0	80.0	87.5	100.0	100.0	86.1
Court trial rate	10.0	19.4	8.2	4.0	11.0	4.9	9.7	12.6	9.5
Court trial conviction rate	73.8	90.0	42.1	87.5	77.1	87.5	71.4	88.2	76.1
Plea (orig charge)	1.1	5.2	5.2	8.9	1.9	2.2	3.7	11.9	3.5
Plea (change NG to G)	34.1	36.1	43.7	45.5	16.9	25.2	33.0	38.5	32.9
Guilty plea rate	37.1	41.8	51.4	56.4	19.1	28.2	39.1	53.1	37.8
Overall conviction rate	80.4	90.2	84.6	83.6	83.5	91.1	83.1	95.9	84.1

SOURCE: California Bureau of Criminal Statistics computer tapes.

Table C-9

SUPERIOR COURT FELONY DISPOSITIONS BY BRANCH OFFICE, 1971: ALL FELONIES

(In percent)

Disposition	Branch Office								County-wide
	Los Angeles	Long Beach	Santa Monica	Van Nuys	Torrance	Norwalk	Pomona	Pasadena	
No. cases disposed	11,671	2,133	2,415	3,466	5,325	5,352	2,492	2,150	35,009
% of countywide	33.3	6.1	6.9	9.9	15.2	15.3	7.1	6.1	100.0
Dismissed (diverted)	4.9	3.2	5.4	3.7	3.6	4.0	4.6	3.9	4.3
Dismissed (Int of Jus)	2.9	2.0	4.6	3.2	2.7	1.2	3.1	4.9	2.8
Dismissed (§1538.5 PC)	1.7	1.5	1.8	1.2	2.0	1.2	2.9	3.1	1.7
Dismissed (§995 PC)	3.3	1.0	2.8	1.9	1.8	1.2	3.3	5.7	2.6
SOT rate	29.2	15.9	18.1	11.6	33.6	29.8	18.6	14.4	25.0
SOT conviction rate	77.5	88.2	71.7	68.4	85.2	82.4	71.1	68.9	79.0
Jury trial rate	3.7	6.1	2.9	2.3	1.8	2.2	2.5	2.0	2.9
Jury trial conviction rate	48.6	83.1	77.5	76.9	77.1	69.8	67.2	86.1	64.9
Court trial rate	5.9	8.1	2.9	2.1	8.8	2.9	5.3	4.7	5.3
Court trial conviction rate	47.2	72.8	69.0	48.7	54.8	57.1	63.9	58.4	55.0
Plea (orig charge)	7.0	22.3	17.3	26.7	20.3	15.4	25.7	23.9	16.2
Plea (change NG to G)	41.4	39.9	44.1	47.4	25.6	42.3	34.0	37.4	39.1
Guilty plea rate	50.8	64.3	64.9	76.9	47.6	60.0	62.6	63.8	57.8
Overall conviction rate	79.5	90.1	83.2	88.0	83.7	88.9	81.7	78.8	83.4

SOURCE: California Bureau of Criminal Statistics computer tapes.

Table C-10

SUPERIOR COURT FELONY DISPOSITIONS BY BRANCH OFFICE, 1971: POSSESSION OF MARIJUANA

(In percent)

Disposition	Branch Office								County-wide
	Los Angeles	Long Beach	Santa Monica	Van Nuys	Torrance	Norwalk	Pomona	Pasadena	
No. cases disposed	1325	336	448	524	754	881	396	348	5012
% of countywide	26.4	6.7	8.9	10.5	15.0	17.6	7.9	6.9	100.0
Dismissed (diverted)	5.8	6.0	4.5	3.4	3.7	4.0	5.8	3.5	4.7
Dismissed (Int of Jus)	5.1	3.9	5.1	3.2	3.1	1.7	5.8	8.1	4.2
Dismissed (§1538.5 PC)	5.4	2.7	5.6	2.3	6.0	2.4	5.8	8.9	4.8
Dismissed (§995 PC)	6.3	1.2	6.9	2.7	3.2	1.7	7.8	12.6	4.9
SOT rate	35.3	14.9	19.6	16.8	32.4	34.9	25.8	14.4	27.9
SOT conviction rate	68.1	84.0	65.9	63.6	76.6	77.5	56.9	60.0	70.7
Jury trial rate	1.9	2.7	0.7	0.4	0.3	0.6	0.8	0.3	1.0
Jury trial conviction rate	20.0	77.8	33.3	100.0	50.0	60.0	33.3	100.0	42.0
Court trial rate	4.4	3.9	4.0	1.0	6.9	2.5	4.8	3.2	4.0
Court trial conviction rate	44.8	69.2	72.2	40.0	51.9	63.6	68.4	72.7	56.6
Plea (orig charge)	4.9	23.8	16.5	30.9	23.7	13.4	18.7	20.1	16.4
Plea (change NG to G)	30.9	41.1	37.1	39.3	20.8	38.9	24.8	29.0	32.3
Guilty plea rate	38.0	69.0	56.1	72.7	46.3	54.5	46.1	50.9	51.1
Overall conviction rate	66.0	87.3	72.9	84.6	75.9	84.6	65.4	62.5	74.5

SOURCE: California Bureau of Criminal Statistics computer tapes.

Table C-11

SUPERIOR COURT FELONY DISPOSITIONS BY BRANCH OFFICE, 1971:   POSSESSION OF DANGEROUS DRUGS

(In percent)

Disposition	Los Angeles	Long Beach	Santa Monica	Van Nuys	Torrance	Norwalk	Pomona	Pasadena	County-wide
No. cases disposed	1388	442	277	551	805	1571	540	389	5963
% of countywide	23.3	7.4	4.7	9.2	13.5	26.4	9.1	6.5	100.0
Dismissed (diverted)	5.5	2.0	6.1	4.5	4.2	4.8	5.9	3.1	4.7
Dismissed (Int of Jus)	3.2	3.2	4.0	1.8	2.5	1.5	4.4	7.5	3.0
Dismissed (§1538.5 PC)	3.4	3.6	3.6	2.0	2.9	1.7	5.6	3.9	3.0
Dismissed (§995 PC)	4.3	1.4	1.4	1.6	1.7	1.0	3.7	5.7	2.5
SOT rate	29.6	15.8	18.4	8.0	34.0	28.7	19.1	11.1	24.3
SOT conviction rate	72.0	87.1	58.8	81.8	85.4	82.5	66.0	55.8	77.5
Jury trial rate	2.0	1.6	1.1	0.5	0.0	1.5	0.7	0.0	1.1
Jury trial conviction rate	39.3	85.7	66.7	33.3	0.0	65.2	100.0	0.0	57.4
Court trial rate	5.0	4.8	1.8	1.5	4.4	2.7	3.5	3.9	3.6
Court trial conviction rate	58.6	81.0	80.0	50.0	57.1	51.2	57.9	53.3	58.8
Plea (orig charge)	6.6	28.3	27.8	39.6	27.6	16.6	27.2	27.0	20.9
Plea (change NG to G)	40.4	39.4	35.7	40.5	22.7	41.4	29.8	38.1	36.9
Guilty plea rate	49.7	69.1	67.7	83.8	52.5	61.0	60.6	67.1	60.7
Overall conviction rate	76.2	88.5	81.5	91.6	85.5	88.4	77.0	75.6	83.3

SOURCE: California Bureau of Criminal Statistics computer tapes.

Table C-12

SUPERIOR COURT FELONY DISPOSITIONS BY BRANCH OFFICE, 1971:   BURGLARY

(In percent)

Disposition	Los Angeles	Long Beach	Santa Monica	Van Nuys	Torrance	Norwalk	Pomona	Pasadena	County-wide
No. cases disposed	1751	332	393	615	892	663	427	329	5402
% of countywide	32.4	6.2	7.3	11.4	16.5	12.3	7.9	6.1	100.0
Dismissed (diverted)	4.9	3.0	4.3	3.6	3.3	3.9	2.8	4.3	4.0
Dismissed (Int of Jus)	1.8	0.3	2.0	2.1	1.6	0.3	1.2	4.6	1.7
Dismissed (§1538.5 PC)	0.5	0.9	0.5	0.7	0.8	0.3	1.2	1.8	0.7
Dismissed (§995 PC)	1.9	0.6	2.3	1.6	0.9	0.5	0.7	4.6	1.6
SOT rate	28.7	19.6	18.3	9.8	32.6	23.4	12.9	9.4	22.8
SOT conviction rate	86.9	87.7	84.7	76.7	90.7	86.5	74.6	71.0	36.2
Jury trial rate	2.4	8.7	1.0	1.3	1.2	1.2	2.6	1.8	2.2
Jury trial conviction rate	42.9	82.8	75.0	87.5	63.6	37.5	54.6	100.0	62.2
Court trial rate	3.9	10.2	2.8	1.3	7.1	1.4	3.8	1.8	4.0
Court trial conviction rate	46.4	79.4	81.8	62.5	61.8	22.2	56.3	50.0	58.3
Plea (orig charge)	9.1	22.3	17.1	25.5	24.9	19.9	36.3	34.0	20.0
Plea (change NG to G)	46.7	34.3	51.7	54.2	27.7	49.2	38.6	37.4	43.1
Guilty plea rate	58.7	58.4	71.8	82.6	54.4	71.9	77.1	74.6	65.7
Overall conviction rate	87.9	91.9	91.2	92.4	90.3	93.7	90.6	84.4	90.0

SOURCE: California Bureau of Criminal Statistics computer tapes.

Table C-13

SUPERIOR COURT FELONY DISPOSITIONS BY BRANCH OFFICE, 1971: ROBBERY

(In percent)

Disposition	Branch Office								County-wide
	Los Angeles	Long Beach	Santa Monica	Van Nuys	Torrance	Norwalk	Pomona	Pasadena	
No. cases disposed	834	156	146	185	328	242	98	120	2109
% of countywide	39.5	7.4	6.9	8.8	15.6	11.5	4.7	5.7	100.0
Dismissed (diverted)	2.3	3.2	3.4	4.3	1.8	0.8	1.0	5.8	2.5
Dismissed (Int of Jus)	3.6	1.3	12.3	2.2	3.1	1.2	4.1	0.8	8.4
Dismissed (§1538.5 PC)	0.6	0.0	1.4	0.0	0.0	0.0	0.0	0.0	0.3
Dismissed (§995 PC)	1.9	0.6	2.1	1.6	0.6	0.0	0.0	1.7	1.3
SOT rate	23.4	9.6	11.6	8.7	31.7	17.4	8.2	9.2	19.4
SOT conviction rate	82.1	93.3	70.6	75.0	86.5	90.5	87.5	63.6	83.3
Jury trial rate	9.1	14.1	13.0	7.6	8.2	6.2	11.2	5.8	9.1
Jury trial conviction rate	59.2	90.9	100.0	71.4	81.5	80.0	54.6	85.7	73.3
Court trial rate	9.2	14.7	2.1	3.8	19.2	2.1	9.2	3.3	9.1
Court trial conviction rate	41.6	69.6	33.3	42.9	61.9	40.0	77.8	75.0	53.9
Plea (orig charge)	4.0	12.8	4.1	11.9	5.2	14.9	18.4	15.8	8.1
Plea (change NG to G)	45.9	43.6	50.0	60.0	30.2	57.4	48.0	57.5	46.9
Guilty plea rate	51.0	58.3	56.0	75.1	36.0	72.9	67.0	77.9	56.4
Overall conviction rate	80.1	91.4	78.7	89.3	82.9	94.6	87.6	92.0	84.8

SOURCE: California Bureau of Criminal Statistics computer tapes.

Table C-14

SUPERIOR COURT FELONY DISPOSITIONS BY BRANCH OFFICE, 1971: ASSAULT

(In percent)

Disposition	Branch Office								County-wide
	Los Angeles	Long Beach	Santa Monica	Van Nuys	Torrance	Norwalk	Pomona	Pasadena	
No. cases disposed	564	77	107	163	254	244	126	80	1615
% of countywide	34.9	4.8	6.6	10.1	15.7	15.1	7.8	5.0	100.0
Dismissed (diverted)	5.9	9.1	5.6	5.5	3.9	4.1	2.4	3.8	5.0
Dismissed (Int of Jus)	4.8	0.0	3.7	6.1	6.7	0.8	2.4	7.5	4.3
Dismissed ($1538.5 PC)	0.0	0.0	0.0	0.0	0.39	0.0	0.8	0.0	0.1
Dismissed ($995 PC)	1.6	0.0	0.0	1.2	0.8	0.4	0.8	0.0	0.9
SOT rate	29.8	20.8	17.8	11.7	36.2	34.0	15.1	15.0	26.5
SOT conviction rate	81.6	81.3	84.2	57.9	91.3	88.0	89.5	75.0	84.1
Jury trial rate	7.5	13.0	10.3	4.3	4.7	5.3	5.6	7.5	6.7
Jury trial conviction rate	35.7	100.0	54.6	57.1	75.0	46.2	71.4	83.3	55.6
Court trial rate	14.0	22.1	7.5	4.3	18.1	7.0	14.3	17.5	12.8
Court trial conviction rate	53.2	76.5	37.5	42.9	39.1	52.9	77.8	64.3	53.9
Plea (orig charge)	2.5	1.3	7.5	14.1	5.9	8.6	18.3	12.5	7.1
Plea (change NG to G)	34.0	33.8	47.7	52.8	23.2	39.8	40.5	36.3	36.6
Guilty plea rate	38.8	38.6	58.4	70.8	30.3	50.4	60.2	50.7	46.0
Overall conviction rate	75.3	90.0	83.2	82.5	75.8	88.0	89.4	80.5	80.6

SOURCE: California Bureau of Criminal Statistics computer tapes.

Table C-15

SUPERIOR COURT FELONY DISPOSITIONS BY BRANCH OFFICE, 1971:   FORGERY

(In percent)

Disposition	Branch Office								County-wide
	Los Angeles	Long Beach	Santa Monica	Van Nuys	Torrance	Norwalk	Pomona	Pasadena	
No. cases disposed	576	112	94	127	220	158	85	109	1481
% of countywide	38.9	7.6	6.4	8.6	14.9	10.7	5.7	7.4	100.0
Dismissed (diverted)	7.3	0.9	1.1	3.9	5.9	3.8	3.5	4.6	5.1
Dismissed (Int of Jus)	2.3	0.0	2.1	3.2	1.4	1.3	0.0	0.0	1.6
Dismissed (§1538.5 PC)	0.0	0.0	0.0	0.0	0.9	0.0	1.2	0.9	0.3
Dismissed (§995 PC)	1.9	0.0	0.0	0.0	0.0	0.0	0.0	2.8	1.0
SOT rate	19.6	8.0	10.4	6.3	16.4	13.9	10.6	7.3	14.5
SOT conviction rate	77.0	88.9	80.0	50.0	86.1	54.6	66.7	50.0	74.4
Jury trial rate	0.7	2.7	4.3	0.0	1.4	1.3	1.2	0.0	1.2
Jury trial conviction rate	0.0	100.0	75.0	0.0	66.7	50.0	100.0	0.0	58.8
Court trial rate	2.1	0.9	1.1	0.0	7.3	1.3	4.7	2.8	2.6
Court trial conviction rate	16.7	0.0	100.0	0.0	37.5	100.0	100.0	66.7	43.6
Plea (orig charge)	13.5	42.9	23.4	48.8	33.2	30.4	44.7	51.4	28.7
Plea (change NG to G)	52.6	44.6	57.5	37.8	33.6	48.1	34.1	30.3	45.0
Guilty plea rate	71.4	88.3	81.7	90.2	71.0	81.6	81.7	85.6	77.7
Overall conviction rate	88.0	98.2	94.6	93.4	89.9	91.5	95.1	91.4	91.0

SOURCE: California Bureau of Criminal Statistics computer tapes.

Table C-16

SUPERIOR COURT FELONY DISPOSITIONS BY BRANCH OFFICE, 1971: POSSESSION OF NARCOTICS

(In percent)

Disposition	Branch Office								County-wide
	Los Angeles	Long Beach	Santa Monica	Van Nuys	Torrance	Norwalk	Pomona	Pasadena	
No. cases disposed	321	45	63	98	85	127	32	47	813
% of countywide	39.2	5.5	7.7	12.0	10.4	15.5	3.9	5.8	100.0
Dismissed (diverted)	5.3	0.0	3.2	4.1	2.4	1.6	9.4	2.1	3.8
Dismissed (Int of Jus)	4.7	0.0	9.5	4.1	5.9	0.8	0.0	4.3	4.0
Dismissed (§1538.5 PC)	6.9	2.2	0.0	2.0	3.5	6.3	6.3	6.4	5.0
Dismissed (§995 PC)	5.3	0.0	9.5	5.1	3.5	3.9	0.0	19.2	5.5
SOT rate	34.6	26.7	22.2	10.2	40.0	29.9	18.8	19.2	28.6
SOT conviction rate	78.4	66.7	64.3	80.0	79.4	81.6	100.0	100.0	79.1
Jury trial rate	1.9	2.2	4.8	0.0	2.4	0.8	0.0	2.1	1.7
Jury trial conviction rate	50.0	0.0	100.0	0.0	100.0	100.0	0.0	100.0	71.4
Court trial rate	3.1	6.7	3.2	1.0	11.8	3.9	6.3	2.1	4.2
Court trial conviction rate	60.0	66.7	50.0	100.0	70.0	80.0	100.0	100.0	70.6
Plea (orig charge)	2.5	13.3	9.5	14.3	9.4	7.9	25.0	8.5	7.8
Plea (change NG to G)	35.8	48.9	38.1	59.2	21.2	44.9	34.4	36.2	39.4
Guilty plea rate	40.5	62.2	49.2	76.6	31.3	53.6	65.5	45.7	49.1
Overall conviction rate	72.0	84.4	70.5	86.2	74.7	82.4	93.1	69.6	76.9

SOURCE: California Bureau of Criminal Statistics computer tapes.

Table C-17

SUPERIOR COURT FELONY DISPOSITIONS BY BRANCH OFFICE, 1971: SALE OF NARCOTICS

(In percent)

Disposition	Branch Office								County-wide
	Los Angeles	Long Beach	Santa Monica	Van Nuys	Torrance	Norwalk	Pomona	Pasadena	
No. cases disposed	960	184	240	308	468	438	257	227	3082
% of countywide	31.2	6.0	7.8	10.0	15.2	14.2	8.3	7.4	100.0
Dismissed (diverted)	4.4	1.1	7.9	2.9	2.6	3.4	2.7	6.2	3.9
Dismissed (Int of Jus)	3.4	2.7	2.5	4.6	4.3	0.7	5.1	2.2	3.2
Dismissed ($1538.5 PC)	2.6	1.6	0.4	3.6	2.6	1.1	2.7	2.6	2.3
Dismissed (§995 PC)	3.8	1.1	2.5	3.3	3.6	1.8	3.9	2.2	3.1
SOT rate	37.1	21.7	23.3	15.3	48.5	54.1	26.9	28.2	35.6
SOT conviction rate	88.5	95.0	83.9	78.7	92.5	93.3	88.4	90.6	90.1
Jury trial rate	3.5	3.8	4.6	5.2	1.5	2.5	2.3	3.1	3.2
Jury trial conviction rate	70.6	71.4	90.9	93.8	100.0	90.9	83.3	100.0	83.8
Court trial rate	5.2	13.6	1.3	1.6	7.5	5.3	6.6	4.4	5.5
Court trial conviction rate	56.0	76.0	66.7	20.0	65.7	73.9	76.5	70.0	65.5
Plea (orig charge)	2.4	11.4	8.3	10.4	6.4	5.3	13.2	8.4	6.6
Plea (change NG to G)	37.6	42.9	49.2	53.3	23.3	25.8	37.0	42.7	36.9
Guilty plea rate	41.8	55.0	62.4	65.6	30.5	32.2	51.6	54.5	45.2
Overall conviction rate	81.8	89.0	89.1	83.3	83.1	90.8	83.2	88.3	85.0

SOURCE: California Bureau of Criminal Statistics computer tapes.

Appendix D

SENTENCING PATTERNS OF INDIVIDUAL JUDGES

Table D-1

FELONY SENTENCE RATE BY SUPERIOR COURT JUDGE AND OFFENSE CATEGORY,
LOS ANGELES COUNTY, 1970

(In percent)

Branch Office or Court Division	Judge[a]	Offense						
		Possession, Dangerous Drugs	Burglary	Possession, Marijuana	Robbery	Forgery	Sale of Narcotics	All Offenses (weighted)[b]
Los Angeles	1	45	53	30	79	66	87	53
	2	23	35	21	83	40	92	39
	3	25	38	18	76	63	61	38
	4	19	9	3	70	38	77	25
	5	13	26	16	82	38	67	30
	6	8	22	6	84	25	50	24
	7	48	46	47	86	65	87	56
	8	45	39	26	47	49	65	42
	9	18	32	4	58	62	64	31
	10	14	17	5	48	15	33	18
	11	54	44	58	85	49	63	56
	12	19	36	10	58	18	81	31
	13	15	17	6	51	48	48	23
	14	25	41	56	44	48	67	43
Long Beach	1	7	60	20	97	60	82	42
	2	58	82	44	76	83	100	69
	3	62	69	53	89	72	98	69
Santa Monica	1	13	24	1	48	21	54	21
	2	30	30	18	57	29	65	33
	3	36	47	24	75	45	85	46
Van Nuys	1	27	45	31	80	54	76	44
	2	19	45	11	68	50	63	35
	3	6	33	10	69	24	53	25
Torrance	1	20	52	4	94	34	89	39
	2	11	51	13	87	32	61	34
	3	17	39	24	80	35	69	36
	4	48	65	31	96	63	87	58
	5	28	37	19	85	44	71	39
Norwalk	1	28	36	6	75	40	66	34
	2	42	57	30	75	64	71	51
	3	34	57	28	90	68	80	51
	4	25	49	22	66	65	59	40
Pomona	1	18	49	19	79	46	67	38
	2	27	50	28	90	66	93	48
Pasadena	1	30	38	20	69	46	66	39
Countywide	All 35	28	42	20	75	43	72	39

[a]To avoid unduly small samples, only judges who have sentenced 300 or more defendants (over all offense categories) are included here.

[b]See Appendix E for an explanation of weighted averages as used in this study.

158

Table D-2

PRISON RATE BY SUPERIOR COURT JUDGE AND OFFENSE CATEGORY,
LOS ANGELES COUNTY, 1970

(In percent)

Branch Office or Court Division	Judge[a]	Offense				
		Burglary	Robbery	Forgery	Sale of Narcotics	All Offenses (weighted)[b]
Los Angeles	1	8	26	18	8	12
	2	10	52	13	7	17
	3	7	48	0	0	11
	4	0	19	0	11	5
	5	3	42	0	0	8
	6	4	26	6	0	7
	7	4	35	0	11	10
	8	4	12	0	7	5
	9	2	27	0	6	6
	10	2	7	0	0	2
	11	5	57	14	11	16
	12	5	22	4	6	8
	13	3	17	0	11	6
	14	11	15	8	21	13
Long Beach	1	6	27	5	11	10
	2	20	11	15	11	16
	3	9	26	6	21	14
Santa Monica	1	5	38	10	9	12
	2	12	20	14	11	13
	3	0	31	0	9	7
Van Nuys	1	4	37	13	14	13
	2	7	22	4	9	9
	3	5	30	6	10	10
Torrance	1	4	34	4	6	9
	2	16	48	10	14	20
	3	2	20	0	0	4
	4	9	51	12	56	26
	5	2	17	0	4	5
Norwalk	1	2	13	0	2	3
	2	2	20	0	5	5
	3	10	38	3	18	15
	4	12	28	12	13	15
Pomona	1	7	28	2	21	12
	2	5	33	21	8	13
Pasadena	1	8	41	9	5	13
Countywide	All 35	6	28	6	10	10

[a]To avoid unduly small samples, only judges who have sentenced 300 or more defendants (over all offense categories) are included here.

[b]See Appendix E for an explanation of weighted averages as used in this study.

Appendix E

THE WEIGHTED AVERAGE

The motivation behind the development of weighted averages as employed in this study[1] was the need for statistical control as it arose in addressing variations in rates of rejection, termination, and sentencing among the Branch Offices. The need arose inasmuch as some differences were expected to exist simply as a function of differences in the characteristics of the cases handled by the Branches, whereas our interest was not in such variations, but rather in the differences that would cause identical cases to be handled differently.

Consider, for example, the comparison of branch rejection rates shown in Table E-1. Here we have two branches, A and B, each of which, for simplicity of argument, receives complaints for only two offenses, burglary and bookmaking. We find that Branch A has an overall rejection rate twice as high as that of Branch B, yet when we look at the rates for individual offenses, we find each Branch rejects 50 percent of its burglary complaints and 10 percent of its bookmaking complaints. The differences in the overall rates can be attributed simply and entirely to the relative frequencies with which the two offenses occur at the two Branches.

As mentioned, our interest is not in differences attributable as above to the characteristics of cases. Hence it was desirable to control for characteristics to which such differences might be attributed. (It is important to note that in order to attribute a Branch difference to some case characteristic, the distribution of that characteristic must differ among the Branches.) The case characteristic to which Branch differences might most readily be attributed is the *charged offense;* hence this was controlled for throughout this analysis. Another characteristic to which differences might well be attributed is the *prior record of the defendant.* As these data were not readily available at earlier stages, we were able to control for it only at the sentencing stage. This was not considered a disadvantage, however, because only at that stage is the effect of prior record thought to be very large.

One method to achieve statistical control is to sample only cases with the same characteristic(s). This has two potential disadvantages.

1. The sample sizes may be insufficient for the precision desired, as was frequently the case in this study. Often there were simply not enough occurrences of a single offense, especially for a single category of prior record, within each Branch.

---

[1] Primarily in Section VII and Appendix D.

Table E-1

SAMPLE COMPARISON OF BRANCH REJECTION RATES

Branch	Burglary			Bookmaking			Overall		
	Total Com-plaints	Com-plaints Rejected	Rejec-tion Rate (%)	Total Com-plaints	Com-plaints Rejected	Rejec-tion Rate (%)	Total Com-plaints	Com-plaints Rejected	Rejec-tion Rate (%)
Branch A	400	200	50	100	10	10	500	210	40
Branch B	100	50	50	400	40	10	500	90	20

2. This procedure characterizes each Branch solely on the basis of a single offense. It was desirable to have a more broadly based measure.

It is of course possible to select several such samples. This procedure increases the total sample size and broadens the base. However, unless the samples are somehow combined, this method provides us merely with a collection of measures, none of which is any more precise than would be obtained by the former procedure. The method we have employed combines the measures obtained from several such samples into a single broadly based measure, which is more precise than any of the single measures on which it is based and which maintains the control achieved by the separate samples.

We now present a development of the procedure:

Let us assume that there are I branches and J offenses to be considered.[2]

Let p_{ij} be the population rate[3] for an offense of type j at Branch i.

Let $\{w_j\}$ be an arbitrary set of weights assigned to the various offenses such that $\Sigma_{j=1}^{J} w_j = 1$.

Define

$$W_i = \sum_{j=1}^{J} w_j \, p_{ij} \, ,$$

where p_{ij} is the rate in the population for offense j at Branch i. This is then the population weighted average.

Based on samples of each of the J offenses from Branch i, W_i is then estimated by

---

[2] The development described here controls on offense; the procedure for prior record or for both offense and prior record is entirely analogous.

[3] That is, the rejection, termination, or sentencing rate.

$$\hat{W}_i = \sum_{j=1}^{J} w_j \, \hat{p}_{ij} \, ,$$

where $\hat{p}_{ij}$ is the rate in the sample for offense j at Branch i.

This $\hat{W}_i$ is then the sample weighted average, and it is this which is presented in the various tables of the text.

In order to understand the precision of each such estimate, $\hat{W}_i$, the variance of each was estimated by the following:

$$\widehat{\mathrm{Var}\,(\hat{W}_i)} = \sum_{j=1}^{J} w_j^{\,2} \, \frac{\hat{p}_{ij}\,(1 - \hat{p}_{ij})}{n_{ij}} \, ,$$

where n_{ij} is the number in the sample of offense j at Branch i.

In order to determine the statistical significance of observed differences between two Branches i and i', the following test statistic, assumed to approximate closely the standard normal distribution, was employed:

$$\frac{\hat{W}_i - \hat{W}_{i'}}{\sqrt{\mathrm{Var}\,(\hat{W}_i) + \mathrm{Var}\,(\hat{W}_{i'})}} \, .$$

We now turn to discuss the actual choice of weights employed. At the rejection and termination stages only offense was to be controlled for. The weights assigned at these two stages are the relative frequencies with which complaints of each were received during the period January 1 to November 11, 1971. The actual values of these weights are as follows:

Offense	Weight
11910 HS	.26358
11530 HS	.25619
459 PC	.26251
487.3 PC	.12022
211 PC	.09750

At the sentencing stage, weighted averages were first obtained for each offense by weighting the rates within each prior record. A weighted average of these, with weights now assigned to the offenses, then combined these into a single weighted average, which thus controlled for both prior record and offense.[4] The assignment

---

[4] Note that this average could be obtained in a single stage by considering rates within each pairs of prior record and offense and weighting by the product of the weights assigned to each element of the pair.

of weights to both prior record and offense was defined implicitly by the marginal distribution of the sample under consideration. For example, in comparing Branch prison sentence rates for possession of dangerous drugs, the weight assigned to the prior record "none" is the relative frequency of "none" as it occurs for possession of dangerous drug cases in this sample.

Weighted averages occur in the following tables:

Control Variable	Table	Item
Offense	48	Last row
	57	Last column
	58	Last column
	59	Last column
	60	Last column
	65	Entries
	66	Last column
	67	Last column
	68	.Entries
	69	Last column
Prior Record	72	Entries
	73	Last column
	74	Last column
	75	Last column
	76	Last column
	D-1	Entries
	D-2	Entries
Prior Record and Offense	72	Last column
	D-1	Last row
	D-2	Last row

BIBLIOGRAPHY

Studies Dealing with the General Topic of Prosecution Behavior or Performance

Abrams, Norman, "Internal Policy: Guiding the Exercise of Prosecutorial Discretion," *UCLA Law Review,* Vol. 19 (1), 1971, pp. 1-58.

Grossman, B. A., *The Prosecutor: An Inquiry into the Exercise of Discretion,* University of Toronto Press, Toronto, 1969.

Hamilton, W. A., "Modern Management for the Prosecutor," *The Prosecutor,* Vol. 7 (6), November-December 1971, pp. 472-475.

Kaplan, John, "The Prosecutorial Discretion—A Comment," *Northwestern Law Review,* Vol. 60, 1965, pp. 174-193.

Klein, Richard, "District Attorney's Discretion Not To Prosecute," *Los Angeles Bar Bulletin,* Vol. 18 (4), March 1971.

Lippman, David, "Some Perspectives on Research and Prosecutors," *The Prosecutor,* Vol. 5, 1969, pp. 257-260.

McIntyre, D. M., and David Lippman, "Prosecutors and Early Disposition of Felony Cases," *American Bar Association Journal,* Vol. 56, December 1970, pp. 1154-1159.

Miller, F. W., *Prosecution: The Decision To Charge a Suspect with a Crime,* Little, Brown, and Company, Boston, 1969.

Newman, D. J., *Conviction: The Determination of Guilt or Innocence Without a Trial,* Little, Brown, and Company, Boston, 1966.

The President's Commission on Law Enforcement and Administration of Justice (Nicholas B. Katzenbach, Chairman), *Task Force Report: The Courts,* U.S. Government Printing Office, Washington, D.C., 1967.

Work, C. R., "A Prosecutor's Guide to Automation," *The Prosecutor,* Vol. 7 (6), November-December 1971, pp. 479-480.

Empirical Studies of Local Criminal Justice Systems

Bing, S. R., and S. S. Rosenthal, *The Quality of Justice in the Lower Criminal Courts of Metropolitan Boston,* Lawyers' Committee for Civil Rights Under Law, Boston, 1970.

Blumstein, A., and Richard Larson, "Models of a Total Criminal Justice System," *Operations Research,* Vol. 17 (2), March-April 1969.

Jennings, J. B., *The Flow of Arrested Adult Defendants Through the Manhattan Criminal Court in 1968 and 1969,* The Rand Corporation, R-638-NYC, January 1971.

Kalven, Harry, Jr., and Hans Zeisel, *The American Jury,* Little, Brown, and Company, Boston, 1966.

Oaks, D. H., and Warren Lehman, "The Criminal Process of Cook County and the Indigent Defendant," *University of Illinois Law Forum,* Vol. 1966, 1966, pp. 584-737.

Subin, H. I., *Criminal Justice in a Metropolitan Court: The Processing of Serious Criminal Cases in the District of Columbia Court of General Sessions,* United States Department of Justice, U.S. Government Printing Office, Washington, D.C., 1966.

Studies of the Los Angeles Criminal Justice System

Graham, Kenneth, and Leon Letwin, "The Preliminary Hearing in Los Angeles: Some Field Findings and Legal-Policy Observations," *UCLA Law Review,* Vol. 10 (4 and 5), March and May 1971.

Stein, L., "Prosecutorial Discretion in the Initiation of Criminal Complaints," *Southern California Law Review,* Vol. 42, 1968-69, pp. 519-545.

INDEX

ABOUT THE AUTHORS

Peter W. Greenwood is Director of the Criminal Justice Research Program at The Rand Corporation and principal investigator on studies focusing on police investigation and dangerous habitual offenders. He holds M.S. and Ph.D. degrees in Industrial Engineering from Stanford University and is currently a third-year law student at Loyola University. During the past few years he has directed a number of major research projects in education and criminal justice, including a major assessment of U.S. Office of Education programs designed to bring about changes in local school district instructional practices, studies for the Commission on Bankruptcy Laws evaluating the impact of proposed changes in bankruptcy laws and procedures on the public and the bankruptcy system, and an interdisciplinary study of the criminal prosecution process in Los Angeles, funded by the U.S. Department of Justice. His principal professional interests focus on the operation of the criminal justice system and its proper role in society and on determining how the legal system can be used to implement social policy reforms.

Sorrel Wildhorn has headed studies in the fields of criminal justice and energy policy research since 1968. He received degrees in aeronautical engineering from New York University and is a senior policy analyst at The Rand Corporation. Mr. Wildhorn is presently directing a new study of the ways of measuring performance in the criminal prosecution, defense, adjudication, and sentencing process. He is the coauthor of *How to Save Gasoline: Public Policy Alternatives for the Automobile*, the coauthor of a forthcoming book on *The Private Police*, and has authored a number of publications in the areas of national security and criminal justice.

Eugene C. Poggio has been a statistical analyst who has worked in a variety of areas at The Rand Corporation. He received a B.A. in mathematics and statistics from the University of California at Berkeley, an M.A. in mathematical statistics from Columbia University, and is currently completing a Ph.D. in statistics at the University of California, Berkeley. His special field of interest is nonparametric statistics.

Michael J. Strumwasser, Deputy Attorney General of California, is engaged in civil trial and appellate practice in the Public Resources Section of the Department of Justice, representing California in resources and environmental litigation. He has served as Special Consultant to the California State Energy Resources Conservation and Development Commission, participating in its formation and organization and directing its legal staff. As Resident Consultant to The Rand Corporation from 1966 to 1970 and 1971 to 1972, he was involved in studies of the Los Angeles criminal justice system, the U.S. Patent Office, and Air Force command and control systems. He received the M.S. and J.D. degrees from the University of California at Los Angeles and is a Member of the California Bar. Mr. Strumwasser's contribution to the present study was made before he joined the staff of the Department of Justice, and the views expressed here do not necessarily reflect those of that Department.

Peter De Leon is on the staff of The Rand Corporation, working in criminal justice education, transportation, research and development, energy research and national security. He received the M.A. in Political Science from the University of California at Los Angeles, studied international relations, public administration, and systems analysis in the Ph.D. Program at U.C.L.A. and at the London School of Economics and Political Science, and is currently writing his doctoral thesis at the Rand Graduate Institute for Policy Studies. He is the author of a number of publications related to public policy analysis.

SELECTED LIST OF RAND BOOKS

Bagdikian, Ben H. *The Information Machines: Their Impact on Men and the Media*. New York: Harper and Row, 1971.

Bretz, Rudy. *A Taxonomy of Communication Media*. Englewood Cliffs, New Jersey: Educational Technology Publications, 1971.

Cohen, Bernard and Jan M. Chaiken, *Police Background Characteristics and Performance*. Lexington, Massachusetts: D. C. Heath and Company, 1973.

Dalkey, Norman (ed.) *Studies in the Quality of Life: Delphi and Decision-Making*. Lexington, Massachusetts: D.C. Heath and Company, 1972.

DeSalvo, Joseph S. (ed.) *Perspectives on Regional Transportation Planning*. Lexington, Massachusetts: D. C. Heath and Company, 1973.

Downs, Anthony. *Inside Bureaucracy*. Boston, Massachusetts: Little Brown and Company, 1967.

Fisher, Gene H. *Cost Considerations in Systems Analysis*. New York: American Elsevier Publishing Company, 1971.

Jackson, Larry R. and William A. Johnson. *Protest by the Poor*. Lexington, Massachusetts: D. C. Heath and Company, 1974.

Leites, Nathan and Charles Wolf, Jr. *Rebellion and Authority*. Illinois: Markham Publishing Company, 1970.

McKean, Roland N. *Efficiency in Government Through Systems Analysis: With Emphasis on Water Resource Development*. New York: John Wiley & Sons, 1958.

Novick, David (ed.) *Current Practice in Program Budgeting (PPBS): Analysis and Case Studies Covering Government and Business*. New York: Crane, Russak and Company, Inc., 1973.

Novick, David (ed.). *Program Budgeting: Program Analysis and the Federal Budget*. Cambridge, Massachusetts: Harvard University Press, 1965.

Pascal, Anthony, *Thinking About Cities: New Perspectives on Urban Problems*, Belmont, California: Dickenson Publishing Company, 1970.

Quade, E.S. *Analysis for Public Decisions*. New York: American Elsevier Publishing Company, 1975.

Quandt, William B. (ed.) *The Politics of Palestinian Nationalism*. Berkeley, California: University of California Press, 1973.

The RAND Corporation. *A Million Random Digits with 100,000 Normal Deviates.* Glencoe, Illinois: The Free Press, 1955.

Sharpe, William F. *The Economics of Computers.* New York: Columbia University Press, 1969.

Sackman, Harold. *Delphi Critique: Expert Opinion, Forecasting, and Group Process.* Lexington, Massachusetts: D. C. Heath and Company, 1975.

Turn, Rein. *Computers in the 1980's.* New York: Columbia University Press, 1974.

Wildhorn, Sorrel, Burke K. Burright, John H. Enns, and Thomas F. Kirkwood. *How to Save Gasoline: Public Policy Alternatives for Automobile.* Cambridge, Massachusetts: Ballinger Publishing Company, 1976.

Williams, J.D. *The Compleat Strategyst: Being a Primer on the Theory of Games of Strategy.* New York: McGraw-Hill Book Company, Inc., 1954.

Wirt, John G., Arnold J. Lieberman and Roger E. Levien. *R&D Management: Methods Used by Federal Agencies.* Lexington, Massachusetts: D.C. Heath and Company, 1975.

Yin, Robert K. and Douglas Yates. *Street-Level Governments: Assessing Decentralization and Urban Services.* Lexington, Massachusetts: D.C. Heath and Company, 1975.